BUSINESS PLANS THAT WIN VENTURE CAPITAL

BUSINESS PLANS THAT WIN VENTURE CAPITAL

Terrence P. McGarty

WILEY

JOHN WILEY & SONS

New York   Chichester   Brisbane   Toronto   Singapore

Library of Congress Cataloging in Publication Data:
McGarty, Terrence P., 1943–
    Business plans that win venture capital / by Terrence P.
McGarty.
        p. cm.
    Bibliography: p.
    Includes index.
    ISBN 0-471-50180-8
1. New business enterprises—Planning.   2. New business
enterprises—Management.   3. New business
enterprises—Finance.
I. Title.
HD62.5.M38 1989
658.1'1—dc19   88-27609
                                                          CIP

Printed in the United States of America
10 9 8 7 6 5 4 3 2 1

To my mother, Dorothy,
who gave me life and love
and
To my grandmother, Hattie,
who gave me wisdom and insight

PREFACE

This book is the outgrowth of a long process of working with a great number of small start-up companies as well as consulting with large corporations in the development of new businesses. Each time a group performs the task of developing the business plan, they must ask themselves, "What should be done and what should be included?" This book is directed at answering that question.

More importantly, a need exists for financial information. The development of personal computer technology has allowed the business planner to assess and develop the business concept quickly and to provide detailed financial answers. This book is built around using the personal computer as an essential ingredient in business planning.

This book is directed toward the entrepreneur and his or her associates involved in the establishment of a new business. More particularly it focuses on the technical, analytical entrepreneur who wants to develop a business and business plan within the context of the technical disciplines in which he or she has been trained. This book builds upon the base of understanding that most things can be presented in a systematic fashion and that, in using the structure of such a system, the strengths and weaknesses of an idea can be effectively evaluated and improved.

The book's objective is to describe the business plan and the business planning process. It is not a text on marketing or finance. It does, however, challenge the reader to address these issues as far as they apply to the development of the new business. Most importantly, this is not a replacement for professional assistance in such areas as law or accounting. It is a guide to seeking out and obtaining such assistance.

In my own experience, the business plan signals the end of a process as well as the beginning of another. The plan is the result of developing the basis of a business. It can be prepared only after entrepreneurs have proven to themselves that a market exists and that there are real customers for the product. The plan is complete only when the business has begun getting customers and producing the product. At that point it becomes the beginning of the business.

This book is a result of many long efforts with start-up companies that had a clear understanding of several of the components that were necessary to put a business together, but did not understand all components, or perhaps even misunderstood several. Engineers may be great technical experts, and even great salespeople, but they are, in some cases, poor financial and marketing people. Even more so, the entrepreneur may be a poor manager. This book has one main focus: Get the knowledge of what is needed and back that up with good people. In the last analysis, the success factor of start-ups is people.

The author would like to thank many of the people who helped with his understanding of new business, specifically the following presidents and officers of companies: Lou Gerstner of American Express, Steve Ross and David Horowitz of Warner Communications, Peter Hankin of OTC, Peter Beck of Digital Access Corporation, Bart Stuck of Teltron, Gerry Clancy of DSO Systems, Fred Sutton of RCA, Ed Hughes and Carl Lindholm of Motorola, Mari Ulmer of BBI, and Art Caisse of Cohesive and now Data America. The author would especially like to thank Gus Hauser, president of HCI, for his guidance and inspiring leadership, along with his questioning and enlightening approach to business. He has provided me with a unique experience: watching the theory in this book successfully put to practice. In addition, special thanks go to Jim McGrath, with William E. Simon, Marcel Mihaeloff, and Ollie Curme of Battery Ventures for assistance on many of the cases. Special thanks to Mounir Chakarji, who helped with all the figures and tables. All, in their way, contributed to this effort.

TERRENCE P. McGARTY

Waterville Valley, New Hampshire
March 1989

CONTENTS

PART III

9. FINANCING THE VENTURE   281

10. CONCLUSIONS   319

APPENDIX   SAMPLE BUSINESS PLAN   327

REFERENCES   359

INDEX   363

BUSINESS PLANS THAT WIN VENTURE CAPITAL

PART I

1

INTRODUCTION

The business plan is the cornerstone of any successful business venture. It articulates the business's purpose—selling its product to the consumer—and how it intends to achieve that goal. The business plan also presents a forum to reposition the original business concept and, if necessary, to reposition the entire business or even to abandon it without dramatic losses.

This book presents the business plan as an evolving process. The plan grows with the business; it is not meant to be a one-time effort, but to evolve into the strategic planning process of the company. However, in its early stages, the business plan represents the totality of the company.

This chapter presents an overview of the book. It discusses the business plan in a broader light than merely as the initial embodiment of the business. The reader must keep in mind that the plan is not only an articulation of the business at a single point in time, but is also the ongoing strategy to best accomplish the goals of the business.

OVERVIEW

A new business requires the preparation of a business plan. In many cases those people involved in the plan's preparation will focus on putting the plan in the correct format, thereby neglecting the substance of the plan. The result: Form takes precedence over substance. This book presents a form, but emphasizes the substance of the plan to a greater degree. Indeed, the form should take a back seat to the articulation of the business, its rewards, and its risks. In this book we convert the plan into a process that allows the plan developers to focus on substance. Experience with this process has demonstrated that, by following it, the plan and its goals can be clearly articulated and rapidly accomplished.

New businesses may start with a group of individuals in either an entrepreneurial setting or a corporate setting. A new business is more than a new product. A new product typically takes life in an existing organization, or at least in a structure that has the support of an existing organization. A new business as described in this book has no such support system. It is a new life that springs forth with the need to develop the product as well as the business's infrastructure.

A large amount of literature on new product planning exists today, but the new business encompasses many more dimensions (see Drucker [2], Liles, and Urban and Hauser). A new product plan typically assumes constraints on distribution channels, product mixes, existing corporate capabilities, and other fixed environmental factors. The business plan generally fixes few if any of the constraint variables, and is driven by the intention of setting up a new and independent entity.

One of the most important developments of the past ten years is the evolution of the service business (see Lovelock or Drucker[2]). Service businesses have not received the amount of attention that they should in the business planning process. As the United States's economy changes, such service business, especially those based on electronic services, will proliferate. Because many new business opportunities already lie in this area, this book pays a great deal of attention to this segment of the business world. Throughout the book we emphasize the similarities between the service and goods businesses.

This book deals with two types of products: goods and services. As we shall see, any business is characterized by the product that it offers the market. The goods product is a piece of hardware such as a modem or computer game. The service product is more intangible. It may be an enhanced communications service, such as a protocol conversion network or the selling of reservations to rock concerts. We shall discover the many similarities and dramatic differences between the two types of products as we focus on developing the business plan.

THE PROCESS

As we've pointed out, the development of the business concept from idea to reality is an evolving process; it is not the immediate result of the preparation of the plan. The business plan itself is just one of several steps in that process. The importance of having a process is that it allows the developer to focus on the information and strategic decisions that must be made in order to fully develop the business. This section discusses the other steps in the implementation of a new business and where the business plan fits in that process.

The process of developing a business has the following steps:

Business definition phase
Draft business plan
Business plan
Detailed market/product/operations plans
Strategic plan convergence
Implementation and operation

Let's now consider the elements of each of these steps.

Business Definition

The first step in our process, the business definition phase, is usually the most difficult to implement. In this phase the product is defined and the business's role in the context of an existing industry is identified. This phase is the most highly iterative part of the development process.

The principals who will subsequently manage this business should take a strong role in this effort. Lack of focus is often at the core of business definition problems. Consider the following example: A start-up company was composed of a group of engineers who had all worked for a large regulated telecommunications company. They recognized the need that would exist for many new telecommunications products as the industry became deregulated. When they first assembled, their thoughts were directed toward a business to develop special-purpose software for the newly formed telephone companies. When asked by a venture capitalist what their product was, they answered that they developed software. When pressed, the answer became: we will do anything the customer wants.

After six months of trying to sell "anything the customer wants," the engineers got back together and decided that they needed to focus on a hardware product. They focused on systems to perform certain protocol conversions of telecommunications signals, thinking that they could sell this new product idea. After a year they had manufactured products. Unfortunately, no one purchased any of the new products. The company was still not certain what business it was in. However, they were willing to customize the products at the customer's request. The customer was uncertain because of lack of consistency or standardization. The company struggled on.

In this example, a group of talented, motivated people wanted to start a new business, but they failed to establish the focus of the business. Their energy was spent on starting the business, not on perfecting the product. The business possessed the vital components—market need, a demand, and talent—but the principals were confused as to what business they were in. This example highlights the need for clear, focused planning from the beginning of the venture. Thus, the first step in the business development process is the business definition. Entrepreneurs need to ask themselves, "What is our product? Why are we making it? What business are we in?" It is essential to be able to articulate these facts clearly when entrepreneurs approach potential customers.

As a second example, consider a start-up company that had recognized the need for a satellite technology to provide for low-cost bypass communications to the business community. The company further recognized that two business roles had to be provided in order for the business to succeed. The first was that of the hardware provider, who would develop the hardware goods that would interface with the customer's network. The second role was that of the service provider, who would provide the network control, operations, installation, and maintenance.

This start-up company wanted to be both the provider of the hardware and the operator of the system. It wanted to vertically integrate at the outset. The firm faltered at the beginning because the customer was confused as to what role the company was playing. It lacked the basic ingredient of any start-up: focus. The keys to success are a good product, focus, and, of course, luck. Without the first two, no amount of luck will suffice to save the company. This company has since developed a strong focus as a hardware provider and is prospering. Thus, the business definition must be clear and achievable with the resources available.

These two examples depict a venture's need to have at the earliest stages a clear focus on the business so that all further steps can be accomplished. In the business definition phase, the first set of questions that should be asked are:

- What is our product? Is it a good or service?
- What business are we in? Are we manufacturing, OEMing (e.g., original equipment manufacture, using someone else's equipment and enhancing it), or reselling?
- What is our relationship to the end user of our product? Are we planning to use a direct sales force or a different distribution channel?
- What will we do and what will we not do?

The last question—especially concerning what the business will not do—is the most important at this stage. All too often the starting business encompasses more than it reasonably can.

During the business definition phase, issues arise concerning the product, the business, relationships, and the extent of the business. We discuss these issues as they relate to the example just presented.

Product

What is the product? Is it a telecommunications terminal or a data communications system? Who are the customers and what are their needs? If the customer were a communications service company, then the hardware supplier could OEM the equipment to the service company, who in turn could provide full service to the end user.

The product description should be brief and to the point. It should describe the product so that the customer will be able to grasp it readily and understand why it is needed.

Business

Whereas the product is what the company makes, the business it is in is a reflection of how the firm relates to the others in its industry and, in turn, to its customers.

As an example, a company that makes television sets also runs a hospital television rental and leasing business. The business of the company is really the manufacturing and distribution of television sets to retailers, and does not really include the service to the hospital. Typically, a serious problem arises when a service business develops in a manufacturing organization. The manufacturing people have interest in selling their product, and so tend to induce the service people to exclusively buy their product (not necessarily at the market rate). The service company is thus in the position of having to accept the mark-ups of the manufacturer; in addition, it does not have the flexibility to control the piece of hardware that it is receiving to best match the needs of its customers.

In this case, the company is really a consumer goods manufacturer that includes a service business that it uses as a distribution arm rather than a separate service organization. Thus, this start-up venture is crippled from the outset because it can never be the business that it must be to survive.

Relationships

Understanding what the product is and what business the company is in are only the first steps in the business definition. Just as important is the need to define the business's relationships within the industry and to the end user.

Questions such as "Who is the end user? How does the company relate to the end user? What sort of distribution channel should be employed?" are essential at this time. The end user of the product is too often forgotten. The entrepreneur too frequently considers who he or she is selling the product to, not who the end user will be. Understanding the end user is critical to understanding the entire distribution chain.

Consider the following example, which highlights the issue of how best to identify the end user, and in turn target the customer. A database distribution company found that the end user of its business information database was the business professional, but that the professional had no access to the database because the company had information specialists act as intermediaries in the process. The reason for this was that the database providers usually had to deal with an intermediate database distributor, such as Knight Ridder's Dialog, who in turn marketed the product to its traditional market: librarians. The result was that the end user was denied access to the service. The distribution company recognized this problem and found that, through a direct mail approach and using its own computer system, the end users could directly access the service. Thereafter, the company kept better quality control of its product and could customize the product for its separate market segments.

Extent

Extent is the issue of what the business will do and what it will not do. Consideration of this issue is essential in that it puts bounds on what is to be attempted in the execution of the business.

Extent is the issue that typically leads to overreach and, in turn, disaster. The Atari experience under Warner Communications is an example of a case where extent became confused. The product's rapid success led to a mindset that falsely indicated to the company that their business world was not just entertainment, but any electronic product that could eventually get into the home. This bred Atari Tel, the venture into the telephone business, which was developed in the face of increasing competition on a price-alone basis. The home computer division was developing more than a dozen different computers, the video division was developing new video creation and production techniques, and an educational institute was developing new ways of teaching, new methods of artificial intelligence, and other elements of the educational process.

As Atari expanded in so many different directions, the company grew from $26 million in 1979 to $2 billion in 1982. The company's focus became lost, however. The excursion into the area of manufacturing and marketing telephones resulted in major losses due to foreign competition, which created a commodity product of low-cost phones consumers found very attractive. In contrast, Atari developed phones designed by Porsche and priced five to ten times above peak market price. Price turned out to be the key market factor. Atari had overextended itself too rapidly. The result was a pretax loss of over $600 million, and the near demise of the company.

Extent is a statement of what the business is and is not. It defines the boundaries of the entrepreneur's reach. It is a focus that must be followed.

Draft Business Plan

The draft business plan is the entrepreneur's first effort at placing the business concept on paper and attaching market estimates and financial values on the business. The purpose of the draft business plan is to provide its creators with a format to work with. The draft plan will contain the following elements:

Product and business definition

Market size and description

Distribution and sales strategy

Management and operations plan

Development plan

Draft financials

Competitive analysis

The firm's principals discuss these seven elements—generally outlined in a presentation format prior to being developed into a formal business plan—until they agree on what the business is and what the holes are that must be filled in the business plan process. If the draft business plan is drawn together early, as it should be, two of the major holes will be defining the market size and the target market. Typically, these estimates appear in the final business plan.

The financials should be blocked out in considerable detail during this first stage. As we shall see later, the financial will be a guidepost along which the business plan develops.

Business Plan

The third step in our process, the development of the business plan, is the step which we examine most closely in this book. It is the most crucial step and requires that the business be well understood and a team assembled to implement the business.

The business plan is the cornerstone of the new business. Whether it is a stand-alone new business or an internal corporate new business, the same plan must be drawn. The business plan contains details on the following items:

The product or business definition

The market, including target definition, size, pricing, and distribution alternatives

Competition, including competitive strategies and key distinctive competence to succeed in this industry

A development plan indicating what additional items must be accomplished to enter the industry

The operations and management plan demonstrating who is going to do what in the business

Financials to indicate the revenue, capital, expenses, income statement, sources and uses, and balance sheet

A funding statement of how funds are to be raised, the amounts, and the dilution of equity anticipated

We shall go into these items in further detail throughout the book.

Detailed Plans

Once the business plan has been developed, a follow-up set of detailed plans is needed in the areas of operations, marketing, product development, and financial/budgeting. These plans may or may not be required at the same time as the business plan. Most entrepreneurs do not prepare these plans; the result becomes an added expenditure during the business growth phase. That added expenditure will result in a need for more capital and a reduction of the owners' equity. Thus, although these plans are not essential to get funding, experience indicates that they are bargaining chips in the business valuation (e.g., how the new venture is valued and, in turn, what it is worth to the investor). We shall see that the valuation of the company is a critical issue, and how these plans help structure the valuation strategy.

As an example, consider a group of entrepreneurs who have developed a unique way to provide bypass communications using a fiber optic system in a large urban area. They devise a business plan and seek financing. The plan does not include any detailed market commitments from customers, nor does it present their key barrier to entry: obtaining a special agreement from the city. The venture capital company looks at the plan in absence of the marketing plan and values the company based solely upon the labor expended up to this point. They value it at $800,000. For $400,000, they want 50 percent. Had the entrepreneurs developed a detailed market plan with these commitments, the value of the company would have exceeded $4,000,000. Thus, the $400,000 would mean only 10 percent of the firm's value.

The venture capitalist tries to mitigate against as many risks as possible. As Silver has stated, there are five types of risks in a start-up venture:

Development risk: Can the product be developed?
Manufacturing risk: Can it be made if developed?

Marketing risk: Can it be sold if made?

Management risk: Can it be profitable if sold?

Growth risk: Can it grow if managed?

Detailed plans should address each of these risk areas separately and should attempt to provide the venture capitalist with a more secure feeling about the company.

In addition, detailed plans should be drawn up to address each of the key operational areas of the business. These plans then become a part of the day-to-day tactics of the business. They are similar to the financial budget that is the watchdog of the day-to-day financial operations. Typically, the plans to be drawn up are:

Product Operations Plan

The product operations plan details the development cycle of the new business as well as all its tasks using a Project Management Control System (PMCS) approach. It shows the critical paths in the firm's development. It also provides for a reporting system that ensures development is monitored as the system grows. It extends itself to the operations phase in which the manufacturing issues are discussed.

Marketing Plan

The marketing plan addresses the risk of who will buy the product and how the sales force will be targeted to the firm's best advantage. The marketing plan:

1. targets market segment toward the distribution strategy.
2. positions the product and the promotional campaign to raise awareness.
3. prices the product by market segment and a presentation of the unique selling features.
4. establishes by segment the needs and benefits of the product.
5. describes the marketing channel, including distribution,

fulfillment, and other sales functions, including customer service and the billing philosophy.

6. contains customer lists and binding or nonbinding commitments, targeting customers the sales force will call on first and demonstrating the entrepreneur's experience in the field.

The key goals of the marketing plan are to target and qualify the customer and to provide the pricing and positioning to affect sales. Due diligence by all the firm's principals and even an outside consultant are essential to the marketing plan. Direct customer contact during the business plan stage ensures that the selling propositions are correct.

Product Plan

The product plan is a detailed description of the product's development. It defines the product in detail and is the basis of the financials detailed in the financial development plan. The plan should be detailed to the level that, as an incoming team is assembled, it can readily implement the product and have a clear vision as to where this new company is headed.

Again, it is essential to remember that the product and marketing plans have to address the same issues. If the customers say they really want something else, then the entrepreneur should listen and modify the plan appropriately.

Financial Development Plan

The financial development plan contains the detailed set of operating plans for the company that lay out the revenue, expenses, and capital requirements as well as all other pro forma operating statements (e.g., income statement and the like). These plans represent the operating budget for the company as it proceeds through its early stages of development.

The four plans discussed represent the day-to-day operating guides for the company. They easily derive from the business plan and are the responsibility of the appropriate business department heads to prepare, monitor, and manage.

THE OUTLINE OF THIS BOOK

This book is divided into three parts. The first, comprised of Chapters 1 and 2, addresses the overview of the business plan. Chapter 2 presents the general concept of the plan, detailing the outline and the financials that are key to its presentation as a business opportunity.

Part II is a detailed look at the business plan and each of its components. Chapter 3 discusses defining the concept of the business or product. As the first step in the development of the plan, its careful presentation in a few short words is essential to grasping the attention of the funding sources.

Chapter 4 discusses the market. For technical entrepreneurs this section may be the most difficult. It stresses the need to define the target market and how the entrepreneur intends to reach that market. It relies on the gathering of facts concerning the market and on direct contact with customers to accurately assess the need and demand for the product. Finally, it addresses the distribution strategy, which is the means of getting the product effectively to the end user.

Chapter 5 is an important chapter in that it discusses competition. Michael Porter's *Competitive Strategy* and *Competitive Advantage* discuss the competitive environment in extensive detail; this chapter does not replace such excellent works. Rather, it focuses on how the entrepreneur should assess the competition, what factors are needed to be successful, and how the entrepreneur intends to accomplish this goal in developing the business.

Chapter 6 presents the development plan. Typically, entrepreneurs still must develop certain key elements of the business. It may be a new product, service, or some key ingredient that gives them the competitive edge. If this were not so, an ongoing business could merely finance itself through debt or a public offering. This section of the plan addresses how the development will be completed, what the risks are, and how these risks will be handled.

Chapter 7 presents the ongoing operations and management. This proposal tells the investor what the expenses, capital, and management team will look like for the ongoing business. It represents the entrepreneur's understanding of how he intends to operate the business.

Chapter 8 summarizes the financial portions of the business plan. In this book, we take the position that this set of financials is developed as we progress. For example, Chapter 4 develops the revenue, Chapter 7 the capital and expenses. Chapter 8 combines these building blocks with income statements, sources and uses, and balance sheets in preparation for dealing with the sources of capital. In this chapter, we develop the key leverage points from the financial point of view.

Part III of the book deals with what to do after the plan is complete. Chapter 9, which describes how to finance the firm, may be the most important chapter for the entrepreneur. Experience has shown that many entrepreneurs have approached venture capitalists with no understanding of the worth of their proposals and how the capital could be raised. Obviously, entrepreneurs who have a grasp of these realities are at an advantage. This chapter starts with a set of techniques for valuing the firm. It then discusses at length the options of financing, including common, preferred, convertible debentures, warrants, options, and pure debt. The chapter then demonstrates the impact of each, allowing the entrepreneur to integrate this information into the financial management of the firm. The essential strategy in raising capital is for the entrepreneur to be in control. That is, the entrepreneur should be in control of the sources of funds by suggesting the strategy and counteroffering, using information on the impacts of the counter offer.

Finally, Chapter 10 draws together all the elements of the business plan.

SCHEDULES AND TIMING

One of the major concerns that relate to the business development process is scheduling of events. Understanding the sequence of events and the time it will take to see these events come to pass often helps the entrepreneur understand where he or she may be with respect to the progress expected from the business.

A set of key events will occur in the course of the business development. These events are:

1. Business concept
2. Business definition
3. Draft business plan
4. Customer contact
5. Customer preliminary commitment
6. Prototype product
7. Business plan
8. Company valuation
9. Financing
10. Business development effort
11. Business commencement

These eleven steps are always present in some form, and almost always in the same sequence. The first step, development of the business concept, starts the business process. Then comes the business definition, the first attempt by the entrepreneur to place his or her ideas on paper. That stage may take two or three months.

Next comes the effort of creating the draft business plan, which is the first truly difficult step. It may take weeks to months, and the business may even end at that point. Most business failures tend to occur at this stage. If they survive, they move on to the next steps: customer contact and commitment. The contact phase may take two to six months; customer commitment may mean a three- to six-month additional effort.

The next step is the product prototype development. Conceptualizing this prototype, which may vary from a simple concept model to a full working system, could take three to six months. This stage occurs in parallel with the other development efforts.

At this point the business plan and the company valuation can

TABLE 1.1 Key Event Schedule

Event	Duration (months)
Business concept	0
Business definition	3–6
Draft business plan	2–4
Customer contact	2–6
Customer commitment	2–6
Prototype	3–9
Business plan	1–3
Valuation	1/2–1
Financing	6–12
Development	12–24
Commencement of business operation	

be prepared. This may take up to six weeks, after which the company can proceed to seek financing using its plan, prototype concept, and market commitment. These elements will all play a role in the valuation of the company and the equity that will be retained by the owners.

The financing of the company often takes from six to twelve months. It is not a short process, and any entrepreneur must understand it. He or she will be forced to visit many potential sources of funds and will be referred to many more. The process, which is iterative and does not always converge rapidly, rarely takes less than six months. Thus, the entrepreneur must be willing and able to hold out financially for that period. Interim sources of financing may help, but they may slowly eat away at the equity base. This phase will be the most difficult part of the start up.

The final step is the commencement of the development process and the actual beginning of the business operation. The development effort will take from twelve to twenty-four months. Table 1.1 depicts these key steps and the time schedule. Day one of the real business starts at its completion.

2

BUSINESS PLAN OVERVIEW

This chapter presents the overall structure of the business plan. The purpose of developing the structure in detail is to provide a framework for addressing all of the key questions that may be asked as part of the business's development. This chapter is a prelude to Part II, which provides the detail for each of the portions of the business plan.

The overview of the business plan in this chapter provides a structure. It is important to understand that structure at the outset, and to understand that the plan addresses questions asked by investors, managers, and the customer.

Three key elements comprise a business plan:

The business concept
The environment
The financial factors

The first element describes the business. As discussed in detail in the last chapter, it is important to remember that the plan must have a clear idea of the firm's product.

The second factor, the environment, includes the market, the competition, and the general conditions in the related marketplace. The essential ingredient of this element is information. The entrepreneur must have sources of information to ascertain the environmental factors. These sources are best obtained first hand, if at all possible. This means speaking to potential customers, speaking to the competition, and being generally aware of the business factors in this industry. Such factors may be the financial community's willingness to finance businesses of the type being proposed.

The third element is the set of financial factors that describe the business and its financing, as well as its return to investors. Entrepreneurs are often intimidated by the financial factors and try to avoid them, relegating their preparation to a third party. However, it is essential that the entrepreneur have these factors well understood. With the advent of automated spreadsheet software, such as Lotus 1-2-3 and other personal computer-based products, the entrepreneur can now play a direct role in the development of detailed financials. This chapter presents the framework for these financials and further develops the key elements in a spreadsheet format.

OUTLINE OF THE BUSINESS PLAN

The business plan document should be as compact as possible and should state clearly all the salient facts. The first page should be an executive summary that gives the key facts of the proposed business and what type of financing is being requested. Many authors, including John W. Wilson, D. J. Gladstone, and Gregory Kravitt, have described how to develop the plan. We have expanded upon their efforts by including not only the questions but the form, the process, and the description of how to accomplish that process.

The plan should not be a long dissertation on the business, nor an all-inclusive consultant's report. The better plans are direct, with the facts presented in a concise bulleted format and the prose kept to a minimum. Many exceedingly verbose plans give investors the impression that the entrepreneur intends to keep the business on paper where it is safe and secure rather than in the market where it can be tested.

The business plan should contain the following sections:

Executive Summary (one page)

The executive summary briefly pulls together the key business and market factors and highlights the financial factors that make the business attractive.

Section 1: Business Definition

The business definition is a detailed statement of the business and the product. It must be clear and concise, leaving the reader with an understanding of the product or service, and the role of the proposed company in providing the goods or service.

Section 2: Market

The market section presents all of the necessary information regarding the target market, with adequate reference to how that information was determined. It also allows the reader to assess the total revenue potential for the business based on the market size, the sales effort, and the pricing of the product.

Section 3: Competition

The competition section is the critical area that allows the entrepreneur to show why the proposed concept differs significantly from other businesses, yet will be successful and generate the revenue and profit proposed. This section identifies all competitors, direct and indirect, and shows why the proposed business is a major improvement on existing methods of providing the product or service.

Section 4: Development Effort

The development efforts associated with the new product are all too often given little emphasis in the business plan. In this section, the full development efforts must be detailed and should indicate accomplishments and what tasks are still to be completed. The detail should be concise but adequate to indicate that management has anticipated any major delays.

Section 5: Operations and Management Plan

The operations and management of the business are key to understanding its ultimate success and profitability. The plan should include how the business is to be managed, and what resources, labor, and capital are required. This section also sets the pace for the expense and capital requirements of the business.

Section 6: Financials

Having described the revenue in Section 2 and the expense and capital in Section 5, this section of the plan expresses the details of the overall financial picture of the business. For investment and valuation purposes, this is the most important section. Throughout this book, we provide significant detail as to how to develop and use this information to strengthen the business.

The total length of the plan should be kept to 25 to 45 pages, depending on how much depth is considered necessary for the financials. It is recommended that a separate document outline the financing alternatives; it is a negotiating tool and should not be given away at the outset. We shall discuss the structure of that document later.

Table 2.1 presents the detailed outline of the business plan developed in this book. Note that the outline is a set of questions. These are the questions that the venture capitalist will ask when the entrepreneur presents the business plan. These questions are those that have been the most frequently asked and answered by those entrepreneurs who have succeeded and those also most frequently avoided by entrepreneurs who have failed.

Part II of this book goes into the detail necessary to develop answers to all of the questions asked in the outline in Table 2.1. Some of these questions may not have to be answered, depending on the business and the state of the business in the mind of the investment community. In addition, the entrepreneur can answer many of the questions in a combined fashion, ensuring that the plan remains a manageable size.

THE EXECUTIVE SUMMARY

The business plan as outlined depicts the total set of questions that must be answered in order to adequately defend the business during the funding and development phases. However, an-

TABLE 2.1 Business Plan Outline

1. Business Definition

   Nature of the Business
   > What is the business?
   > What are its functions?
   > What does it do and for whom?

   Product
   > What is the good or service provided by the business?
   > Why is it needed?
   > What is the product and what is it not?

   Industry Roles
   > What industry is this business in?
   > What are the normal roles in this industry?
   > What role does this business play?
   > Is it a standard role?
   > If it is a new role, why is it needed?
   > Who does what to whom, and why?
   > Why are these roles needed?
   > What is the product distribution channel?
   > How does pricing change in the distribution channel?

   Distribution Channel
   > What is the flow of product from source to end user?
   > What is the position of the business in the channel?
   > What are the existing and new channels?
   > How does the benefit statement relate to positioning of the product?

   Product Need
   > Why is this product needed?
   > What does it enhance or displace?
   > What benefit does it provide?
   > Is there an unmet need?

2. Market Plan

   Definition of the Market
   > Who will buy the product?
   > What need are you satisfying?
   > Why are they buying it?
   > What is the size of the market?
   > Are there multiple market players?
   > Where will they get the money to pay for it?
   > Is this an enhancement or a displacement?
   > How rapidly will the market grow?
   > At whose expense will the market grow?
   > What is the initial market size?

TABLE 2.1 Business Plan Outline (continued)

What will be its final size?
What is the total market?
What is the projected market share?
Who has the other share?

Positioning
How do you want your product perceived?
Why is your product different?
What are the product benefits?
How do you inform your customer of the product?
How are you signaling your competitor?
Are you going head to head, or is this a niche?
Are you delimiting your product?
What makes you unique as a company?

Pricing
What is your unit sale?
What is your unit sale price?
What is the basis of your pricing?
What pricing flexibility do you have?
How do you price across market segments?
How do you price across business segments?
How does the price compare with competitors'?
What are the margins in the distribution channel?

Distribution Strategy
What are the distribution channels?
What are the interdependencies in the channels?
Who are the players in the channels?
How will the product be distributed?
What are the costs of distribution?
Are there alternative channels?
Is there a separate fulfillment channel?
How is brand recognition preserved?

Sales Plan
What is your sales strategy?
What is your promotional plan?
What is the timing of the plan?
What is the sales organization?
Is retention marketing essential?

Barriers to Entry
What makes the product unique?
How long would it take to copy and market?
What are the success factors in this business?
Is there a barrier to exit on the consumer side?
What are the barriers to entry for competition?

TABLE 2.1 Business Plan Outline (continued)

How long is there a competitive edge?
What is the product life cycle?

Revenue Potential
What are the market size, penetration, and price assumptions?
What are the churn assumptions?
What are the revenue-by-product assumptions?
What are the total revenue assumptions?
What are the key revenue assumptions?
Can you provide a detailed revenue model?
Can you segment revenue by product and market?

3. Competitive Analysis

Key Success Factors
What are the key success factors in this business?
How do they differ in the technical and market areas?
What are their weights of importance?

Competing Industries
Who are the competitors?
Are there similar or displaceable products?
What does this product enhance or displace?
Can you list the competing industries and companies?
How much revenue is in the market now?
What is the present distribution of market share?
What are the key competitive product benefits?
What are the markets served?

Business Success Factors
What are the key factors to be successful in this business?
Can you correlate these factors with each of the competitors?
Have you considered possible coalitions?
Can you list strengths and weaknesses of company and competitors?
Can you position competition in terms of operational vs. marketing
strength?
Can you position this business in that matrix?
Can you specify the competitive strengths and weaknesses?

Competitive Strategies
What are the strategies of the key competitors?
How can they be combatted?
How is your product positioned against the competitor?

4. Development Plan

Technical Description
How will the product be developed?
What is the architecture?

TABLE 2.1 Business Plan Outline (continued)

What are the key hardware and software factors?
What elements had to be developed?
What are the technical risk areas?
Is there an established technical base upon which the product is built?
What is the basis of the technical development?
What is the development organization?
What are the size and scope of the development?

Schedule
What has to be done to develop the product?
What is the breakdown of the development tasks?
What is the schedule?
What is the key development path?
What is the development organization?
What materials are required?
How do you intend to control and monitor development?

Development Milestones
What are the key milestones?
What are the design reviews?
What is the review procedure?
What control procedures are used to manage the development?

5. Operations and Management Plan

Organization Chart
Who does what and why?
What is the chain of command?
Who are the key people?
What is the review procedure?
How does the organization grow with the business?
What are the personnel costs?

Operations
How is the developed product deployed?
How is transition from development to operations handled?
Who does the manufacturing and what are the costs?
Are there any subcontractors?
How are operations goals measured?
Is there an operations management control system?
How are personnel requirements related to operations?
What are the personnel growth requirements?
What are the personnel ratios of sales per employee, revenue per employee, profit per employee, etc.?
How do these ratios compare to industry standards?
What are the capital requirements?

TABLE 2.1 Business Plan Outline (continued)

6. Financial Plan

Development Costs
What is the schedule and detailed cost breakout?
What are the capital requirements?
What is the cost by development task element?
What is the cost by organizational element?
What is the summary of costs?
What are the salaries, overheads, etc.?

Revenue
Do you have a detailed revenue model?
What is the revenue by segment and market?
Is there sensitivity to key variables?
What are the variabilities of revenue to pricing?
What are high, medium, and low scenarios?

Capital
What are the capital requirements by segment?
Do you have a schedule of capital asset introduction?
Do you have depreciation schedules?

Expenses
Do you have a full list and model of operating expenses?
Do you have a breakout by organization?
Do you have a breakout by function?
Do you have a relationship-to-revenue model with fixed and variable factors?
What are the direct and indirect expenses?
What are the key ratios of expense, including overhead?

Pro Forma
Do you have a summary of revenue, expenses, depreciation, and net operating income?
Do you have a treatment of taxes to determine profit?
Do you have a balance sheet to present asset/liability flow?
Do you have an analysis of equity vs debt funding?
Do you have cash flow analysis, incremental and cumulative?
Do you have sources and uses statements showing funding impacts?
Do you have key ratio analysis and comparison to industry standards?

Summary
Have you presented key ratios, such as IRR, ROI, ROA, ROE, etc.?
Have you included analysis of cash flows for public offering?
Have you included structures of funding deals and implications?
Have you included working capital requirements and plans to meet them?

other element of the plan—the executive summary attached to the plan—carries the most weight. This part of the business plan will be read by potential investors, and will cause them to either keep reading or pass over it in favor of another. Most investors receive from 10 to 50 plans per week; a detailed reading of all is impossible. Thus, a carefully prepared executive summary that grabs investors' interest is essential. This summary contains the following elements in as brief a form as possible:

1. Business overview
2. Financial highlights
3. Financial needs
4. Present business status
5. Key achievements
6. Key personnel

1. Business Overview

The business overview is a brief statement of the business, the product, and the market. It must readily convey what is to be sold to whom and why. This is the point in the document where you must succinctly state the uniqueness of the product. For example,

> The business will provide both customer premise equipment and central office equipment to support a switched 56Kbps transmission service to users of data circuits. We have applied for a patent on the product, which will be distributed through OEM relationships with the top three PBX manufacturers as well as with agreements with the top three RBOCs.

Note that this statement contains a significant use of jargon. Such acronyms as OEM (for Original Equipment Manufacture), PBX (for Public Branch Exchange, or local telephone switch), and RBOC (for Regional Bell Operating Company, such as Bell Atlantic) are used freely. The entrepreneur may want to explain these terms in more detail, depending on the sophistication of the investor.

2. Financial Highlights

The financial highlights are the major parameters that make for business success. They may include revenue, profits, margins, cash flows, and return on investment. As an example:

> The business reaches a $50 million revenue base in five years with a 24 percent pretax profit margin. The peak negative cumulative cash flow is $3.5 million in Year Two. The business has an IRR of 27 percent and NPV at a cost of capital of 25 percent of $12 million.

Again, note the standard terminology for the investor in such terms as IRR (for internal rate of return) and NPV (for net present value). It is generally not necessary to expand on these abbreviations because the typical sophisticated investor is familiar with them.

3. Financial Needs

Financial needs statements describe the business's requirements for capital with which to grow, and the desire of the company to part with equity to support these needs. The statement may present a strawman financing schedule, which acts as a baseline for financing. For example:

> The company is valued at $6 million using an NPV approach. The first round of financing needed is $1.5 million; the company is willing to provide 25 percent equity for the funds. The company has secured agreements from several RBOCs to purchase the beta test equipment for a total of $1 million, which will assist the financing through the beta test phase. Subsequent second-round financing is required and will be sought in 18 months.

4. Present Business Status

This report includes a brief description of the corporation, major employees, and shareholders.

5. Key Achievements

This listing details the achievements of the company, which may include patents, contracts, prototypes, or development facilities. A simple statement may be:

> The company has applied for a patent on its three key technologies. It has a predevelopment contract with three telephone companies for 35 units valued at $1 million. The company has hired the engineer who holds the patent, as well as the key marketing and sales vice president. The company is presently funded by $100,000 of equity from the principals, and has working capital generated from three consulting contracts from two telephone companies.

6. Key Personnel

This list should include management and the Board of Directors. Management must be proven experienced for the tasks required, and the board should demonstrate sufficient business breadth to support the company.

THE BUSINESS MATRIX

As we have discussed, businesses are divided between producing goods or services. In addition to these two differentiators, two others lead to the definition of the business matrix concept that we shall build upon in the other examples in this book. These dimensions—the capital and labor intensiveness of the business—help to characterize the business and allow the entrepreneur to determine where the business fits into the overall industry spectrum.

Capital intensiveness, a measure of how much capital is required to develop and operate the business, is figured by the ratio of revenue per asset dollar or the asset dollar per employee. For high capital intensiveness, the revenue per asset dollar is small, as it is in the cable television (CATV) business or the telecommunications business. The intensiveness on the capital side is strongly affected when financing is considered by the tax policy that may be in place at that time. CATV, for example, relies upon limited partnership financing to support its growth. Without favorable tax advantages, less incentive exists for investment in these ventures.

Labor intensity, a measure of how many people are required to operate the business and to generate revenue, is the ratio of revenue per employee, expense per employee, and income per employee. Each year *Fortune* magazine presents a detailed set of ratios for these types of companies.

Thus, we can consider the business matrix as an assessment and ranking of goods or service businesses by their labor/capital intensiveness on a scale of low to high. For example, we can have a labor/capital mix of H/H (High Labor/High Capital), H/L (High Labor/Low Capital), L/H (Low Labor/High Capital), and L/L (Low Labor/Low Capital). The following are examples of companies that fit these categories:

L/L: Satellite Communications Company

This company has developed a satellite communications service that allows interconnection of computers through a small satellite terminal and a proprietary protocol converter. The company modifies the software to accommodate any user, and allows the user to access the network at a rate that is 15 percent less than the comparable AT&T rate.

The company has a revenue per employee of $100,000 and a revenue per asset dollar of $0.85—high intensity of both labor and capital. The company needs both people and capital. Such a company is at a high risk because it must balance both of these limited resources.

L/H: Turnkey Communications Company

This company adds software to standard off-the-shelf computers so that they may act as message switches, packet assemblers, and disassemblers. The company has little capital; it is all purchased for a specific client and is considered inventory rather than capital. It does have significant labor for assembly and software development.

In this case, the revenue per asset dollar is $25.50 and the revenue per employee is $98,000. Thus, the firm's range for labor intensiveness is a revenue per employee two to three times the average employee salary.

H/L: Fiber Optic Network

This company provides a telecommunications service to bypass the local communications carrier. It has to establish itself with a significant capital base but, once established, it needs limited employees in order to operate. This example has a revenue per asset dollar of $0.95 and a revenue per employee of $400,000.

H/H: Bed-and-Breakfast Reservation

This company has established a reservations service for the bed-and-breakfast industry. It uses a pyramid sales force who are not employees; they all work on commission. Thus, the revenue per employee is very high: $550,000. The capital requirements are also very low: a revenue per asset dollar of $150.00. However, the company has a limited barrier to entry. As we shall discuss in Chapter 5, such businesses are readily challenged by competitors with low-cost labor who need little capital.

Table 2.2 depicts the four types of businesses and the typical ratios that apply to the Revenue/Employee and Revenue/Asset. For example, the H/H case shows that if these ratios are $200,000 per employee and $1 per asset, then this is a highly capital-intensive business that requires a very professional staff. The businesses that fall within this category are usually difficult to finance because the overall risk may be too high for the typical venture capitalist.

TABLE 2.2 The Business Matrix

		Labor Intensiveness	
		LOW	HIGH
Capital Intensiveness	LOW	Revenue/ Employee<$150K	Revenue/ Employee>$200K
		Revenue/ Asset<$1	Revenue/ Asset<$1
	HIGH	Revenue/ Employee<$150K	Revenue/ Employee>$200K
		Revenue/ Asset>$3	Revenue/ Asset>$3

CONCLUSION

This chapter presented an overview of the business plan structure. The key fact to remember is that the plan has a form that is often as important as its contents. The plan must clearly present the concept, and must articulate the business objectives and the financial returns. It represents the people as well as the business.

The plan is the description of how the business is to be operated. The executive summary is the most important part of that plan. The summary must be carefully executed so as to attract the attention of the investor. The plan must also be prepared so as to position the offering to the proper investor. As we shall see, the plan may be written differently to attract a venture investor as compared to a private corporate placement. In the latter case, the investors may be interested in a strategic fit of the new business within their overall corporate strategy. The venture capital investor is interested in a shorter-term financial gain. The implementation strategy of the business may differ in these two areas.

PART II

3

BUSINESS DEFINITION

The business definition section of the business plan, the first formal section, follows the executive summary, which provides the overview of the business. The objective of the business definition section is to reiterate the purpose of the business and describe the product in some detail. In particular, this section sets the pace for the remaining sections, which build on the business and product concept, explaining in detail the customers, competition, operations, and financials. This chapter presents the key elements of the business definition as viewed by the potential investor, as well as by the entrepreneur.

It is critical that the first section of the business plan convey the reasons the proposed business is a sound one. Writing the business and product definition statement forces entrepreneurs to shift focus from the product to the business itself. If they fail to make this shift, they may miss many of the subtleties that are essential for success in that business. As we shall see, two entrepreneurs with the same product may, however, find themselves with two different businesses. Their resulting strategies for marketing and meeting the competition thus may be drastically different.

NATURE OF THE BUSINESS AND PRODUCT

To understand the business, it is necessary to understand the relationships among the industry, business, and product. For example, the company may be in the telecommunications industry, in the bypass communications business, offering a high-speed data modem product. In contrast, another company may be in the telecommunications industry, with a position in the bypass communications business, and provide an end-to-end communications service with network management.

The product is the intended focal point of the business. It may be a computer board, a database, a fiber optic network, or a public access terminal. You have to have a product before having a business. Kenneth Andrews discusses this difference between product and business in his book, *The Concept of Corporate Strategy*. We shall see how this also fits into the concept of the competitive strategy as discussed in Michael Porter's *Competitive Advantage*.

The business describes what is to be done with the product. For example, if the product is a business database that resides on magnetic memory, then you may want to pursue several businesses with that product. The first is to sell that product to a database distributor such as Dialog and let them do the rest. The second business is one where you deal with a broker such as NewsNet or MCI Mail, who would allow access to any end user. You will develop a sales and marketing scheme to attract a potential customer base. The third business places the database on your own computer using CD-ROM technology, and again you do the sales and marketing. In the latter case, you have vertically integrated all of your product in the distribution channel.

In particular, the product is what you intend to sell and the business is how you intend to sell it. Often the means by which the business is structured is determined by the product potential. The entrepreneur may have a new product and intend to establish a standard business. For example, the new company may have a more efficient data concentrator switch for high-speed data. The business then is to manufacture and sell them direct to OEM or end users.

The industry, on the other hand, represents a standard broad classification of where the business is with respect to other businesses in the United States and elsewhere. One typical classification is the Standard Industrial Codes (SIC codes) used for classifying industry segments. As another example, consider a business with a standard product but with a new business flair—perhaps a publisher of financial data on companies and stock quotations. The product is well known and has a high market acceptance. The business will distribute the product electronically rather than via paper, which is the business that Dow Jones and Quotron are in. A new version using radio transmission rather than telephone has been developed by Lotus Corporation to add to its spreadsheet products.

Example One

Telmation, a start-up company, has developed a data communications interface board that provides for the access to local telephone lines by high-speed data terminals. The access permits dramatically lower costs of operations for service to the end user. Using the service, the end user is charged $0.10 per minute of access, compared to a dedicated line that is charged at the rate of $400 per month.

Telmation can decide to be in either of two businesses. The first business is that of a board manufacturer to the local operating companies. In that case, it may develop the board and sell it to the operating companies. The BOCs (local Bell Telephone Operating Companies, such as New England Telephone) will then have the responsibility to market the service and the hardware. The second business is that of a service provider. Telmation may decide to develop a local switching center that allows customers to dial directly into the service, as did MCI in the voice telephone business.

These are two strategically different businesses. The first is a simple hardware manufacturer. In that case, the risk is limited and the competition may find it easy to enter the market. The product may have a short life cycle. In the second case, the business is that of a service provider; the cash needs are great and the customer is locked in. The revenue stream from the second is larger and the service has a much longer life cycle.

This example portrays the essential difference in the nature of businesses with the same product. The entrepreneur must carefully position the business to meet market needs as well as to obtain financing for the venture.

PRODUCT DEFINITION

As you'll recall, the first step in developing the business plan was the need for a product and the determination of the business. Once this step is complete, the plan must include a detailed description of the product. This description must be detailed enough so that the investor can visualize its development risks in some detail, as well as envision its market potential and competitive advantages.

Thus, the product description must be somewhat detailed, but not to the extent that it is a full technical description of the product. If the product is a computer board, then the description should include its functionality, the type of hardware employed, and the extent of the software that will make this a unique product with a large market.

If the product is a service, the description should include a high-level view of the system's architecture, and specify what is expected of the user interfaces as well as the overall service features and functions.

In the case of both a good and a service, the product definition should include all features and functions that make it unique. For example, consider a new on-line data access service that a company wants to develop. The features and functions may be described as:

Ease of direct access to the system by an automatic log-on procedure for the user.

An artificial intelligence front-end support service to assist the user in selecting databases and in searching the database for the desired reference. This AI-based front-end system allows for simple user dialog to the system and supports a natural language query and response.

Automatic logging of information into local reference files is provided to the user so that usage of local PCs may be supported.

In contrast to the features and functions, the product description should include a high-level architecture. This section may include a description of the elements of the system and the major parts of the software. To continue with the example, the system architecture has the following key elements:

The system uses a VAX 9200 machine with 25 GB of direct access memory and is supported by disk drives for full data storage.

The system uses an AI Expert System Shell developed by the company especially for the untrained user. It has been tested in an academic environment as part of one of the founder's doctoral thesis.

The system is networked together using an X.25 packet network.

The plan should not include extensive details about the system; the investors will follow up on these issues during the due diligence process. In addition, the detail will be provided in the full-system architecture document, as described in Chapter 1.

Thus, the product, whether it be a good or service, is characterized by two elements: its features and functions and its architecture.

Consider a second example of the product definition. A company was founded to develop protocol conversion devices that allow for any word processor to talk to any other. In the product definition, the features and functions may be described as follows:

The system has the capability to translate document editable files between the IBM, Wang, DEC, and IBM PC/PS systems in real time.

The system interface acts as a file server to the systems and can be addressed directly, as would any file server, via a local area network.

The system uses a windowing server that allows for the direct access to the server and for real-time transfer of the editable document.

The architecture description may read as follows:

The system uses Motorola's 68030 chip for the main processor and has direct access to both Ethernet and token ring systems.

The system software runs on UNIX in C language and can be modified by I/O drivers, the source code of which will be provided to the end user on request.

The system can be addressed by remote access via a dial-up modem port. This feature allows for real-time updates of software modifications. It also allows for remote diagnostics on the system for improved customer support.

It should be noted that the description for both a service and a good may be developed without significant detail, but that both are heavily filled with technical jargon. This is unavoidable. If the potential investor insists on simple explanations, one must consider what help that investor may give in later stages.

INDUSTRY ROLES

Having established the business and the product in some detail, the business plan should include a discussion of the industry roles. This concept is frequently left out of many business plans. In essence, the industry role statement focuses on the roles various players in the business must act out for the business to be effective. That is, for a product to get from development to the end user, there will be several players in the chain whose roles are assumed. If they do not act according to their roles, the effectiveness of reaching the end user—and in turn reaching the desired business goal—is in doubt.

Consider the following example. A reservation service has been conceived that will provide bed-and-breakfast establishments with an on-line reservation service and assist them in reaching a much larger market. This service uses a small computer in each B&B location and relies upon the telephone company to provide the necessary high-speed data lines. In order to provide an effective service, the company must be able to assure the B&B establishments that their payment will be guaranteed.

Thus, in this simple example there are many assumed relationships:

1. The company is providing a service that will reach potential customers through direct mail and advertising.

2. The company is expecting that the telephone company will be able to provide high-speed data lines. However, in many locations the telephone companies are small independents; such technical capability may be very limited.

3. The company assumed that a credit card company would allow them to become one of their service establishments. Since the company has no track record in the business, a required bond had to be established.

As you can see, the simple assumptions could lead to a business that may not be successful. The company does not only have to look at its role but the capabilities and assumed roles of those on whom they rely.

UNIQUENESS AND TIMING

The reader of the plan must develop an understanding of the business, product, and market, then ask, "What is unique that makes this opportunity worthy of the financial risk?" Typical reasons are as follows:

We are first in the market.

Our product is cheaper.

Our product has better features.

The other products don't work.

We have a better technical team.

We know how to market better than the others.

The list can be continued, but what is necessary is to be specific and not to generalize. In the case of a fiber optic bypass company, their competitive edge was three contracts with carriers, a ten-year right-of-way to the city's subway ducts to lay their fiber, and a management team experienced in the business. They had revenue, controlled expenses, and people. That is what gives the leading edge to a business.

The issue of people must be addressed head-on at the beginning of the plan. Describe the assets that you have in your people, the uniqueness that they will bring to your business.

Timing is also an important element in this first section of the plan. As you have defined the business, you must also provide reasons why it is important to do it at this moment. Timing is driven by four major factors:

Product Lifetime Limited

A product may meet a need, and that window of need may be limited. The limit may be a market-imposed limit or and externally defined technological limit. For example, just before telephone deregulation, there was a need for telephone users to dial a string of access numbers to obtain an MCI service. A company was founded to provide the product to MCI. It grew from an annual sales of $1 million to $76 million in three years. Then it collapsed. This was an external market window, since the need disappeared when equal access came on.

Competition Directly Active

The company may have a good idea, but it may be known that the competition will not be far behind. One example is that of Apple versus IBM, where IBM may often provide early announcements of new products to stimulate the market and retain market share. This is a typical IBM strategy and a small company may find a niche for a new product but the product lifetime and product entry timing must be considered carefully.

Price Pressure

Price pressure may allow for immediate entry into a market. However, that may be a limited draw that also will disappear. For instance, RCA had a company called Cylix that developed based upon the fact that local calls were being subsidized by long distance. Using satellites, Cylix could provide cheaper long distance service. They then had an arbitrage advantage. However, with deregulation, the equation changed and the business tumbled until it was repositioned by a new management apart from RCA.

Window of Opportunity

In 1977, Scientific Atlanta (SA) found that it had a chance to develop satellite antennas for the cable television business to broadcast signals from a company called HBO. Within a four-month period, HBO's subscribers grew from 45,000 to over one million. SA decided that it was profitable to provide low-cost satellite dishes, and the rest is history. Had the chairman of SA not perceived the market and responded quickly, it may have been lost to another company.

Clearly, it is essential to describe in your business plan why timing is important and why your business must be developed now.

CONCLUSION

The business and product definition provides a reader of your plan with the clear understanding of what the business will do and in what industry it intends to compete. Your statement of this set of factors must provide the reader with a clear and unambiguous understanding.

4

MARKET

The market section of the business plan describes what the entrepreneur has learned as a result of being exposed to the product's potential users in the context in which the business will be executed. The market section combines a set of strategies, detailing very solid names and numbers of customers. The market must be targeted to a great degree to ascertain if it truly exists. If it does, the entrepreneur must decide how best to sell to that market.

All too often the market does not materialize; the entrepreneur will wonder what went wrong. This area, then, is the most critical. The financials can be predicted fairly well on the basis of capital and expenses, but the business hinges on the market and its accompanying revenue. In this section we not only develop a formal methodology, but we also stress the importance of getting commitments from potential customers to validate the existence of the market.

This chapter is an overview of the many issues covered in the more classic marketing texts, such as those by Kotler and Mc-Carthy. In specific, we will discuss many of the elements of market research without giving the details. These details are contained in the texts by Bellenger and Greenberg, Boyd et al., and Luck et al.

TARGET MARKET

The first step in developing the marketing presentation is a description of the target market. The target market is characterized by defining who is going to buy the product. The definition has to be specific enough so as to not encompass too diffuse a base, but broad enough so as to reach the total market. The definition of the target market is a result of a lengthy process of talking with potential customers, surveying, performing market research, and getting letters of intent from the potential customer base. The business plan reports on the results of this process; it does not detail all of the steps in this process. Thus, in the plan, the target market definition is succinct and to the point. In a subsequent due diligence process, the entrepreneur may take the opportunity to investigate the results of the studies performed.

We first present an overview of the market, then develop the process that leads towards the resulting target market. This approach will be the same for both the consumer and commercial markets. Our approach uses a set of filters to delimit the target market along very specific lines, starting with a total potential customer base that is very broad.

The market is developed along the following lines: First, the total potential market, characterized by all those users who may have the slightest interest in the product, is developed. Second, using a limitation called the demographic filter, we obtain the addressable market. The demographic filter delimits the total market by using measurable elements such as age, computer type, or other definable limits. Third, using psychographic or interest factors, a feasible market—based on an interest to buy, a willingness to change, or other softer questions—is developed. Fourth, we use a conversion rate to develop the convertible, or target, market. The conversion rate is based upon the theory that any new or existing product has a life cycle, and that only a portion of the feasible market may have an interest in a particular year. This segment of the market represents those customers who actually will buy in that specific year. The conversion rate is based on the adoption theory to be discussed (see Philip Kotler's *Marketing Management*). Fifth, using the market share number or that percentage of the target market that the company hopes to attain, we determine the actual number of customers or units on a year-by-year basis. The key to developing the target market is to understand this process and to ensure that all limits (the five steps described above) are applied. We show this process in Figure 4.1.

Figure 4.1 demonstrates the target market development process in detail, showing the five steps and four filters (shaded areas) that are applied. To summarize:

Step 1. Total Potential Base: Knowing the product and business as developed in Section 1 of the plan, we develop the overall set of possible users. For example, if the product is a consumer market, the total base may be the number of consumers, the number of households, or the number of women in households. In the case of a commercial business, the total potential may be the number of banks and financial institutions.

Step 2. Addressable Market: Using the appropriate market research tools (to be described in this section), we may use limiting factors, such as age, sex, or computer type and location to delimit the total potential market and derive the addressable market.

Step 3. Feasible Market: User preference based on highly subjective factors such as price, interest in the product, intent, and even political orientation are used to further delimit the market size.

Step 4. Target Market: Having determined the set of users that are both demographically and psychographically acceptable, we then determine which of those users are interested at what time. That is the basis of adoption rate theory. Similar to the concept of diffusion rate theory in engineering literature, it describes how new products diffuse their way into the marketplace. The results of this process give a year-by-year estimate in the target market—that is, those users in each year who would actually be interested in purchasing the product. At this point, we know who, where, when, and how many.

Step 5. Market Share: Until this point, the numbers have all been fairly quantitatively derived. The target market

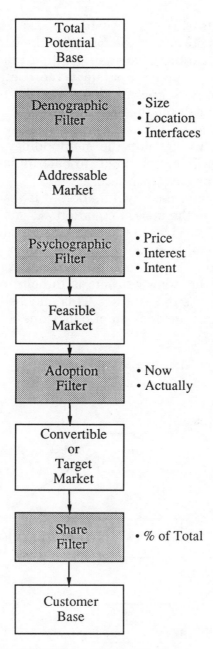

FIGURE 4.1 Market Breakout

is the totality of the customer base. The market share is that portion of the base that the company believes it can capture. We shall see that this number is dependent upon the strategy the company takes, the competitors present already in the market, and the cost of gaining the market share.

In this section, we develop the methodology to support this process, allowing the entrepreneur to determine the target market and, in turn, the customer base.

To fully understand the target market, it is essential to understand the players in the market equation. At one end is the supplier of goods and services to the company developing the product. Thus, if the company is making a modem device, it has a supplier in the company who supplies LSI (large-scale integration) circuits. At the other extreme is the end user, the person who will actually use the product. This may be a secretary who uses the device for transmission of data from her desk. Between

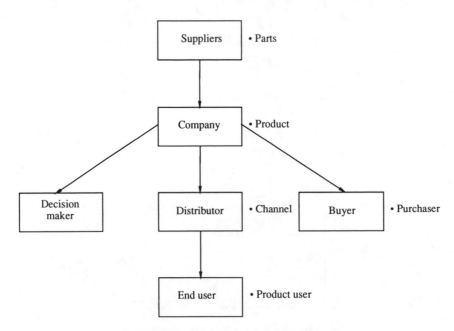

FIGURE 4.2 Target Market Chain

the supplier and the end user are several key players. Figure 4.2 depicts these players, from the supplier down to the end user. The company must deal with a distributor, who in turn deals with the buyer on behalf of the company. In addition, a company decision maker may or may not be the buyer of the product. Thus, the typical set of players are:

1. Supplier: The provider of the primary inputs to the product. These inputs are not necessarily essential to the product, and the company may have alternative sources of such inputs. As indicated, these products could be telecommunications services, computer chips, or cabinets. However, the company must recognize that its competitive strategy will depend on how the competition uses the supplier relationships and if the competition can obtain cost or price advantages.

2. Company: The company itself.

3. Distributor: One or several players whose role is that of the company's representative in the distribution process. The distributor may take the role of integrator of the company's product, salesperson for the company, or merely the physical distributor.

4. Decision Maker: The person or entity that decides on the product, has the responsibility and authority for signing the purchase order, and ensures that the product is used.

5. End User: The person who will actually use the product. This person will not necessarily be the decision maker, but may eventually have a significant role in influencing the decision maker.

This chain of individuals in the target market is essential to understanding the overall target market. In the development of any questionnaire and target market definition, the first step is the determination of this target market chain. That is, the target market definition must include not only the number of end users (who will determine the market size), but a description of the decision maker who will determine the effort associated with the sales effort. For example, consider an on-line database. The decision maker may be the company's information specialist, whereas the end user may be all of the marketing and engineering staff. In that case, 100 to 1,000 end users may be affected by one decision maker. This factor may drive the overall marketing strategy.

Consider the example of the modem company. The distributor may be the local telephone company business systems sales office. The buyer may be the procurement officer for the company, or the office automation executive. The decision maker, however, may be the chief financial officer of the company. In developing the target market, the entrepreneur must understand this chain so as to most effectively characterize the target market.

This chain may also be broken in a different fashion by repositioning or repricing the product. The classic case is Federal Express, a company that, by pricing the product properly, allowed the secretary to be the decision maker, while the secretary's manager was the actual end user. Federal Express changed the channel of decision makers and made for rapid expansion of their total market volume and sales.

The target market allows for the estimation of the total number of units that may be sold. The number of units is limited by the total end users and their unit consumption, as well as the impact of the decision maker on the consumption.

The definition of the target market will vary from commercial applications to consumer applications. In the next section, we investigate both applications as well as the techniques used to validate the target market.

Consumer Market

In a consumer application, the target market is defined in terms of the number of people who would buy the product. This group in turn is defined by its demographics and psychographics. Typically, one starts with the entire population on an annual basis, and then begins to delimit the numbers by the factors discussed. Let us begin the filter process with the most typical demographic factors, which are:

Age
Geographic location
Sex
Education
Occupation
Marital status
Age of children
Profession

A typical demographic profile could be: male, 25–40 years old, with income in excess of $50,000 per year, college educated, in a managerial position. With this profile it is then relatively easy to target that consumer; you have an understanding of his external characteristics.

The psychographics of the potential buyer are less quantifiable by external observations and other external characterizations. Psychographics describe the buyer's likes and dislikes, interests and activities. They are used for the eventual positioning of the product in the consumer's mind. In a demographic segment, it is possible to further segment the target market by combining demographics with psychographics.

A typical psychographic profile might read: The customer is an active, community-involved person, with an interest in outdoor sports. She also tends to be highly competitive and goal-oriented, and to think in non-traditional modes.

This description can be used to target the potential buyer through a direct mail campaign, through media advertising, and to establish the most effective distribution by comparing the demographics of the readership lists with the target market. Such comparisons of demographic factors can be used throughout the distribution chain.

As an example, if this target market characterization is for a new financial product offered by a large bank, then it suggests that the following actions be taken:

• Advertise in publications such as airline in-flight magazines, *Business Week, The Wall Street Journal,* and *Inc.*

- Provide a toll-free telephone number to sophisticated service representatives to transact the process.
- Use the American Express mailing list for a direct mail campaign.

The process used to determine the demographic and psychographic filters and the corresponding market elements have been developed significantly over the past decades. In the consumer case, the process is usually through direct or primary market research, which is done by a firm with the resources to perform the tests and analyze the results.

The types of market research vary widely, but the process is somewhat consistent. The product is presented to the consumer, who is asked to evaluate the product. The consumer is asked questions that provide demographic and psychograhic data as well as product-specific questions, such as purchase intent, benefits, needs, and price information. These questions will take a variety of forms.

The key question imbedded in all of the research is the intent to purchase. The demographic questions are supplemented with questions regarding travel, family closeness, and jobs. The researcher then collects the responses; the results are cross-tabulated along several lines. For example, the demographics may be tabulated with purchase intent (given as very high, high, moderate, low, no interest) and the age of the questionnaires. Table 4.1 depicts the result of a questionnaire on a new product that was presented to a sample cross-section of consumers. A total of 700 people were questioned; it was assumed that they were randomly chosen and represent a typical cross-section of the U.S. population. The table shows the results of a cross-tabulation (cross-tab) of the interest (Very High, High, Moderate, Low, and Not Interested) versus the age of the respondent.

By observing the survey results in Table 4.1, you can make several important observations. First, only 50 out of 700 interviewees said that they were very interested in the product. However, the market researcher will focus on those who indicate not only a very high interest, but also a high interest. Thus, 170 out

TABLE 4.1 Sample Cross-Tab (Number of Respondents)

Age Group	No.	Intent				
		VH	High	Mod	Low	NI
18–25	250	5	55	65	75	50
26–38	110	30	25	25	25	5
39–48	120	10	30	40	30	10
49–64	110	5	10	45	35	15
65 +	110	0	0	35	55	20
Total	700	50	120	210	220	100

of 700 appear to be available. Of those in that category, most are in the age groups 26–38 and 39–48. (This is true despite the large number in the 18–25 age group, since their percentage is lower.)

This group of 170 is the target market. It does not say that the target market, so defined, is the only market. What it does say is that the target market, so defined, is the most likely market.

The process of market research is quite extensive. Here are some of the ways the data discussed above are obtained:

- Focus groups, meetings, or large groups of randomly selected consumers.
- Mall intercepts of consumers in shopping malls and other areas.
- Mail questionnaires to a large group.
- Telephone interviews.
- Baseline group of standardized and projectable samples of average consumers. This is done by large firms who use a set group for testing. The major factors in such testing are the sample size of the group and its projectability. The larger the sample, the better the results, given that market research is an uncertain art. Sample sizes of 300–900 people are typical. Testing using these procedures helps to determine the demographic and psychographic factors. Later in this chapter we present a set of typical questionnaires containing detailed

questions that address all of these factors, in addition to those other factors that help to ascertain need and benefit.

Commercial Target Market

The same set of demographic and psychographic filters can be applied to the commercial market. However, the difference is that the consumer market usually starts with all customers, then filters down to more standard demographic and psychographic factors. In the commercial area, the starting point is not that broad. It usually does not start with all companies, but with some segment of industries that are addressed by the product. In addition, further customizing of the industry base is performed by direct potential customer contact. On the commercial side, there is a three-step market research effort.

Step 1. Preliminary possible customer calls to assess rough-guess responses. These allow for direct access to the customer and are typically directed by a process of open-ended questionnaires. Such questionnaires ask questions that may be used in a later stage to develop closed-end questionnaires to help sharpen the target market.

Step 2. Quantitative/qualitative market research through focus groups and telephone interviews. This step provides for more detailed questions of the potential customer base. It sharpens the focus and helps to determine the end user, the decision maker, and what factors are necessary to determine who they are and how many of them are in the total universe of samples.

Step 3. In-depth customer marketing calls and presentations of the product, which help refine the focus and the product, and assist in positioning the product as it is introduced into the market.

This process is best described by example. A large company, which had been a major manufacturer for many years, decided to get into the communications network service business. The service concept was conceived and brought to friendly customers for informal discussions. The response led to an understanding that the real product in a service business was not hardware, but the computer software and customer service that was required to provide ease of access and high availability.

This conclusion resulted in a redefinition of the service. The company hired a market research firm to contact a large number of companies to find out what type of industries, what functions in the companies, and how large a company would have interest in the service. That is, they explored the demographics of their consumer base. This was to be the target market.

In a parallel effort, the company sent a group of managers to deal with a broader base of potential customers in one-on-one marketing calls. A marketing call is not a sales call, but is more than a focus group session. It deals with the customer as a customer who would be a sales contact, and attempts to sell the service although there is as yet no service to sell. The result of this marketing call was the ability to put together a sales presentation for the marketing and sales staff.

Thus, for a commercial application, the demographics that result from the above process might be the following:

1. *Industry Segment.* What type of industries are appropriate? These may include the financial services industry, the transportation industry, and the manufacturing industry. We suggest that typical SIC classifications be used; this method will assist in processing data and in using on-line databases.

2. *Company Size.* Within the industry, the company's size in terms of its total revenue is often a key factor in determining whether it may be an appropriate candidate. Thus, the market researchers segment the questions to allow for interest and cross-tabs on revenue.

3. *Location.* The company may be national, international, regional, or even local. These factors are typically useful for

applications that include networking of various elements. In addition, the issue of location may have to be subdivided into areas by different locations. For multilocation companies, the decisions may be local, or they may be centralized at corporate headquarters. The answer to these types of questions will play a significant role in developing sales strategy and the distribution channel.

4. *Number of Employees.* The research on the company should also include the number of employees. As we discussed in evaluating businesses by high labor or capital content, we should also be able to evaluate our customer in a similar fashion. Thus, if we are proposing a product that improves productivity, we should know the number of employees as well as knowing their roles in the firm's day-to-day operations.

5. *Number of Plants.* Knowing the location of the companies is the first step in evaluating the need for coverage. We also must know the number of plants and their operations. As with the employee productivity factors, we should also understand our customer's capital plant productivity and ways the product may enhance that productivity.

6. *Functional Area in Company.* The type of companies should be studied in detail. Understand their organizational charts and the function of different elements of the organization. This understanding will assist you later when you examine needs and benefits.

In the opening example of this section, the target market was characterized as follows:

$500 million per year or more in annual sales

20 or more locations

5,000 or more employees

Computer, service, communications, and distribution industries.

Sales, customer service, and field service functions.

Using this information, we determined the size of the market in terms of end users and growth. This determination can be performed using many of the on-line database systems, such as the Dialog system. Feeding this type of information into those on-line systems will provide the researcher with details on the companies, their revenues, locations, and employees. In addition, such services as Dialog may even provide the researcher with preformatted labels to be used in more detailed customer contact.

One of the more classic mistakes in estimating the market is evidenced in the case of Satellite Business Systems, originally a joint venture between IBM, Aetna, and COMSAT. In the early days of the business (1974), the industry witnessed dramatic projections of the growth of data communications, with over 50 percent of all communications being of the data type by 1985. In 1985, however, the actual figure was 4 percent. The result was a system that did not foresee the IBM-PC, the expansion of data speeds on twisted pair, or the breakup of AT&T. The system was designed as a network optimized for bypassing the old AT&T network using an all-data mode and for the most part neglecting voice transmission (96 percent of the business). To date this error has cost almost $1 billion. This market was driven by a dream rather than the harsh realities that, for the most part, people do not change large investments quickly.

Let's examine the second part of the commercial market characterization—what we call the psychographics. This process involves describing the company's type of "personality." The company's personality may be characterized by the way it approaches its computer systems, its personnel policy, or by the general character of its executive decision process. The latter may be the key to understanding the customer and his needs, and in turn making the sale. For example, the decision maker and buyer in a company may not be the end users. In fact, there may be three people, or three committees. These factors are psychographic characterizations that are important qualifiers.

Let's look at an example. In a new communications service business, the data was to enter the company through its MIS (management information systems) center. The center was an

IBM "shop," with the MIS director thoroughly trained by IBM. The new system required a new communications front end that was not an IBM product, but was IBM-compatible. The decision maker was the group executive, the buyer was the vice president of sales, and the end user was the sales force. The MIS director was the stumbling block. The system did not go in. This was a psychographic factor that further delimited the market.

As we have seen, the target market is described in both psychographic and demographic terms. It can be then sized using these terms against the universe of all companies. This process then yields the target market size.

Another approach in determining market size for the overall business is to start with the major drivers of the business, then to segment down from there to the subgroups that would represent the target market. Let us take as an example a company that wants to make a modem replacement for medium-speed data communications. The product requires that both the customer as well as the phone company obtain the hardware to operate the system. The overall driver for this market is the set of all companies and users that have modems at this time. In addition, the growth of the market can be measured against the growth of the modem market.

This second approach to market size estimates is described in the following manner:

1. Start with the total market driver, such as the known modem market. This information, called the gross or total potential market, may be determined from the open market research literature.

2. Determine the addressable market—that fraction of the gross market that would have the product available based upon certain demographic factors. The availability would be limited by such factors as phone company or circuit availability. Note that the approach taken here is identical to that taken in the company-driven approach that we have developed.

3. From the addressable market, determine the feasible market—the fraction of the addressable market that would

first find the service appropriate based upon the set of psychographic factors. Again, this process requires that we develop the customer's profile from the research efforts that we have described.

4. Use the feasible market and the adoption curve shown in Figure 4.3 to determine the convertible, or target, market. The curve is broken into five major segments:

    Innovators: 2.5% of the total

    Early adoptors: 13.5%

    Early majority: 34%

    Late majority: 34%

    Laggards: 16%

    The horizontal axis can be plotted in time, and the rate of adoption developed. In a five-year adoption curve, the median point is at 2.5 years; the other points follow directly. Figure 4.3 depicts the adoption curve for the typical market. In (a), the curve is depicted as a function of time. The area under the curve from one period to another depicts the percentage of users who will adopt the product in that interval. Thus, the interval of maximum adoption rate is in the center of the curve. Part (b) shows the cumulative of the curve in (a), depicting the effect over time to total adoption. Using the equation for this curve as depicted in Urban and Hauser, *Design and Marketing of New Products*, the details of the adoption rate and adoption cycle time can be included in the development of the target market.

5. Using the target market, a market share number determines the actual size of the market. This number is often subjective, based upon the business's goals as an estimate of the impact of the potential competition.

The result of applying this approach to determining the market size is that we now have a dynamic market profile that includes a generally verifiable and measurable profile of users. This profile will be useful in the due diligence process as well as in the operations of the business. It allows the entrepreneur to

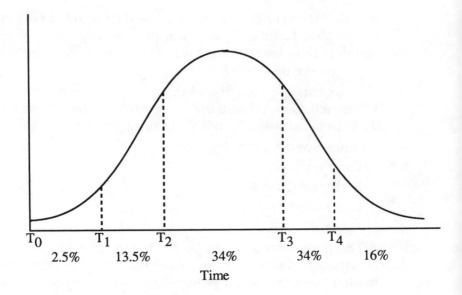

(a) Adoption Rate Curve

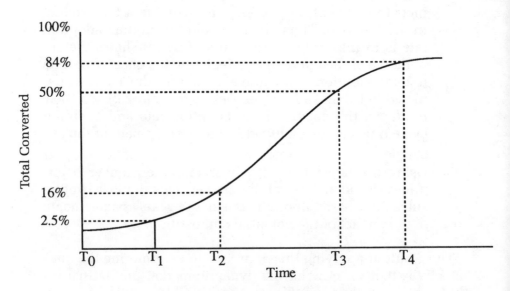

(b) Cumulative Adoption Rate

FIGURE 4.3   Adoption Rate Theory

continually cross-validate his or her assumptions about the target market, how effectively the market is evolving, and the business's market share.

Example

Consider a modem company that will develop a high-speed (9.6–64 Kbps) bypass device (one that allows for service without the support of the local telephone company). This device will be used by companies who have IBM-type computer systems and many data entry devices—for example, companies such as Federal Express, Purolator, Emery, and United Parcel Service that dominate the overnight delivery industry. The end user is the entry clerk, and the decision maker is the MIS director. The device will replace the existing dedicated high-speed data lines; it will significantly reduce costs for the system. Thus, the decision makers are well known, and the total market is the set of all data communications users. Then, using the above logic, we obtain:

Total Market

This is the base of all modems in the United States. This total number of modems may be determined from the databases described in Chapter 2.

Addressable

The appropriate set is determined by the need for the data rates specified, or whether the price is appropriate. The appropriate percentage is determined from the available base by asking such questions as:

Do you need 56Kbps or greater?

Do you use your data circuits 25 percent of the time or less?

Do you have an IBM-compatible system?

Feasible

This is the fraction of the addressable market that would be interested in using the terminals. They would be determined by asking questions such as:

Would you buy the terminal now?

Would you change-out your old terminal?

Would you change terminal manufacturers?

Would you save money with this service?

If the answers are positive, then we have the penetratable market. These are the potential customers that have a need, a clear benefit, and a willingness to consider the product.

Target

In this business example we assume a five-year adoption curve following typical market characteristics from past modem experience.

Market Size

In this example we further assume a 20 percent market share based upon our knowledge of our four major competitors. Based on that knowledge, we believe that such a share is achievable.

The total market used for sales projections is then a product of these segments. Let M represent the market size in units. Then let:

T represent the total market driver

PAD represent the fraction addressable

PAF represent the fraction addressable of those feasible

PP represent the fraction convertible of those addressable

S represent the fraction obtainable based upon share

TAR the target market size

Then we have:

$$M = T*PAD*PAF*PP*S$$

and

$$TAR = T*PAD*PAF*PP$$

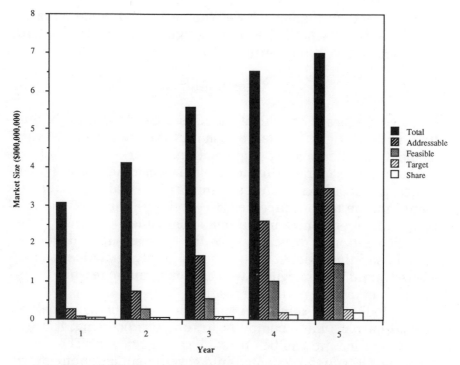

FIGURE 4.4 Market Size Development in the Modem Market. This figure depicts the dynamic nature of the five elements of the market and how they develop over the product's lifetime.

For example, Figure 4.4 depicts the market numbers for the described modem business. Notice that in Year 5 we have a total market of 7 million units. However, the target market is only 200,000 units; a 50 percent share yields only 100,000 units. The key marketing question then becomes, "How, if at all, can we change the percentages that delimit the target market size?"

The major problem that many new business developers have is that they fail to understand the market delimiters that we have just developed. Market research done by industry watchers rather than professional market researchers often fails to predict these factors. A classic example is the multi-tenant unit communications business, which tried to sell integrated communications services to large building owners. Industry watchers' failure to understand these factors resulted in a target market 100 times the actual number. Those who performed much more detailed market research determined significant factors showing that the business did not truly exist.

Segmentation

We have discussed the target market's characterization in multiple terms. A less detailed division of the market into natural elements is called market segmentation. A market's segments are the naturally separate divisions of the customer base. For instance, in our service business example discussed above, the segments are the large companies ($4 + billion), the medium companies ($1–4 billion), and the small companies.

Segmentation is driven by how the company intends to market and sell the product, not by some purely analytic breakout. There should be strategic as well as demographic reasons to segment a market in a particular fashion.

Let's look at an example. A small computer company makes a special-purpose microcomputer for image processing. It uses a LISP compiler and can be operated as an AI device. The market for this unit is first segmented into government and non-government areas. The non-government area is divided into direct sales and OEM sales. Thus, the market has three segments, each selected as a result of the way the company wants to strategically market the product as well as how the market is divided quantitatively.

NEEDS, USES, AND BENEFITS

The main issues associated with selling a product are the reasons the end user has a need for the product, the product's use, and its benefits. These factors all lead to positioning and pricing the product, and in turn creating in the customer's mind an essential need to obtain the product being offered.

In his book, *Our Crowd*, Steven Birmingham says that the true salesman is one "who sells something that they don't have to someone who doesn't need it." The reference is to the investment bankers who sold parts of companies, such as railroads, to wealthy individuals. They didn't own the railroads nor did the buyer of the stock want a railroad. Yet the bankers received 5 percent of all their placements, and this 5 percent deal built the empires of investment banking. Yet the truth of this statement is that what the stock buyers wanted was further wealth; the possibility of added wealth is the actual product the bankers sold. From this truth come the needs, uses, and benefits.

We briefly discussed the concepts of needs, benefits, and uses in Chapter 3. The same concepts hold here. They are:

Needs: The internal requirements of a customer to have and use the product.

Benefits: The advantages that accrue from the product.

Uses: Those things that an end user does with the product to elicit the benefits.

The business and product concept are initiated as a result of the entrepreneur's understanding of the product's possible uses. This knowledge may come from exposure to the business or personal activities of the end user. For example, video games came about from observing that students at MIT were spending great amounts of time playing computer games on the large mainframe computer. It was understood that there could be no consumer product if the delivery mechanism was a large-scale computer such as the one at the Institute. Thus, the need for this form of entertainment was recognized. The benefits were few in view of the delivery mechanism. This problem was overcome by the low-cost Intel 6502 microprocessor chip that permitted the game to be put into what became the Atari 2600, a new distribution channel for the games.

The method of validating the three elements of need, benefit, and use are the same as those of the other market elements. Testing with end users in focus groups is essential. Listening to what the customer wants and interpreting those wants leads to a better chance of survival and growth. Let's examine the questions in market research efforts in a consumer area and in a commercial area. The questions test for the elements of need, benefit, and use.

Market Research Questionnaire: Commercial

The typical market research questionnaire for commercial applications is shown in Table 4.2. This first questionnaire is called open-ended because it asks questions in an open-ended fashion, allowing the interviewee to provide the answer in whatever form is appropriate. This type of questionnaire allows for investigations of new products during the early stages of development in a fashion that addresses many issues that may not otherwise occur to the researcher.

Five major issues must be addressed by the market researcher when developing such a set of questionnaires. These are:

- What are the objectives of the research? For example, in this questionnaire, the researchers are investigating the feasibility of the product concept and how best to develop follow-up research to more clearly determine the target market. This questionnaire is not appropriate for the final market targeting.
- What are the key issues? Are the issues those of functionality of the device, price versus performance of the service, or who best to sell the service to?
- What is the best way to structure the questions? For example, do you ask about price at the beginning of the questionnaire, then ask about needs and benefits, or do you reverse the order? In addition, where do you describe the potential product?
- How is the questionnaire to be administered? This is a key issue. The questionnaire discussed in this section is administered in a focus group, where significant interaction can occur. Other questionnaires can be administered by phone or by mail.
- How are the results to be processed? If the results are to be summarized in a rewritten format, then the questionnaire can be very free flowing. If, on the other hand, the results are

TABLE 4.2 Questionnaire: Commercial

BACKGROUND INFORMATION

1. Usage Information

   Data

   What are the product's uses?
   What are the to/from locations?
   What are the data speeds and how are they related to total use?
   How much use is there in min/month/speed?
   What are the interface requirements?
   What carriers are used?
   What is the expected annual growth rate?
   What type of data equipment is used?

   Voice

   What is the monthly usage in minutes?
   What is the monthly cost?
   How many trunks are there?
   What are the number of employees?
   What are the to/from locations?
   What is the expected annual growth rate?

2. Computer Systems

   Types
   Locations
   Database size
   Expected annual growth rate
   Packet communications use
   How much use per month?
   What is it used for?
   Number of PCs per location
   Data speed on terminals
   Data terminal usage per month

3. Competition

   Which long distance companies do they use?
   What is the amount of traffic and the expense?
   Why was it chosen?
   Who chose it?
   How long did it take them to decide?
   What was the deciding factor?

to be tabulated, then the questionnaires must be much more specific. In the questionnaire discussed in this section, the results are to be left in a free format for the later development of a more detailed closed-end format.

Example

A company wants to offer a new data bypass solution via a fiber optic cable system around New York City. The company has selected a set of 150 companies where they will ask questions about data as well as voice usage (see Table 4.2). It is structured along four areas: data use, voice use, computer use, and the competition. The questionnaire results will be used to obtain the market size, its growth, and pricing information as we have outlined in the previous sections.

Let us consider this questionnaire in some detail. First, the questionnaire is called an open-ended questionnaire. This is the most difficult type to analyze. All of the questions are open-ended; the interviewee may give any answer that comes to mind. Thus, there is no limited set of responses. The questionnaire results may be reduced to statistical data, but it will require considerable effort.

The questionnaire, implemented through direct customer contact, is given to a market researcher who sets up an appointment with the potential customer and then proceeds to ask questions and record answers in a free-flowing fashion. The market researcher can then assess the results. He or she may then use these results to fashion a closed-ended questionnaire for a more detailed follow-up.

The plan at this point must be able to state carefully the three elements and to validate them through research efforts. It may be possible for a business that is repositioning an existing product to use prior research results in this area.

Let's return to the questionnaire in Table 4.2. Its objective is to help the researcher understand the target market in some detail, but it does not assume in advance the market segmentation factors. Thus, the questionnaire is divided into five sections. The first provides information on the interviewees, which will be useful for follow-up contact. The other sections are as follows.

Usage

This section allows for a free-flowing dialogue on both data and voice usage. Note that the questionnaire starts with data usage, since that is the driver of the business. It asks about local and long distance (intrastate and interstate) usage.

Internal Switch Capabilities

This section further qualifies the potential customer on his system's advanced switching capabilities. In the actual administration of this questionnaire, it was found that many of the questions could not be answered by the interviewee, which indicated that the product assumed a sophistication that exceeded the customer's capabilities. This was a key observation that results from such an open-ended questionnaire.

Computer Systems

Since the service is for computer users, further research may require segmentation on the type or model. This factor first surfaces in the computer systems section.

Competition

The final section attempts to assess the customer's viewpoint on what competitors could provide the service.

Market Research Questionnaire: Consumer

We can now consider a second questionnaire example; in this case it is a closed-ended type. This questionnaire was developed to address the needs of a specific market, and to help in further refining the product's target market. As does the commercial questionnaire, it addresses the five key questions:

1. What are the goals? The goals of this research will be much more quantitative. The results will be used to target the market, position the product, and determine the price. The results will also help develop the overall promotional strategy for the business.

2. What are the key issues? The major issues are, who is the customer and who is the customer's customer? The qualifications here are determined by the demographics of the ultimate end user of the product.

3. How should we structure the questions? The questions should be as unambiguous as possible, and should be administered by the simplest means possible. The answers should be all multiple choice or fill-in of specific data.

4. How is it to be administered? The choice of administration is based on cost and size of the sample. In this case a telephone approach was used.

5. How are the results to be processed and evaluated? The results will be the basis of market estimates, so it is essential that they be as accurate as possible and contain little anecdotal material.

Example

Let us now consider the example of the business that administered this questionnaire. In this questionnaire, shown in Table 4.3, we are using a closed-ended approach (i.e., all the questions are multiple choice). This questionnaire is directly reduced to a statistical analysis of the market and its sizing. It is important to remember, however, that this questionnaire is a result of the open-ended approach wherein the sets of choices have been carefully selected. If this were not the case, then the answers may not be appropriate.

The company being investigated in this questionnaire is considering developing a bed-and-breakfast reservation service. Its end users are B&B operators, but the firm must also understand the nature of the decision makers: consumers. Therefore, many of the questions address the demographics of the end user as well as of the consumer. This questionnaire was administered through the mail using a set of mailing lists for the B&B industry. These lists were obtained through books listing these locations. There were 750 questionnaires mailed and the response was 10 percent, or 76—a very high response rate for the B&B business.

TABLE 4.3 Questionnaire: Consumer

QUESTIONNAIRE
BED AND BREAKFAST INTERNATIONAL INC.

Instructions: This questionnaire will be used to develop a new service business concept. We at BBI would appreciate your assistance. You do NOT have to identify yourself. Please answer all the questions as best you can; your answers will help many in the B&B industry. Thank you for your help.

PART I: Please indicate the location of your B&B, and provide us with some vital statistics.

1.1 State:

1.2 Zip code:

1.3 Number of rooms:

1.4 Average rate per room per night:

1.5 Average occupancy rate (%):

1.6 Occupancy rate by season:

    1.6.1 Summer:
    1.6.2 Fall:
    1.6.3 Winter:
    1.6.4 Spring:

1.7 Average number of nights per stay:

1.8 Method of payment (%):

    1.8.1 Cash:
    1.8.2 MasterCard:
    1.8.3 Visa:
    1.8.4 American Express:
    1.8.5 Other:

1.9 Method of reservation (%):

    1.9.1 Letter:
    1.9.2 Phone:
    1.9.3 Reservation Service:
    1.9.4 Other:

1.10 Customers' method of finding B&B (%):

    1.10.1 Advertising:
    1.10.2 Personal referral:
    1.10.3 B&B guide book:
    1.10.4 Referral service:
    1.10.5 State or local chamber of commerce:
    1.10.6 Drop-ins:
    1.10.7 Other:

TABLE 4.3 Questionnaire: Consumer (continued)

1.11 Type of customer:

  1.11.1 Age (enter % in each group):

    1.11.1.1 20–30:
    1.11.1.2 30–40:
    1.11.1.3 40–50:
    1.11.1.4 50–60:
    1.11.1.5 Over 60:

  1.11.2 Type of profession (enter % in each group):

    1.11.2.1 Professional:
    1.11.2.2 Self-employed:
    1.11.2.3 Retired:
    1.11.2.4 Managerial:
    1.11.2.5 Other:

  1.11.3 Estimated level of income (enter % in each group):

    1.11.3.1 Under $30,000:
    1.11.3.2 $30,000 to $50,000:
    1.11.3.3 $50,000 to $100,000:
    1.11.3.4 Over $100,000:

  1.11.4 Marital status (enter % in each group):

    1.11.4.1 Married, no children:
    1.11.4.2 Unmarried:
    1.11.4.3 Married, one or two children:
    1.11.4.4 Married, more than two children:

  1.11.5 Employment status (enter % of those married):

    1.11.5.1 One employed:
    1.11.5.2 Both employed:

1.12 Returns (enter % of customers who are returns):

1.13 Growth (enter your growth rate per year):

1.14 What year did you begin business?

1.15 How long has the present management been in operation?

PART II: Please answer all of these questions based on your personal opinion. Select one of five listed answers. These answers will be used to determine how best to develop a service to meet your needs.

2.1 If a national reservation service was developed, would you be interested in joining it?

[ ] Extremely interested
[ ] Very interested
[ ] Interested
[ ] Not interested

TABLE 4.3 Questionnaire: Consumer (continued)

2.2 If the service had a computer terminal as part of its operations, would you like to use it?

[ ] Extremely interested
[ ] Very interested
[ ] Interested
[ ] Not interested

2.3 Please rank the reasons why you would use a reservation service (1 is the most important):

[ ] Increase occupancy
[ ] Obtain better clientele
[ ] Guarantee rooms
[ ] Pre-screen
[ ] Raise rates
[ ] Automate accounting
[ ] Guarantee payments
[ ] Provide better control over long-term occupancy

2.4 If the reservation service had a rating service accompanying it, would you be interested?

[ ] Extremely interested
[ ] Very interested
[ ] Interested
[ ] Not interested

PART III: If you are interested in receiving a summary of the results, please include your name and address:

Name:

B&B name:

Address:

City/State/Zip:

Phone:

Please include any additional comments:

A selected set of 252 respondents were telephoned on a random basis with a 50 percent response rate to a phone interview. Thus, the total response was 126. This figure was sufficient to obtain a sampling of the total base of 10,000 B&B establishments.

The questionnaire in Table 4.3 has three parts. The first part sets out to identify the B&B user as well as the revenue potential from the typical B&B. In addition, it addresses the needs for such a service as the one proposed. Part II of the questionnaire gets more deeply into these needs and ranks them. The most important question is 2.1, which determines customer interest. All the cross-tabs can be done on this question, allowing for a determination of the target market as well as the need and benefits.

Statistical Validity

The typical market researcher will not only focus on the questions, but will also look more closely at the sample size and quantify the validity of the answers. That is, using a base of 126 sampled out of 10,000, the researcher will give limits as to what level of reliability will be attached to the answers, given the sample size. That level of detail is adequately covered in other texts, so is not a part of this book. The reader is cautioned, however, to review that literature in detail, before relying too heavily on the quantitative results.

POSITIONING

Positioning, a term discussed at length in marketing texts, is the concept of stating how the company wants the purchaser to view both the company and the product. It will become a pervasive concept in the promotional campaign of the company.

A typical positioning statement for a communications service company might read as follows:

The most advanced and reliable high-speed portable communications network service, providing national service at competitive prices.

Let us analyze this positioning statement.

1. The company is providing a communications network service. This means that there is more than just an end-to-end transmission of data—it is a service company providing communications.

2. The communications type is limited to high-speed data communications. The system addresses the portable communications user marketplace, so the need addressed is that of portability of high-speed data channels. In contrast to the first observation, which is expansive, this is a limiting factor for the business.

3. The company wants to make itself unique by stating it is the most advanced and reliable. This may mean that the firm intends to position itself against the competition on the basis of these features.

4. The business is national. This is a description of the scope and the total market that is potentially served. It may delimit the business to those companies that want international service. However, that need may not be very high.

5. The price is called competitive. The business will not try to undercut the prices of the competition; in other words, to provide the other features, the company has not found a way to reduce the prices and compete on price. It also says that the alternatives to this service, such as telephone lines, will not be cheaper, but may be comparable.

From this positioning statement, these five observations say a great deal about the business. You can see that it is important that the business plan contain the positioning statement. It says how you view your business in the context of the market and the competition.

PRICING

Product pricing can be based upon one factor or a combination of three factors: competition, cost, or use.

1. *Competitive Pricing.* In this case, a set of competitors may be in the market. The business may look at competitors' prices and their offerings, then price the product at a point

that balances value with price. In markets of this type, pricing may rapidly degenerate into a commodity pricing war. For example, in the long-distance communications area, a fiber optic company started in a region that had limited high-speed data facilities and was rapidly growing. At first the firm could price at the going rate of the telephone company, less a suitable discount. As other competitors came into the market because of this potential for high profits, the result was commodity pricing. The product could not be distinguished from one maker to another.

One of the other factors a new company must consider before entering a market and using competitive pricing is that the buyer expects two discounts. The first discount is based upon the buyer's need to change to your service, or even to buy it if a safer and more routine alternative exists. This may be a 10 percent reduction from the price of the existing alternative service. This is called the switching discount factor. The second discount factor is the risk factor cost on a buyer if he buys your product and you do not survive. This may have a greater cost discount factor of 12 percent. Thus, you may have to price your product 22 percent or more below the going rate if you cannot distinguish your product from the rest of the pack.

2. *Cost Pricing.* This approach is based upon your desire to maintain a margin on your product above cost. Hardware manufacturers try to follow this trend, although it can be quite difficult to do, particularly at the early stages where costs are high due to low volume. You may be forced to price to market (e.g., what the customer is willing to pay), to the competition, or to the displacement level (e.g., what it costs to displace the present provider of the product).

3. *Use Pricing.* This pricing scheme is most favored by service companies who can position the service with regard to benefits, and in turn can tell the customer how much they are saving by using the service. The service must avoid the commodity position for this plan to work effec-

tively. As with the other market factors, the pricing issue must be tested with the purchasers.

The other dimension of pricing is the price itself. This is called the pricing structure, and includes the way the customer pays. Consider the following example. A communications service company will provide a portable data communications service that will help the end user communicate from any location using an RF modem. There are several ways to get $100 per month per user on average, which is the use pricing level. These schemes are:

1. *Fixed Price.* In this case, the end user is charged $100 per month. The advantage: billing is simple and the user knows the charge. The disadvantage is that not all users use the same amount of data. Some may have incentives to hog or jam the network. Under this scheme they may be encouraged to do so. Some may decide to resell excess capacity.

2. *Fully Variable Pricing.* In this case the user pays for every system variable: the number of messages, the geographical coverage, the priority level, the time-of-day usage, and the size of the network interconnect.

3. *Discount Pricing.* Large users may need to discount the price. This scheme works with hardware as well as service businesses. The discount price is based upon the customer's commitment to purchase large volumes, over long periods of time, or on some exclusive basis.

4. *OEM (Original Equipment Manufacturer) Pricing.* This plan works where there is a middle man who adds value to your product. OEM pricing is similar to discount pricing, but has lower distribution costs. For example, the company can sell its computer terminal at one price directly to an end user, and at a lower price to an OEM company who may add software to the machine and sell it with some value-added service. The reason for the two

price levels is that the OEM reseller provides for their own distribution to the end user, thus saving the company added expenses.

Thus, pricing has two dimensions: type and structure. One can imagine fully variable use pricing as well as fixed cost pricing. The pricing schemes also may vary by business segment. The pricing will be important as we develop the revenue model. The price along with the market segments and size determine the overall revenue potential for the business.

DISTRIBUTION

One of the most difficult issues for a start-up company is distribution, or how the product will reach the end user. The simplest distribution is direct sales, where the company has its own sales force that makes door-to-door sales to the end user. This system requires that the company develop the sales force and target the buyers, decision makers, and end users in the target companies—often a very expensive process. Alternative distribution channels are then sought.

Distribution encompasses the entire process of getting the product from the factory to the end user. It is comprised of the following elements:

- Marketing: Determining the need and targeting the customer.
- Sales: Presenting the product and the price, and obtaining closure.
- Promotion: Raising awareness of the product and its benefits.
- Fulfillment: Delivering the product and following through with the sale.

Multiple distribution alternatives present themselves to the entrepreneur. These alternatives depend upon the type and size of the market as well as the interplay between the three key players: the end user, the buyer, and the decision maker. Take the simple example of two extremes—a commercial product and a consumer product. In the first case, the company has a new communications processor that can be used by telephone companies. Five of these companies represent 90 percent of the market. In each, there is a single point of contact for new network equipment. Thus, it is possible to deal with five people as the total set of decision makers. In this case, a direct sales effort is the only alternative.

In the consumer case, the company has made a new computer terminal for the consumer to access many videotex databases and to bank at home. The estimated market is two million terminals in the first three years. Clearly, direct sales are not feasible. Furthermore, the market is delimited by two factors: the target market of those interested, and those interested who can have access. The market recognizes the service and not the product (the terminal). Thus, distribution could occur through retail stores, in conjunction with database suppliers, or even by direct mail. In this case there are several alternatives, each with associated costs of distribution. (Details on distribution channel alternatives are presented in the works of Louis Stern and Edward Nash.)

The Distribution Channel

To understand the distribution issue, we must first understand the nature of the distribution or marketing channels. The distribution channel describes the process of converting basic raw materials into the product that is consumed by the end user. The distribution channel is composed of the following basic elements:

1. *Supplier.* This is the entity that provides the raw product to the channel. It may be a maker of silicon, LSI circuits, modems, or whatever product or service the company is providing in the chain.
2. *Packager.* This element is the position of the company in the business plan. It packages and adds value to the sup-

plier's raw product, views suppliers as commodity providers, and is the key value-added element.

3. *Distributor.* This element distributes the product to the channel end users. In some cases the company may want to be its own distributor; in other cases there may be multiple layers of distribution. For example, in the computer industry, a company that makes filaments for console lights will sell them to a computer company through a distributor. In that case, the end user is the computer company. The computer company may have its own sales force, so the company is its own distributor.

4. *End User.* This element is the person or entity who will use the product.

5. *Decision Maker.* This is the person or entity that makes a decision to purchase, and may also be the entity through which the product flows to the end user.

Figure 4.5 depicts the distribution channel alternatives that apply to a generic example. Note that the figure contains all of the elements and interrelations just described.

Let's take a closer look at the various alternatives depicted in the distribution channels of Figure 4.5. (Combinations of the strategies outlined below can be very effective, too.)

1. *Direct Sales.* A sales force that has direct contact with the decision maker, the end user, and the buyer. Companies such as IBM have extensive and accomplished direct sales forces.

2. *OEM Sales.* In this case the product is sold directly to a firm that incorporates it into its own product, then resells it.

3. *Distributor Sales.* A distributor buys the product and resells it to a retailer or other sales force.

4. *Agent.* A third party takes on the sales of the product, possibly on a direct sales business. As an example, Motorola has a large direct sales force whose members act as agents

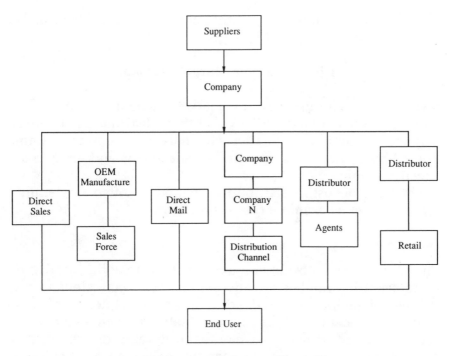

FIGURE 4.5 Distribution Channels

for radio common carriers (RCCs) to bring customers to their service if RCC purchases Motorola's hardware.

5. *Retail*. Direct selling to the retailer, such as Sears Roebuck. Atari was successful in using this approach to gain a breadth of distribution. Direct selling avoids the problem of having to deal with the distributor middlemen.

6. *Direct Mail*. In this approach the company targets its customer via a direct mail campaign. This plan works very effectively if product recognition is high and if the product is easily understood. For example, American Express is a master at direct mail sales.

7. *End User Agents*. This method assumes that the end user will use a product that works in conjunction with another company's product. Each company tries to bundle its product with that sale. Software companies use this tech-

nique in conjunction with computer companies to make sales.

Distribution by Market Segment

Distribution may also vary by market segment. In a business with three segments, it is likely that three distribution channels may exist. The choice of such channels is determined by the firm's ability to reach the market effectively and in a cost-effective manner.

The issue of cost in distribution channels is often a determining factor. Let us examine cost alternatives.

Direct Sales

The direct sales costs depend upon three factors: the number of customers, the number of calls per customer per sale, and the number of people required per call. For example, a software company needs a salesperson and a sales software engineer to call on a client. It takes six months to develop the client; this process may require six calls, each two days long. Each call day requires three days of preparation, resulting in 30 days of effort at the rate of $200 per day for a total of $50,000 per year. A fully loaded cost is $500 per day. Thus the cost of a sale is $15,000. If the product is priced at $100,000, then the sale is productive. Another approach is to pay a 15 percent commission on the sale. This factor is deceptive, however, since it does not include the loaded technical support. As we have mentioned before, sales costs are determined by the three factors of market, productivity, and salary.

Direct Mail

Direct mail is appropriate for reaching a large cross-section of targeted consumers. It works in both the consumer and commercial market. Consider an example. A software company has developed a tool to allow the educated investor to evaluate optimal option pricing schemes and to select options from a large portfolio. The software is composed of an artificial intelligence kernel that makes it easy to use and provides real-time optimal selection of a stock option portfolio. The target market for this product is the upscale, financially active individual investor who has a personal computer. At the time of the plan development, eight million personal computers were in use; of those, 1.5 million were in homes or used for personal use. Of these 1.5 million, 10 percent, or 150,000, were sophisticated investors who had interest in the product.

The product was priced at $995.00, based upon market research. The company approached American Express for access to its mailing list program; the quote per direct mail package was $2.30. The buy ratio—that is, the percent of direct mail pieces returning for purchase—was estimated at 2 percent.

The company direct-mailed 200,000 packages; the return rate was 2.5 percent. Thus, the firm garnered revenue of $5 million from the mailing. The cost of the mailing was $500,000, including preparation. The sales cost was 10 percent, which is quite low for typical direct mail operations. If the company had sold the product at $495 and had only a 1 percent return, then the revenue would be $1 million and the sales cost would have been $500,000, or 50 percent. This extreme case represents the sensitivity of direct mail to overall costs of sales.

OEM Sales

In OEM sales, a company contracts to incorporate its product in another company's product, then agrees to a price per unit sold to the end user. The cost of sales in this case is the cost of selling the OEM company in integrating your product. It is similar to a direct sales approach, but the price at which you sell the product is much lower, and the sale terms can be less demanding in light of warranties and guarantees than a direct end user sale that may be controlled by the Uniform Commercial Code (UCC).

As an example, take a software company that makes a project management control system software product that can be put into a workstation product. The workstation manufacturer wants to add to its CAD/CAM ability by providing an integrated applications package. The software company then has the option of selling the packages one at a time, or licensing the package to the hardware company. The difference is that a sale books the total revenue to the software company's books, whereas the license books the license fee only. It will not change the profit, only the type of revenue.

Retail

In the retail distribution channel, a company has a product that it wants to sell in the retail market. Take the example of the electronic game industry. In this case, the end user is the consumer in the 9–15 age bracket. The possible store chain is Sears Roebuck. The company approaches the Sears buyers in Chicago and tries to convince them to carry their product. Sears may try to persuade the firm to private-label the product for in-store use, or otherwise try to gain some exclusivity. They may also quote a price level for different volumes of sale and include a returns policy for the unsold product. The company may be able to sell the game to Sears at $120 per unit, which Sears then marks up to $295 for in-store sales. Sears may then quote a net of 60 days, saying that inventory held longer than 180 days is acceptable for full return at purchase price.

The cost of retail selling is that of targeting the retailers and of closing the sale. There is also the after-sale costs of keeping the retailer happy if the product is not meeting expectations, or of negotiating a better deal if it is doing well.

Some costs are also hidden. Remember that revenue is booked to the company once the retailer takes custody of the product. This action may occur when the product leaves the shipping dock at the factory. However, the company must have reserves against returns. Let us see how this provision may backfire. In the case of Atari, the company shipped $2 billion of products in 1982. The company did not perform shelf counts, a typical step in the retail business. A shelf count is done by an independent company to determine how the product is moving in retail stores. If the product is not moving, then the reserve account—which is an expense—is increased. In November 1982, the electronic games business softened. Shelf count would have given

Atari an early warning signal. Because no shelf count had been performed, Atari unexpectedly saw a return of 25 percent of store inventory in mid-December, resulting in a $500 million-dollar expense hit. Combined with lowered operating margins due to increased development costs, Atari suffered a $350 million loss for the fourth quarter.

Agents

Agent channels use third parties to sell your product to end users. The agents may be distributors for several companies who go door to door selling a list from companies they have been dealing with for many years. An agent may also be a company that has access to your customer base, or some other relationship to the customer that gives them access.

An example: Motorola, which has a large distributed direct sales organization in its communications business for mobile products. It will act as an agent for carriers to sell the product. An agent agreement typically results in a fee for sale, which may be anywhere from 15 percent to 45 percent. This amount is agreed to by the two companies. Unlike the distributor, the agent does not take title to the goods; it remains with the company until the goods are sold to the end user.

Distributor

A distributor takes the product and its title. When the company sells the product to a distributor, the sale can be booked, unlike sales via an agent. However, the distributor may also have a returns policy, as may the retailer. The same factors apply as do those of the retailer except that the price will be lower than retail prices.

End User Agents

End user agents are a special type of distributor/agent. For example, a large bank has developed a home banking package. The product requires computer terminals to operate the package in the home, but the bank does not want to sell the terminals. It then strikes a deal with a terminal manufacturer to send out direct mail pieces in its promotional campaign, advertising both the terminal and the service. The bank will then get 5 percent of the selling price on all terminals sold through this means. The bank will never take title, but also will not represent itself as selling the terminal. This is more than co-op advertising but less than an agent status.

Table 4.4 summarizes the advantages and disadvantages of each of these approaches, and Table 4.5 depicts the costs of the scheme and the possible margins. Table 4.5 lists the cost drivers for the sales expense for each of the channel alternatives. We shall be using this information in detail in the next chapter. In addition, the table outlines the typical margin on sales associated with each type of channel. This table could be prepared for any business and may provide a basis for deciding on the most desired type of distribution channel.

In all distribution channels, each player has a role. Let's consider generic examples using the structures that we have developed.

Example: Electronic Home Shopping

A company wants to develop a home electronic "shopping mall" that provides a wide choice of goods and services using videotex and full-motion video. The firm wants to get the goods and services to the consumer from a wide variety of service providers.

TABLE 4.4 Advantages and Disadvantages of Distribution Channels

Channel	Advantage	Disadvantage
Direct sales	Well targeted	High cost of sales
OEM sales	Existing force	Loose customer control
Distributor	Existing force	High cost of sales
Agent	Controlled sales	Loose customer control
Retail	Large distribution	High return reserve
Direct mail	Highly targeted	High cost of sales
End user agent	Controlled sales	High cost of sales

TABLE 4.5 Distribution Cost Factors

Channel	Cost Factor	Margins
Direct sales	No companies Sales staff/Co Months/Sale	25%
OEM sales	No OEM Cost Sales staff/OEM Months/Sale	15%
Distributor sales	No distributors Sales staff/Dist Months/Sale Reserve %	30%
Agent	No agents Sales staff/Agent Months/Sale Agent fee	35%
Retail	No retail Sales staff/Retail Months/Sale Reserve %	55%
Direct mail	Cost per piece Number of pieces Buy ratio % Prep costs Cycles/Product	30%
End user agent	No agents Staff/Agent Months/Sale Fee	35%

Several roles arise in this distribution. At one end are the suppliers of the goods and services, such as banks, retail stores, and travel suppliers. At the other end is the consumer. The company recognizes several roles in the distribution channel. They are:

1. *Suppliers.* Basic suppliers of goods and services. These may be the basic travel service providers, such as American Airlines or Hyatt Hotels.

2. *Packagers.* Electronic packagers of industry-specific offerings, such as electronic banking and automated ticketing. Typical in this area may be such banking establishments as Citibank, Chase Manhattan, or Chemical Bank.

3. *Distributor.* The role that the company wants to take on as the local sales force, selling the bundled set of services to the consumer—the electronic shopping mall. The company wants to deal with packagers of electronic services, perhaps American Express, Citibank, Ticketron, and J.C. Penney.

4. *Transmission.* The providers of the communications network to the consumer—the telephone company, the cable television company, or both.

5. *Terminal Provider.* The provider of the terminal to the consumer who accesses the service.

6. *End User.* The consumer.

The distribution channel reflects how these entities coordinate with each other in distributing the goods and services.

Figure 4.6 depicts the channel for the home shopping service. Note that there are many alternative ways the terminal gets to the consumer. Is it via supplier, packager, or distributor? What do the players do and how do they share in the revenue? Who sells the service to the consumer? (In this model, the distributor sells.) Is there a co-op sales effort? What is the role of the packager? (In this case, it is that of merely packaging the product electronically.)

This example raises many of the questions that are present in the development of new businesses. You can see why it's important to clarify each player's role. One of the many problems that can arise is that the consumer confuses these roles. If the end user gets confused as to who provides what part of the service, the market may be lost for all players.

Example: Data Radio Network Service

A company wants to develop a portable communications service that will allow both special-purpose portable devices and radio

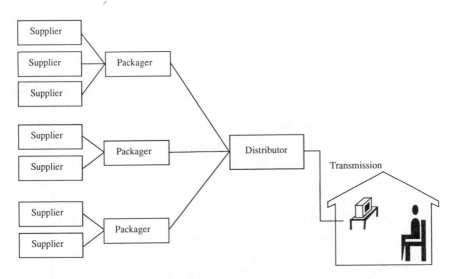

FIGURE 4.6 Industry Roles for Electronic Services Distribution

frequency (RF) modems to communicate over radio signals into a national network. To get the service to work, it is necessary to have both the service and the terminals. The company does not want to manufacture the terminals, only to operate the network. The distribution problem, then, is how to sell the service and ensure that the terminals are available. The second dimension is the segmentation of the market. There are corporate users and individual users. The corporate users are further segmented by corporate size, adding to the distribution alternatives.

The service is the same for all segments of the business. The company must now develop a strategy to reach four segments with two possible user products per segment, opening the way for eight possible distribution strategies. It also opens the way for confusion.

The company decided to divide the corporate users and the consumer users into two segments. The consumer users were targeted by direct mail and through co-op efforts with retail distributors such as Computerland. The corporate users were targeted by direct sales and agent sales. The direct sales allowed the bundling of the RF modem or terminal. The service company provided the manufacturer with 5 percent of the customers' revenue for three years or the life of the customer as a user, whichever was less.

Thus, four distribution channels were selected:

1. *Direct Mail.* Developed to target users who have already expressed an interest in similar types of services, such as pagers or mobile telephones.

2. *Retail.* This channel allows for expansion of the service into a broad base of retail establishments, such as those that are already selling personal computers. For example, the service could be bundled directly with a portable computer at that device's point of sale.

3. *Direct Sales.* This sales channel is targeted to the large corporate user who may have a totally bundled solution and need to access the large corporate network. This type of sale may require a sophisticated sales force that can address the need for integrating the service into a complex network.

4. *Agents.* The agents are those sellers of collateral services. They may be the automobile dealers that sell mobile phones and who may be able to extend the sales to fleets of distribution truck companies, such as United Parcel Service or Purolator.

Figures 4.7, 4.8, and 4.9 depict the distribution alternatives for this case. Figure 4.7 tackles the overall distribution problem. Two suppliers play a role; the first is the basic service supplier, who provides the network and the network service. The second is the hardware supplier who provides the modem device that is placed in the portable computer terminal. Two end user markets also enter the picture. The first is the niche market who wants the modem integrated into the terminal, and who wants to purchase the product as a total system. The second market is the modem market—those want to purchase the modem only and to integrate it into a device of their own choosing. They also want the service.

Figure 4.8 shows how the niche market is addressed. It has a

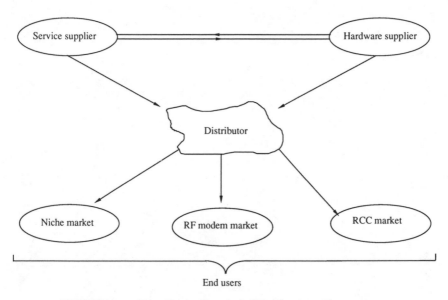

FIGURE 4.7   Data Ratio Network Distribution Alternatives

direct sales force for both the service and the terminal. The sales force is a unified sales force that approaches the customer because the typical customer in this segment is not that sophisticated, and so needs direct support.

Figure 4.9 depicts the different channels for the modem market. This case includes several distribution alternatives: direct sales, direct mail, and a distributor. The reason for the three approaches is the need to reach a wide base of customers whose needs and technical expertise vary significantly.

SALES STRATEGY

The sales strategy is a specific detailed statement of how the distribution strategy will be implemented. Having selected the distribution alternative, the entrepreneur must develop a sales strategy that defines how the sales force in that distribution channel will deal with the end user. The sales strategy should include the following elements:

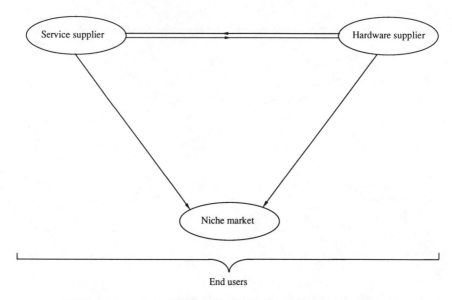

FIGURE 4.8   Distribution Channel: Niche Terminal Market

1. *Product Pricing Alternatives.* Includes the elements of the pricing strategy and details the flexibility of the sales force in exercising the strategy.

2. *Targeting Customers.* Who are the target customers and how will they be approached? Also includes the format and details of the sales presentation.

3. *Lead Generation.* Includes how the sales force determines a good customer and how that information is provided to the salesperson.

4. *Commission Policy.* Perhaps the most critical part of the sales strategy: how the salespeople are compensated for their efforts. All too often the company fails to recognize that the sales commission will directly determine how sales are made. For example, in a service business, the on-going relationship with the customer is critical. If the commission recognizes only a one-time sale, the ongoing relationship will be lost, as will be the customer.

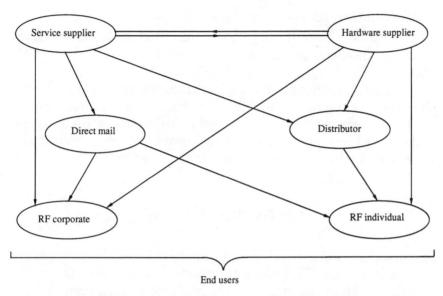

FIGURE 4.9   Distribution Channels: Modem Market

The sales force is totally independent from the marketing force. Marketing is often confused with sales. Frequently, both are confused with order takers. The marketing force positions the product, provides general pricing guidelines, and targets the customers. The sales force must do one thing: sell. They must be motivated and supported because they are the life's blood of the company.

The sales strategy determines how the sales force is to be organized or leveraged off an existing force. For example, a company may develop its own sales force or work through distributors who represent other products. The latter approach often works well for new companies. A direct sales force allows for high and consistent quality of service, but can be quite costly.

The following are the typical sales force strategies:

- Direct: a single sales force to target all companies
- National accounts: a large company's sales force segmented on specific customers

- Distributors: independent agents for sales
- Joint efforts: sales through companies that are larger and have complementary products

The use of such new technologies as telemarketing for lead generation is important in the sales effort. The development of the sales team requires that the sales force be provided with a well-defined product, told to address a well-targeted market, and be provided with leads to succeed in that market.

REVENUE POTENTIAL

The revenue model is the first quantitative model developed in the business plan. The marketing section of the plan must present the revenue potential for the product and, in turn, for the business. The revenue model also is the one most subject to speculation. It will be used to drive the capital and expense models. The revenue model requires that the following items be specified:

1. *Market Size.* Includes the major factors that make up the market. It may be the number of consumers, the number of companies, the number of buildings, or other factors that drive market size.

2. *Market Segments.* The total market must be segmented according to those elements that are treated differently in terms of how they are serviced. For example, if the type of customer is different for two elements of the market, then the market and revenue model must reflect these differences.

3. *Distribution Alternatives.* Further differentiation of the customer base must also be made along the lines of the type of distribution channel employed. The reason for this is that the expense model will include the different expense factors for the different distribution channels.

4. *Pricing.* Pricing is the final factor in determining the revenue on a yearly basis. The developer of the plan may want to segment the market further by pricing strategies, or to aggregate the pricing to an average.

5. *Growth per Segment per Distribution.* The growth of the individual elements of the market (segment and distribution) must be presented annually. This growth includes both the diffusion process associated with a new product introduction, plus the growth associated with the overall market size.

6. *Unit User.* The unit user must be identified, ensuring continued support for that user.

7. *Churn.* The churn represents the loss of existing customers due to moves, relocation, or dissatisfaction with the product. Many business plans do not include this factor. It will result in a large number of new customers that will have to be sold in order to keep the existing base. For example, 20 percent of the U.S. population changes location every year. Thus, in a consumer business, one could expect a 20 percent churn.

The revenue model, then, includes the factors of total number of customers multiplied by the revenue per customer, which generates the total revenue. The planner must know the total market size and the growth of that market with time. In addition, the planner must estimate the penetration of that market by the company as a function of time. In this section, we consider two examples of revenue projections—one for a service business and one for a hardware business. It is important to develop the drivers for the capital and expense requirements that we shall discuss in Chapter 7.

One of the greatest problems with new business plans is estimating the market size and its growth. (Market share estimation is a problem that requires an assessment of competition and marketing expertise; we discuss this issue later.)

The growth of new business follows a well-established cycle. Revenue models must take these cycles into account when developing the total revenue potential for the new business. Markets do not always grow as rapidly as the entrepreneur would like. For example, Figure 4.10 depicts the market evolutionary process for our previous example of the electronic distribution business. Step One in this process shows that, at present, the suppliers see a set of benefits in developing a new distribution channel through an electronic means. If they can develop that channel, it will result in a set of needs that keep the business growing. Remember that the benefits come first, and that needs are developed when the business has proved itself and has demonstrated results. When these needs affect the new distribution, the user of the service perceives the benefits. Then, through promotion and education of the customer, these benefits become needs. The needs then feed demand, and the business grows.

All new businesses follow this cycle. The benefit-need cycle takes time as new products enter the market. If it stops at benefits and never turns into need, the business may falter. The user must become reliant upon the product.

The amount of time this cycle takes also varies. The first com-

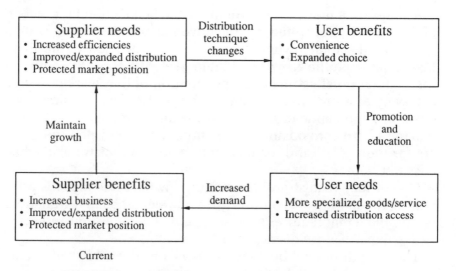

FIGURE 4.10 The Distribution Process Evolutionary Cycle

company may suffer from being too late. An old proverb states that it is better to be a lucky second than a smart first. Business does not reward intelligence—it rewards luck and timing.

The following two examples depict the revenue model structure that we have developed.

Example: Fiber Optic Network Business

A company lays 100 miles of optical fiber in a large metropolitan city. The city now has a market for $1 billion annual data revenue in the T1 band; this is the target market. The revenue is 80 percent among 150 companies, with the remaining 20 percent divided among the other competitors. The company wants to bypass the telephone company. Targeting the top 150 companies, it believes that it can capture a 10 percent market share in ten years, or a total revenue of $80 million plus growth. Annual growth is 12 percent. The company must have all the fiber in place by the end of the second year.

The company can sell direct to the 150 companies, or it can deal with the long-distance carriers who, in turn, would resell the product. These are the two distribution strategies. The firm chooses to sell to the long-distance companies at first because that is an easier sale and they will buy in bulk. The price for the service from the local phone company is $1,000 per month per circuit. There are 80,000 circuits in the city. The company will price its service at $750 per circuit to commercial companies and $500 for carriers. This pricing will assure rapid market entry.

Table 4.6 depicts the revenue model for this business. The capital drivers are the number of companies, the drops per company, and the number of miles of fiber. The expense drivers are the number of companies, the number of new companies, and the miles of fiber. The churn represents the percentage of companies that drop out each year. The company uses a five-year contract, so 15 percent is an adequate percentage.

Example: Computer Terminal Company

A company makes special-purpose telecommunications terminals that allow the user to access remote databases from any lo-

TABLE 4.6 Revenue Model for Fiber Optic Network

Year	Revenue Summary ($000)				
	1986	1987	1988	1989	1990
Miles (trunk)	35	35	35	35	35
Customers	4	21	48	97	157
Locations (sites)	41	182	211	264	330
New bldg entries	30	95	10	17	21
Bldgs entries cum.	30	125	135	151	172
Sites entry	1.38	1.46	1.57	1.74	1.91
New customers	4	17	28	48	60
Entry/customer	7.50	5.98	2.78	1.57	1.10
T1/customer	75	66	34	22	18
T1	300	1369	1654	2156	2788
Bldg entries	30	125	135	151	172
Rev/T1/mo ($)	$500	$543	$594	$650	$692
Transmission rev (000)	$1,800	$8,924	$11,790	$16,822	$23,143
New customers	4	17	30	53	70
Chg/NewCo/T1	3	3	3	3	3
Sign-up rev	$900	$3,207	$855	$1,505	$1,896
New drop	30	95	10	17	21
Cost/drop/T1	0	0	0	0	0
New drop rev	$0	$0	$0	$0	$0
Up-front payment	$0	$0	$0	$0	$0
TOTAL REVENUE	$2,700	$12,131	$12,645	$18,327	$25,039

cation by plugging into a telephone. The terminals are battery-operated, and have an autodial modem and a 10-line display. The terminals also connect into television sets for full display capability.

The market for these terminals is both commercial and consumer. The distribution strategy for the commercial user is to sell the terminals on an OEM basis to a turnkey computer system integrator who is developing a full system for companies to ac-

TABLE 4.7 Revenue for Computer Terminal

Year	Computer Terminal Revenue ($000)				
	1	2	3	4	5
Segment 1 (OEM)					
Companies	50	55	61	67	73
Term/co	1,000	1,000	1,000	1,000	1,000
Term (mkt size, 000)	50	55	61	67	73
% Penetration	5%	10%	15%	20%	30%
Companies	3	6	9	13	22
New cos	3	3	4	4	9
Terminals	2,500	3,000	3,650	4,250	8,500
Rev/term	$150	$150	$150	$150	$150
Segment revenue	$375	$450	$548	$638	$1,275
Segment 2 (Direct Mail)					
Term (mkt size)	1,000	1,150	1,323	1,521	1,749
Cum term	1,000	2,150	3,473	4,994	6,743
% Penetration	2%	6%	8%	9%	10%
Rev/term	$199	$199	$199	$199	$199
Segment revenue	$3,980	$13,731	$21,062	$27,241	$34,805
Segment 3 (Retail)					
Term (mkt size)	500	575	661	760	875
Cum term	500	1,075	1,736	2,496	3,371
% Penetration	1%	3%	5%	8%	8%
Rev/term	$135	$135	$135	$135	$135
Segment revenue	$675	$2,329	$4,462	$8,208	$9,450
TOTAL REVENUE	$5,030	$16,510	$26,071	$36,087	$45,530

cess corporate databases. On the retail side, the company has developed a direct mail approach for those users that it believes have a need for electronic mail. The consumer approach is via computer stores, such as Computerland.

On an OEM basis, the company will sell the terminals for $150. In the direct mail market, it has priced the terminals at $199. In retail stores, the terminal will sell at $235; the company will sell it to Computerland at $135. Computerland has a 100 percent return policy for all inventory not sold after 180 days.

The company has estimated that, on the commercial side, there are 50 target companies with 1,000 terminals per company. The company believes that it will get 30 percent market penetration in five years. On the consumer side, the company estimates that the electronic mail market is one million, and that it will get 10 percent penetration by Year 5, with flat growth thereafter. The retail store market is estimated to have a potential of 500,000, of which the company will get 8 percent by Year 5. Table 4.7 depicts the revenue potential for this business.

CONCLUSION

This chapter presented ideas on the basis of markets and how to sell to the customer. The business plans of many high-tech start-up companies fail to present the market in the correct perspective. Entrepreneurs are cautioned that the same amount of effort supplied to product development must also be supplied to market development. Revenue projections will become the cornerstone of the business. The sales force will rely upon your projections and market definitions. They cannot be expected to develop customers from thin air. Thus, the entrepreneur must develop a business that has a strong and realistic foundation.

5

COMPETITION

The competition section of the business plan combines a statement of the business strategy and how the business will be run with a tactical statement of the day-to-day efforts to position the company against its competition. As we shall see, the competition is not necessarily composed of the obvious competitors.

All too often the new entrepreneur whose firm is the first in the market will say that there is no competition. The new product is the first of its kind; there will be no other competitor. The fallacy in this reasoning is that people have just so much money; they will not create money to buy the new product. They will have to spend less in some area in order to spend money on the new product—the issue of enhancement versus displacement. If one could add up the revenue streams of all the new business plans that have been reviewed by venture capitalists in the past five years, the revenue would exceed twice the present U.S. gross national product. Competition—seen and unseen—eliminates most of these new businesses. The competition is not always the other company who makes the same product. It is a much more complicated set of mechanisms inherent in our economic system.

This chapter is structured around the concepts of success factors and distinctive competencies. These factors are the most important keys to success in the new business. In our approach, competitors must first be identified. The suggested methodology is more expansive than merely viewing the direct competitors. We then address the questions, "What does it take to succeed?

What does this company have that makes it better than the competition?" In that context, we then position the start-up company and its competitors in the competitive matrix.

Now for a brief overview of the logic of this chapter. First, we show how to identify the set of competitors. Second, we detail the set of success factors. These are the factors that any company must meet in order to be successful in the business. For the most part, the entrepreneur will have identified competitors through market development and discussions with the customer. Third, we identify the set of distinctive competencies of the start-up. These factors allow the new firm to compete and to have a sharp competitive edge.

Fourth, we develop the competitive strategies. These strategies build upon the three items discussed above. They recognize what is needed to be successful, what the competition has to compete with, and the start-up company's strengths. They are strategic statements of how the company will enter and survive in the market. Finally, we state the barriers to entry. These barriers are important; they tell investors how strong the start-up's position will be.

In this chapter, our approach follows in many ways the work of Michael Porter. In addition, we refer the reader to Kenneth Andrews's works on corporate strategy, as well as the books by Thomas J. Peters. We end the chapter with a discussion of the value chain concept applied to a start-up company, and show how it can be used as a competitive strategy tool.

COMPETITORS

In a new business, competition may already exist with a similar product or entrenched companies that may already offer the present product. Consider the example of a new company that wants to enter the business of providing electronic shopping, banking, and other home services. The company has a proprietary technology providing videotex plus full-motion video, offered to the consumer through a combination of cable television and telephone. After demonstrating the service, the firm has enjoyed high consumer acceptance. The suppliers of the goods and services to be marketed on the system have an interest in the business as an alternative distribution channel for their products. The business has a set of competitors in several start-up companies funded by larger corporations, but that offer text or graphics only, with no full-motion video.

For this new electronic shopping and banking service, how is the firm to determine its competition? Clearly, the competition is more than just the other videotex companies. It should also include present channels of distribution, since they will continue to provide the consumer with the standard, accepted means of shopping. It also includes catalog shopping services, since they are continuing to grow at a significant rate. This simple example illustrates that competition is not readily defined as those entities directly competing with the new company, but should include all possible competitors.

In this section, we develop a methodology to determine the set of competitors and show how to use external resources to determine them. The assessment of the competitors is of the same magnitude as the assessment of the target market itself.

In the business we've described, several classes of competitors emerge:

1. *Direct.* These firms are the other start-ups who are trying to enter the market. The company must distinguish its offering on the basis of its enhancement over these other start-ups.

2. *Existing.* These elements are the existing distribution channels that suppliers are currently using. The suppliers are accustomed to them, and a switching cost may be applied if they decide to change. Also, the present channels are measured by the efficiency of the channel given by the ratio of sales cost to total sales. This efficiency of a distribution channel reflects itself in the profitability of that channel. If a new channel is introduced, the cost of sales may not change, but the total sales may. This reduction in productivity in this channel may be viewed negatively by

the supplier of goods to that channel. Thus, a significant barrier to entry may inhibit the new start-up company, due to the switching costs associated with the new channel.

3. *Alternatives.* The existing channels of distribution for the shopping channels are the "brick and mortar" stores. They are the edifices that presently represent retailers in their local markets. This representation leads to strong brand recognition and loyalty. However, alternatives exist to the proposed electronic channel. One is the use of a direct mail channel, sending catalogs to a well-targeted audience. This is a proven distribution channel, but it may or may not work, depending on the product mix and target market of the retailer.

Thus, three sets of competitors arise: those that compete directly with the business, those that offer an alternative that may satisfy the need, and the existing method of satisfying the need. It is important to note that there may be a need—an unrecognized need—but the company or consumer does not want to have it satisfied, or the funds available are not adequate to purchase it.

Therefore, to determine the competition, we must determine the need that the product is satisfying, see how that need is currently satisfied, evaluate the cost of satisfying it, and see what is displaced or enhanced on the part of the consumer to satisfy that need. The competition is not analyzed in a vacuum. It is analyzed within the context of the market, the consumer, and the consumer's needs.

As a second example, consider the electronic games business. The consumer's need was entertainment. The target market was the 9–17-year-old. The existing expenditures competing for consumer dollars were records, fast foods, movies, and teen magazines. These items had to be displaced if the business was to succeed.

The size of the target market was 40 million consumers, each of whom spent $500 per year for a total of $20 billion. In 1982, Atari revenues reached $2 billion, or 10 percent of the total market. The competing companies made up an additional $2 billion. So, the games business represented 20 percent of the total. Revenue was displaced from the other markets. It was not an enhanced revenue base. The other markets suffered the loss and responded with increased promotion. Thus, Atari had three competitive sectors: direct competitors, such as Coleco and Activision; existing competitors in the records and movies market; and alternatives, such as clothes and fast food. The games business focused solely on the direct competitors, trying to outdo one another. They failed to address the attacks of their other competitors.

The result was a rapid growth in record sales as consumers became bored with the limited electronic games. As such new promotional television channels as MTV grew, consumers' interest in records grew, and the record business rebounded. The lesson: don't watch direct competition only. (The irony of this strategy was that Warner owned Atari, Warner Records, and MTV. The outcome for Warner was a short-term loss at Atari, but a long-term growth and stability in the alternative businesses. In this case, the top Warner manager, Steve Ross, had taken a long-term view and had very accurately predicted this trend. Ross had managed a short-term loss into a long-term winner).

As you can see, the business plan must include a description of all competitor sectors, including direct, existing, and alternative sectors. Now let's examine the process by which these competitors may be identified. Once you've defined the business and the product, the next step is to assess those companies that are direct competitors. This can be accomplished via:

1. *Market Assessment.* By going directly to the customers, you can develop a list of competitors. The customer, or even your equipment suppliers, may be able to provide guidance.

2. *Databases.* Using the SIC (Standard Industrial Classification) codes for the product and business areas, you can search databases to determine the list of competitors. This approach often expands the list and encompasses compa-

nies that you would not ordinarily consider. Another way to use on-line databases is to search for companies that are addressing the same product area that your company is interested in.

3. *Investors/Venture Capitalists.* In the process of trying to raise capital, investors are closely tied to other start-up companies. These investors are the most valuable source of new competitors. The typical problem that you will face in this area is that the investors do not really know what the company does; they know only what they have been told. For the most part, venture capitalists are not technologically knowledgeable, although they do have a good grasp of market and technology trends. Once this identification process is complete, you can begin to assess the competition.

SUCCESS FACTORS

Success factors are those elements that a company needs to be successful in the business. These factors may be in technical, marketing, operations, or financial areas. The first step is to review the business concept, then to list the areas of importance. Then examine these areas in detail, identifying specific factors of importance. Let's consider several typical areas.

Example

A company wants to get into the business of providing a sales and collection service to large corporations who have distributed sales forces. Companies like Avon, Tupperware, and Mary Kay Cosmetics are typical examples of distributed sales force companies. The extreme is Mary Kay, who has a little over 300 employees but over 30,000 sales representatives. The salespeople really act as agents for the parent company. In these types of businesses, sales often occur at remote locations, where the sales personnel are usually left to perform their tasks using paper and pencil. This process results in a long order cycle and an extended period for receipt of accounts receivable. For example, one of these three companies has over $2 billion in sales, and 120 days' delay on accounts receivable. Thus, if the company could develop a means to automate the distributed sales force's data collection and payment processing, it could save significant interest on financing the receivables.

Recognizing the need and the opportunity, the new company decided to enter into the business of providing a service bureau function to these distributed sales companies. The business requires that the company have a large computer system and a relationship with a major bank that is also an automated clearing house (ACH) to collect funds. The target market is the set of Fortune 1,000 companies who need support to better manage their working capital.

In order to be successful in this business, the entrepreneurs have determined that the following list of success factors are essential. They developed the list by carefully assessing the industry and the market.

- Marketing /Sales
  Large, well-dispersed sales force
  Trained account executive team
  Access to key decision makers
  Established direct mail presence

- Technical/Operational
  Proprietary design
  Software capability
  Communications network capacity

- Operations
  Large field service organization
  Trained maintenance personnel
  Extensive operations software support

• Financial

Commitment to meet peak negative cash flow

In-place management control system

These factors represent a typical set; more general factors can be listed for any start-up business. Typically, a new business will not have success factors in more than two or three of these dimensions. If the company must meet a very long list of factors in many dimensions, the risk associated with the business becomes very high; it becomes doubtful that any company can meet those expectations. If, for example, field service is an important factor, then the company can either develop the capability internally or contract for the service from a third-party firm. In the latter case, the contract can be phased out as the company develops its own capability.

Let us consider an example of how these factors may be developed for a particular business and how, in turn, they may be related to competitors' capabilities.

Example

A company called Digital Pathways Inc. (DPI) has decided to get into the business of providing a national computer communications network linking portable computers via a data radio network. It developed a technology that provides the service at a low cost and in a frequency band that is capable of supporting many instantaneous users. This company's founders have both a hardware and service business background. They recognize that this business requires the combination of skills from both disciplines. They look at the needs of the end user and see that providing communication among these portable computers is a valuable service, but that there are alternatives, such as the telephone. In addition, in order for the system to be effective for users, it must be installed in many locations in a fairly short period of time.

The key success factors for the business fall into two categories: technical/operational and marketing/sales. The following are the elements for each of these areas.

- Technical/Operational Factors

  Exclusive access to a proprietary design.

  Extensive experience in operating a large scale national shared communications network.

  Extensive experience and presence in multiple SMSAs (Standard Metropolitan Statistical Areas) to operate, administer, and maintain a local communications network.

  Established base of software development expertise to support the end user (e.g., communications and applications software).

  End user credibility in the areas of supporting the customer on the technical side and an assurance that the company can provide for a total integration package of all the customer's systems into the operation.

These five technical success factors span the range addressing what the company has within itself to how well the company can interact with the customer's own technical and operational infrastructure. As we shall discuss later in this chapter, every company has a value chain which is an effective tool to evaluate corporate competitiveness. The start up company's value chain will reflect how well it addresses its own technical prowess and productivity. The customer's value chain will mirror that effect and represent revenue opportunities for the company.

- Marketing/Sales Factors

  Established marketing and sales organization on a national scale with access to the decision maker and end user of the service (e.g., systems and service selling skills).

  Experienced customer service infrastructure and experience in operating a national service oriented business.

  Recognized image on the part of the end user as an integrated communications/applications service provider.

  The ability to manage the account interface with specific customer engineered solutions. This includes the ability to understand and integrate into existing customer operational systems.

Established base for billing, problem resolution, etc. on a real time basis to ensure level of service.

These five marketing factors, as the technical, relate to how well the company can not only deal with the customer but also how well it deals with itself. The primary focus is the ability to solve the customer's problem. In this business the provision of communications is not the solution but only a means to it. The company must provide the customer with the ability to integrate the system into an existing service methodology, such as integrating the service into an already existing order entry and receivables system.

The entrepreneurs of DPI have evaluated the absolute measures of success and have in turn graded themselves as to how they fit in the success factors. The grading is initially all qualitative, yet we shall develop a methodology to convert that grading into a more quantitative result. The qualitative approach allows for the statement of the key issues, whereas the quantitative grading allows for a more objective assessment of the strength of the company on any single factor. The following is a qualitative assessment of the position of DPI relative to the success factors in this business.

- Technical/Operational

  Proprietary Design: DPI has a proprietary design but it has also made the decision to sell this to any bidder. This gives the Company organization a lead and access to personnel but does not ensure a barrier to entry.

  Communications Network Experience: DPI has a large corporate communications network but has never made the network available to outside users. Thus it has functional experience but not operational.

  Local Support: DPI has extensive presence in the local markets to support and maintain the system.

Software Level: DPI has developed special purpose software with great success but has not developed large scale end user software.

End User Credibility: The end user has an understanding of DPI as a portable/mobile communications supplier of hardware but has not seen the company as a service supplier.

• Marketing/Sales

Organization: DPI has an extensive and experienced hardware sales organization but lacks the account executive high level contact organization to address many of the key users.

Customer Service: DPI has developed a customer service infrastructure and has demonstrated that it functions quite effectively.

Image: DPI would have to reposition itself as a service supplier of a national network. It is presently positioned as a hardware company.

Customer Engineering: DPI has the capability to integrate customer engineering with a to-be-developed account executive team.

Service Support: DPI does not have the infrastructure to support a billing, problem determination etc. to support the level of service. The expertise is present but an ongoing operation is not present.

DPI has recognized as a result of its discussions with potential customers that there are several competitors or potential competitors in the new market. These competitors are:

IBM
General Electric, GEISCO
Bell Atlantic
Ameritech

The largest potential competitor is IBM. The following is the evaluation of the IBM factors relative to success in this business.

• Technical/Operational

Proprietary Technology: IBM has an agreement with a Japanese company to purchase and operate on a limited basis a shared network. It has had two years of contact with the Japanese company to understand the hardware and is capable of designing it elsewhere.

Network: IBM presently operates and markets a large communications system and network and other closed user group networks.

Presence: IBM has a direct presence in all SMSAs and with its Field Service group can support any system requirement.

Software: IBM will enter the market by backward integrating this service with its software. It has a preeminent position in this area.

Credibility: There are mixed feelings as to IBM's ability to provide the service. It has had multiple technical problems in previous attempts at developing and operating communications systems (viz. SBS and MCI).

• Marketing/Sales

Marketing Organization: IBM has a preeminent Account Organization with direct access to the end user as well as the decision maker.

Customer Service: IBM has a well established customer service organization.

Image: IBM has a mixed image as a communications network provider. It may have to compete with ATT to reposition itself and if it overreaches it may chill the market.

Customer Engineering: There is a well-developed base here.

Support Services: IBM has a well-established base in this area.

The following table, Table 5.1, compares DPI, IBM, and the other competitors along the lines of key success factors. The

TABLE 5.1 Competitive Positioning

Key Success Factors	Data Pathways	IBM	Bell Atlantic	Ameritech	GEISCO
Technical Factors					
Propriet tech	18	14	0	0	0
Net experience	12	15	18	18	16
Local ops	18	18	15	15	10
Software	10	20	15	8	18
User credibility	15	16	15	15	12
Total technical	73	83	63	56	56
Marketing Factors					
Mktg/sales org	10	20	15	15	16
Cust serv exp	15	18	16	16	17
Image	15	16	18	18	12
Cust engr	13	17	11	11	13
Support svcs	10	20	17	17	13
Total marketing	63	91	77	77	71
SUMMARY					
Technical	73	83	63	56	56
Marketing	63	91	77	77	71
Total	136	174	140	133	127

comparison is quantitative. The quantitative determination of each of the elements will be described shortly. The table provides insight into DPI's competitive strength but also provides insight into possible alignment and joint ventures. This is further exemplified in the figure in Figure 5.1 which positions each of the competitors relative to one another on a technical/marketing axis.

Table 5.1 is developed in the following fashion. First, define the key success factors. Then assess the competitors. We shall develop this process in further detail in section 5.2. For each of the success factors, rate the competitors. This rating has been done for DPI and IBM in a qualitative fashion. To create a quantitative result, as was done in Table 5.1, there are two possible approaches.

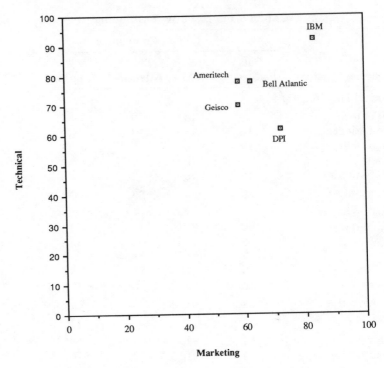

FIGURE 5.1   Position of Competition

Group Assessment

In this approach, a group of competent and well informed reviewers assist in the preparation of the quantitative statements for each of the factors and each of the competitors. Then, each individual rates the level of performance of this factor on a scale of 1 to 5 or 1 to 20, or whatever scale is appropriate. In this sample case, we use a scale of 1 to 20 since five factors were used and the total had a maximum of 100. This process may be further extended to allow each of the assessors to review the work of the others and have a group consensus.

Absolute Measures

This approach requires that the measures of success have a base of an absolute and measurable unit for comparison. For example:

- Proprietary Technology: 5 points for each patent with a maximum of 20.
- Customer Service: 1 point for each SMSA covered by a Customer Service Facility with a maximum of 20 points.

A similar set of quantitative measures can be made up for each of the elements, and these may be determined by a review of the status of the competitors in each area. This approach is generally the more difficult, but it allows for a specific articulation of what quantitative measures are necessary for success in the business.

Once the rating table is complete, it can be depicted on a chart that has dimensions of the technical and marketing ratings. This has been done in Figure 5.1. The upper right corner shows the highest of both ratings. The lower left the lowest. On this chart, we position all the competitors as well as the start up company. This chart then allows us to determine the following:

- Competitive Positioning: How well are we positioned to the competition and in what areas. Specifically, where are the weaknesses of the company?
- Key Competitors: Who are our key competitors and how are we to compete with them. Specifically along what dimension. If we find that we excel in the technical area, and are falling behind in the marketing, how do we best improve the company in that area. In this case, the quantitative approach is of great help.
- Strategic Alliances: Rather than competing, we may wish to for a strategic alliance that may allow us to work with a potential competitor and then in turn be stronger than the major market force. This type of analysis is readily performed and depicted using this approach.
- Strategy Issues: The chart also allows us to develop the competitive strategies that we shall discuss later in this chapter.

The competitive analysis is typically performed in this fashion. First, determine the business's success factors. Then, list the competitors and position them in this matrix of success factors.

Then, rank each competitor's strength in each area. It is possible to rank the competition on the basis of some quantitative measure regarding the success factor. This process then yields the matrix and the competitive positioning chart.

Having established the success factors in the business, and having determined the relative position of the competitors, the company can now set out to determine its market share. The share is based upon three factors:

Competition

The company's expected share will depend upon how aggressively and competently it expects the competition to enter the market and respond to the perceived threat of the company. For example, in the DPI case, IBM is assumed to be a very aggressive competitor who will ultimately attain a high market share. The same would be true of the GE position. However, the two regional holding companies, Bell Atlantic and Ameritech, are expected to be more cautious and more concerned about regional markets.

Capability

The share dependence on capability is assessed directly from the results of the success factors. The company with the greater success factor total will have the greater share of the market. All things being equal, the ultimate equilibrium share should be directly proportional to the success factor of each company, relative to the total of all competitors. This, however, does not include the other two factors discussed.

Required Financial Return

The return on the investment is highly dependent on market share. Thus, to be a significant player, the company must be first, second, or third in the market. This means that the desire to attain adequate profitability requires a high level of market share. This strategy is the essence of the General Electric strategy of being one of the top three players in any business it is in.

Using these three factors, entrepreneurs can determine estimates of achievable market share. The process follows the approach of consulting experts, as was done for the quantitative
assessment of the success factors, and determining share along
the three lines discussed to achieve the summary number.

In our present example, the business has three segments. The
first segment is for a special-purpose terminal directed at a niche
market of users. The second segment is for a data modem device
to be inserted in portable computers and many other devices.
The third segment is a low-end, two-way paging service that addresses a broad-based, but limited service market.

Table 5.2 presents the estimate of the market share of companies in the industry for Years 1 through 5 of the business. It sub-
divides the market from the total, to the addressable, to the feasible, then to the convertible. It then assigns market share to the
company, and to each competitor. Note that, in this example, the
company is the sole player in Year 1 and it reduces its share to
20 percent by Year 5. However, this reduction still allows for a
significant growth in the company's market. Ultimately, it also
shows IBM having the largest market share.

It is assumed that DPI starts with a 90 percent share that is lost
as the business base expands (see Figure 5.2). As the business
becomes better known, and DPI sells hardware to others, com-

TABLE 5.2 Market Share

Year	1	2	3	4	5
Total market (users, 000)	666	810	1,177	1,354	1,836
Percent addressable	20	30	35	40	45
Percent feasible	25	30	35	40	45
Percent convertible	20	30	40	45	80
Convertible market (users, 000)	7	22	58	98	298
Percent share	90	80	65	50	20
Market size (users, 000)	7	18	38	49	60
% IBM	10	15	25	30	30
% AT&T	0	0	5	5	20
% RBOC	0	5	10	15	20
% GE	0	0	0	5	10

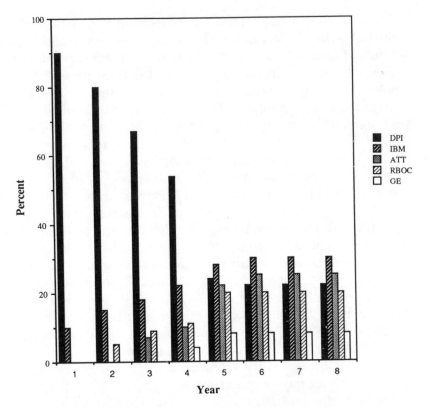

FIGURE 5.2   Market Share Development

petitors enter the market. In addition, the competition grows in share, dominated by its software expertise and its 50 percent hold on the personal computer market. DPI also assumes that it can attract its existing computer base users to the business and retain its share among them.

One of the problems often faced in a start-up business is the determination of market share. As we have seen in the marketing section (Chapter 4), market share is one of the factors that allows for determination of revenue. However, for the start-up business with no defined market, the share is a goal rather than a defined entity. For many existing businesses, the share may be determined using the on-line databases. They allow the market researcher to obtain and analyze detailed market information.

However, for the new business, this may be quite difficult. Thus, market share is a qualitative assessment of expectations. The process developed in this chapter provides a simple and direct methodology that combines the market numbers with the competitive analysis, and permits a quantitative analysis of the share problem.

Market share has been determined to be a key factor in the success of a business. The PIMS study, as described by Derek Abell and John Hammond in their book, *Strategic Market Planning*, indicates that the greater the market share, the greater the return on investment. Thus, it is imperative to assess the business for the ability to obtain a dominant market share. Unlike larger companies, such as General Electric, which only appears in those segments in which it is number one or two in market share, the start-up business allows more flexibility in aggressively getting market share. GE and Exxon have each demonstrated dismal performance in internal start-ups. They are superb in petroleum, light bulbs, and silicone cement. They have not done well in computers or office systems.

Having established the set of success factors and the relative position of the competitors with regard to each of these factors, we can now delineate the strengths and weaknesses. In determining market share estimates, the planner needs to determine—in a very quantitative fashion—why each of the competitors will have the ability to attain the customer base ascribed to them. The result of this process is a clear understanding of the start-up company's strengths and weaknesses.

The strengths and weaknesses of the players described in our example are detailed in Table 5.3. IBM is clearly the strongest player in this business. The only barrier to entry will be the associations with the larger customer base, which IBM has strength in.

This section provides an evaluation of the success factors and how the start-up venture compares to the competition. In this example, we have evaluated a company in terms of its own relationship to the success factors and that of its prime competitor and other competitors.

The competitive analysis, therefore, is a three-step process:

TABLE 5.3 Strengths and Weaknesses

Company	Strength	Weakness
DPI	Direct access to technology	Non-exclusive tech access
	Large direct sales force	HW sales force, not service
	Large national service force	Lack of SW depth
		Lack of operations support
IBM	Direct access to technology	No internal HW capability
	Large sales force	Limited network sales
	Large field service	
	Large operations support capability	
	Strong SW capability	
	Strong communications network expertise	
	Existing network	
	Ability to work on marginal cost basis	
GE	Potential technology access	Lack of direct tech control
	Strong marketing	Lack of network experience in DRN
	Large national network	
	Strong computer expertise	Limited SW capability
	Extensive field service	
	Extensive operations infrastructure	
RBOC	Potential HW access	Lacks direct tech control
	Operations infrastructure	Lacks national network
	Moderate marketing	Lacks national presence
	Field service	Lacks national force
	Computer expertise	Lacks SW expertise

1. Determine the key success factors in the business from both the technical and marketing sides. Try to choose the factors in such a way that they are key and are quantifiable.

2. Choose the set of competitors and rank them along the success factors, comparing them to the start-up company. This task will be subjective but can be assisted by the use of quantitatively measured success factors.

3. Determine the strengths and weaknesses of the competition and the company along the business areas.

This analysis will lead to market share estimates and a positioning of the company relative to the market. It will also lead to the development of competitive strategies to meet the competition, or even to develop joint ventures.

DISTINCTIVE COMPETENCES

The distinctive competences are those elements the company possesses that the competition does not. They are the factors that make the company able to succeed and that position it in such a way as to best deal with the competition. The distinctive competences are those items that the entrepreneur must use to convince investors that the firm will succeed where others will not.

Distinctive competences may include the following:

Proprietary technology protected by patents

Existing direct sales force in place

Long-term leases

Franchises in access to resources

Team of unique technical talent

Commitments from key customer base

Proprietary software developments

The business plan must then map the distinctive competences against the success factors. In the previous section, we did this for the case of the data radio network business. Similarly, we can follow this pattern for many other businesses.

One of the advantages most frequently stated by firms is, "We are here first." As indicated in the last section, the competition may not be only firms that have the same or a similar offering. Merely being the first with a new device does not necessarily guarantee success.

A second popular distinctive competence is, "We have the best people." However, good people can move or disappear in other ways. People are the heart of a business, and good people are rare. Although they are an ephemeral asset, they are truly the most distinctive competence that a company may have. This fact must be brought out. The company needs three key people: the entrepreneur or idea person, the manager or organizer, and the marketing person or seller. These three can make the company and form one of its distinctive competences.

The sets of distinctive competences place the company in a framework with respect to its competition. That is, how does the new company intend to differentiate itself from the competition, and with what tools is it planning to do so? To see how this concept can be reflected in terms of distinctive competences, let us examine the set developed above in more detail.

Proprietary Technology

The key to any new high-tech start-up company is the special technology that it has developed. This is true whether the company is a goods- or service-oriented company. The proprietary technology allows for a short period as sole player in the new business with some control over product pricing. The competition has not yet produced or duplicated the technology and taken cost advantage. The proprietary technology may be a device or system that performs some process that has never been done before, or a device that does it better and/or cheaper.

The protection of that proprietary technology lies in the use of patents or trade secrets. The patent process is a long-term process taking two to five years; it is expensive. It does offer public protection, but only as far as the claims of the patent can be supported. Trade secrets provide total protection only as long as the responsible persons hold them secret.

Many new start-ups try to use patents to leverage their proprietary technology. However, in so doing they expend valuable resources and time while signaling their actions to a set of competitors. Therefore, patents' advantages are debatable. The trade secret approach uses the legal strictures against employees or others exposed to the technology, and tries to keep secret the concept. This latter approach has an advantage in a small firm with limited resources and a market that may have a short fuse in terms of its response time. If the small company has the ability to market the product, then it may be able to capture the market share and defeat the competition early on.

Proprietary technology is often short lived, but it is a distinctive competence at a point in time with any start-up company. The proprietary design must be carefully explained and protected. Let us consider two examples of how this may work.

As a first case, consider a start-up service company that intends to develop a fiber optic network in a large metropolitan area. The key to the business is the right of way (ROW) to allow the company to lay the fiber optic cable along pre-existing cable ducts in a large city, using the local transport authority's access. Five principals form a company to set up a business with this unique way of providing the service. Unfortunately, two of the members have less than the best intentions, and return to their old companies with the idea. The management at the old company tells the dissident employees that it will help the employees with the business if they stay. They do. The result: the idea becomes public, the start-up loses the proprietary concept, and the two employees that left are terminated by their original company on a cutback. The situation results in a lose-lose situation for both the start-up company and those who betrayed the confidence.

In this case, the problem was that the proprietary concept was held as a trade secret, but was not protected by agreements between the principals. The most important aspect of trade secret protection is the need to have control over all those employees who have access to the trade secret via employee or consultant agreements that include a non-disclosure clause and a non-compete clause that allows the use of temporary or permanent injunctive relief.

Consider a second example. A hardware company developed a means of transmitting telephone calls on electrical power lines. The technology was protected by extensive and well-written patents. Unfortunately, the product did not sell. Apparently, it was positioned in the wrong market. Yet the company's assets were sold and the original investors did recover because the patent had clear value. Non-compete agreements allowed the purchaser to be assured of a market window. Specifically, the purchaser repositioned the product, was assured that the idea was protected, and was further assured that any disaffected former employees could not restart the venture and perform an end run around the newly formed product concept.

Thus, distinctive competences in the area of technology allow for not only short-term advantages; they allow for long-term advantages with respect to the value of the business. The proprietary base must be protected in an active and legal form.

Distribution Capability

The second general distinctive competence is distribution. Even if the product is the most effective ever created, it means nothing if it cannot be sold. Thus, access to distribution is a key distinctive competence. Most start-up companies may have a significant lack in understanding the issues of distribution and in gaining access to it. In the commercial area, a firm may need a large direct sales force that is not easily developed. The way around this deficiency is to enter into a joint marketing and sales agreement with an existing sales force of some non-competing company that covers a similar market. This arrangement may cost the company in sales margin; however, it may pay back in gaining visibility and distribution that results in market share. Some companies also enter into joint licensing agreements with companies that want to distribute the product, which can result in a win-win situation for both sides.

On the consumer side, distribution means market presence through retailers and distributors. It means getting shelf space in the right locations and developing a brand recognition in that market. The Atari experience is another example of how, in the early days of the company, distribution was obtained through agreements with Sears and other retail stores. The company obtained very favorable agreements on margin, and agreed to accept any unsold merchandise.

Long-Term Leases

Long-term leases or agreements provide the start-up company with a guaranteed revenue stream that reduces the level of risk in the venture. This may result from the agreement of a large customer to buy a certain quantity of hardware for a specified period of time, or through agreements with customers to purchase the service for several years. On the positive side, the lease guarantees the revenue. On the negative side, it locks the company into delivering the product at that revenue level for an extended period of time, perhaps placing the company in a market position that may not provide adequate cash flow for growth.

Franchises

A franchise represents, in the most general sense, a right to exploit a market, unencumbered by the competition. Franchises typically arise in the context of natural monopolies. They are granted in the areas of cable television, communications systems, and in many service-oriented companies. Franchises represent less than long-term contracts or leases in that they give rights to sell in an unencumbered market, but do not assure that a revenue stream exists.

As an example, a company has developed a new service that provides nursing homes with cable television and educational programming to each room for a daily rate. The homes have given the company a five-year exclusive franchise and have assured the company that the patients will have approved television sets in their rooms. Here is a market without competition. However, the company must still market to the patients on a daily basis.

Unique Technical Talent

In a new business, the need must first be recognized, followed by development of the means to satisfy that need. In some cases, satisfying that need requires the collection of a unique talent base. As an example, several banks with large communications and computer networks needed to interconnect these computers using several protocols. These multiple protocol conversion devices required the talents of a few highly trained specialists because many of the requirements were based upon technical folklore—experience with what worked and what did not—rather than on literature. Very few individuals were available, and the collection of several in one location was even rarer. Thus, the distinctive competence in this case was the unique collection of talent.

Proprietary Software

Software may be patented in certain cases, but for the most part it is considered proprietary. Once the firm has protected this software, it becomes its distinctive competence in that it provides the company with a base against which it can meet the competition head-on. The software must be expandable and must be valued to the end user for an extended period of time. The software should not be just a one-time development effort. A database system is an example of a reusable competence, whereas a custom billing system may not be.

In the business plan, the collection of distinctive competences shows potential investors why this company can hope to compete with those who might already be in the market, or with other established firms that may enter the market. The statement of the competences should be clear and should be carefully judged against the competition. It is important to remember that the competition is not only those firms that are presently making a similar product; it also includes those with the resources to develop and distribute the product to the target market.

COMPETITIVE STRATEGIES

So far in this chapter we have developed the set of success factors, the list of competitors, and what makes the firm different in a positive fashion in this industry. Understanding these, we can then articulate competitive strategies. The strategies, both defensive and offensive, fall into the following areas:

Technical
Marketing/distribution
Production
Pricing

Using these strategies, the company can clearly address the competition based on its assessments and targets for attaining the desired market share. It is important, however, to understand that there are good and bad competitors (see Porter[2], p. 213). A good competitor will compete on the basis of maximizing the return on equity to its shareholders. A bad competitor is a predator whose sole objective is to grab market share independent of return. The latter typically drops prices below cost to get market share. Japanese firms have been accused of the bad-competitor strategy, as have many other American companies. Generally, IBM is considered a good competitor. Even though it has large market share that may make it appear predatory, it acted out its good role in the PC market, allowing Compaq and other companies to establish a foothold and prosper.

Let's now go into greater detail on each of the competitive strategy areas.

Technical Strategies

Technical strategies focus on how the product's unique technical capabilities are to be leveraged and developed to gain market share. Part of the technical strategy focuses on the eventual vertical integration of the product line.

For example, consider a company that wants to develop a network control center (NCC) concept that is primarily software-based. Its distinctive competence is focused in the software area. It must use standard off-the-shelf hardware for the field monitoring equipment. However, it recognizes gaps in the hardware that it is also interested in filling. Thus, it develops the software with hooks that allow for vertical integration of its proposed hardware, but without allowing another hardware competitor to enter the system. Thus, it has established a barrier to entry in a vertical aftermarket by developing a long-term strategic plan that focused on the technical development of the product.

Example

Hewlett Packard has developed a strong competitive lead by using strong technical competitive strategies. It has developed a set of high-quality measurement equipment, and then expanded into the instrumentation computer business. The vertical compatibility of the measurement equipment and the computers has allowed the company to ensure its business base while at the same time expanding the market potential.

Marketing/Distribution Strategies

One of the typical marketing strategies is to recognize that the need for the product may exist in different forms in several key individuals of the buyer's firm. Thus, the marketing strategy must recognize that, with a new product, it is necessary to convince a set of individuals of the new products' merits. For example, a PBX enhancement company recognized that the telecommunications manager has a large expense budget but a low capital budget. The MIS manager has both a large capital and a large expense budget. In addition, the decision maker is the VP of Finance and Administration. So, to sell the PBX enhancement, the firm must position it differently than the PBX which is sold to the telecom person. It is positioned as a data processor enhancement, and the company focuses much of its marketing activities on the VP by establishing a presentation that shows the operating cost savings to the company and the potential return on investment. Thus, the strategy focuses on decision makers and on the users with funds.

Example

IBM has been the quintessential example of the marketing strategist. It has addressed the broad base of customer users, such as the MIS manager, the telecommunications manager, the chief financial officer, the office automation manager, and even the CEO. IBM is really in the service business. It is only happenstance that it manufactures hardware. The firm establishes a relationship with the company, builds on that relationship, and then uses it to expand its product base. This strategy accounts for IBM's success in the PC business—it was not because of technical strength, but marketing power.

Pricing Strategies

For new start-up companies, pricing is a difficult problem. Hardware companies in the commercial field often assume that the price is based on a cost-of-goods margin on the operating statement. Yet, as we already have noted, pricing is really a very flexible item. A start-up may price as high as possible to gain large up-front cash flows, and be prepared to drop the price to a certain level as the competition develops. This is the classic IBM strategy. Yet IBM has also managed to refrain from destructive pricing. The latter was the case in the calculator business, where Texas Instruments dropped the price below cost to get market share and found that they could not raise the price once it had been dropped.

The issues of pricing and competition also suggest who you should compete with. IBM is a good competitor in certain niche areas because they tend to avoid early price drops. Other companies can be suicidal in their pricing and should be avoided.

Example

In the satellite communications business, American Satellite, owned by Contel, has repeatedly competed on price. It has gained market share on the basis of underpricing the competition. The strategy: they could buy market share, then—using the inherent scale economies—maintain margin. Unfortunately, the telecommunications business is a commodity business with replacement from a wide set of alternatives. As American Satellite cut prices, so did AT&T. However, AT&T was well along on the scale economy curve. Thus, American Satellite continued to see margin erosion and took more than 11 years to see a positive margin.

Production Strategies

The key strategic issue in production is to determine how much is done in-house and why. As an example, a small start-up was in the business of developing computer keyboards to be placed in hotel rooms so visitors could access the hotel's database on restaurants, entertainment, and final check-out. The company had a contract for 250,000 units. The device was very straightforward. The company decided that it would develop its own production line instead of sending the boards out to a job shop. It felt that the contract cash flow would pay for the acquisition of the capital plant, which was obtained on a debt basis. Regrettably, the contract fell through, and the company was left with the capital plant and no money left to pay employees. The company was sold off and is now in the custom board stuffing business. The stragegy was sound only if the contract was sound.

In-house production gives a firm some control, but also a great level of risk. The production strategy should be focused on the long-term strategy of the business with an eye to the short-term risks. A cost arises in avoiding the risk and reducing the inside production, but in the early phases it may pay off.

BARRIERS TO ENTRY

When approaching a venture capitalist for funding, the first question asked after the business concept is presented is, "Why can't someone else do what you have just done?" Let's consider a rather complex example. A company wants to get into the business of providing home shopping, banking, ticketing, travel, and other services. The business is called TIES (for Transaction, Information, Entertainment Services). It has developed a proprietary software system with generic interfaces to the product suppliers, and has developed a special input device to be used in the home. To be successful, TIES believes that it must be established in 20 cities within five years. It has a unique technology that allows it to provide full-motion video on demand to the consumer, with no limit on the system load. The firm has obtained the support of a large retailer, a bank, and a regional telephone operating company. Its competition is a joint venture of three major corporations, all of whose revenue exceed $10 billion.

TIES has articulated its competitive strategy as follows:

Provide an enhanced consumer package at modest cost

Rapid market entry with full service to capture market share

Provide a proprietary terminal to reduce switching of services by the consumer

Price at a rate similar to cable television and be prepared to reduce the rate by 30 percent as the competition enters

Use the partners' consumer recognition as an acceptance factor

Use the proprietary video technology to leap-frog the competition

The company is trying to raise $15 million. The venture capitalist asks, "Why can't this service be performed by any other group of people?" TIES answers:

The cost of entry is high, and not all companies are willing to spend $50 million.

The market will support only two or three players, and we will have early market share.

The technical expertise is unique, and we have filed for a patent with broad claims.

The customer would not be willing to switch and to learn a new service.

These answers are barriers to entry. They represent the company's perceptions as to why competitors would shy away from the business. Barriers to entry typically fall into the following categories:

Cost of entry

Technical expertise required

Proprietary technology

Lead time to develop the product or service

Lowered margins as a result of established player reducing prices

Barriers to exit on the customer associated with switching costs

The development and understanding of the barriers to entry will be the key to business success. The barriers to entry will be in the same areas as those of the distinctive competences or the success factors. All businesses must have some barrier to entry. Without such barriers, the business will have no chance of lasting if it is profitable and subject to attack by a large company.

The barrier-to-entry concept is one of the main reasons that service businesses have a difficult time raising funds from venture groups. Take, for example, the BBI (Bed and Breakfast) business discussed earlier. It is a reservation business that develops a software package and agreements with bed-and-breakfast establishments to provide a service. The only barrier to entry is the set of exclusive agreements that the company has with the establishments. If the business concept catches on early, a large company such as American Express or American Airlines may readily enter the market and cream-skim the B&Bs, thus reducing the market share and endangering the business base.

Barriers to entry are more successful in hardware businesses, where there is a prototype of the unit that can be protected by a patent. However, even here the patent may be reversed-engineered or blatantly copied. The small company cannot fight back, and is forced to go after a reduced market share.

The entrepreneur typically views the barrier to entry as the uniqueness of the idea or being first in the market. In reality, the barrier to entry must be much more substantial. It should be legally defendable, and include the high cost of reproducing elements of the design. Software developments for commercial items may have such a barrier to entry. Contracts with a large portion of the market are barriers to entry. Remember, a good idea is easily copied.

VALUE CHAIN ANALYSIS

Having established the concept of competition and developed a methodology for determining and evaluating it, the entrepreneur needs to better understand the process of developing competitive strategies. We have just completed a discussion on the elements of competitive strategy within the context of determining how to be successful in the business. An alternative approach is suggested by Porter when he develops the concept of a value chain. Simply stated, the value chain is that set of steps or processes that a company takes to deliver a product to an end user. The analysis of the value chain entails assessing each step of the chain, determining how that step adds to the firm's profitability, and finally, comparing each of the steps to the competition. The result is a process that allows the planner to detail where specific improvements can be obtained.

Now let's develop the value chain concept for new start-up companies and, in turn, develop a methodology to utilize the results developed throughout this book to improve the competitive strategies. Consider the process of developing and delivering a new product to market. We shall call this the product development cycle. It consists of the following steps.

1. *Product R&D*. This is the early development stage, where the product concept is developed and the prototype is produced. It is also a step in the chain that is required for the ongoing development of new products to keep the distribution channel filled with competitive products. The tasks performed in this element of the chain are the technical aspects of the product, its initial conceptualization, and the steps necessary to bring out the first prototype.

2. *Product Concept Development*. This is a marketing-driven step in the product development chain. It focuses on the normal marketing functions associated with the development of the target market, the development of the pricing strategy, the distribution strategy, and the product positioning.

3. *Systems Development*. This element provides the development of the product from the stage of being a prototype to that of a pre-production unit. This step provides the design to cost, design to manufacture, design to maintainability, and design to integratability into the product. In an on-going business, the total product quality and assurance lies in this area.

4. *Manufacturing*. This step includes all of the functions necessary to create the flow of product from the company. It may include the company's factory, but may also include the use of outside manufacturers. The manufacturing function may be considered as an extended factory, encompassing all of the elements needed to deliver goods or services to the end user.

5. *Operations and Maintenance*. The day-to-day operations of the business are included in this element of the product development chain. These operations include such ele-

ments as customer service, billing, and maintenance of the hardware product.

6. *Marketing and Sales.* This final element includes the day-to-day tactical marketing functions and the day-to-day sales functions.

This product development cycle is depicted in Figure 5.3, which illustrates the relationship of each of the elements in the chain. This figure shows that the R&D function drives both the product concept and the system development functions. Manufacturing supports the operations and maintenance area, as does the product concept. Marketing and sales is the day-to-day, direct contact with the customer.

Each competitor must have the same or similar set of elements in its business operations. Thus, by understanding the operations for their own businesses, entrepreneurs will be able to project the response capability of the competition.

We can further expand this concept by recognizing that each of these elements in the chain has an operational cost associated with it. Specifically, for element i in the chain, it has an expense $E(i)$. This expense is composed of three elements: the revenue driver element, called $RD(i)$, resulting from the need to meet the needs given by the customer base; the productivity factor element, called $PF(i)$, based upon how effectively the company can perform in each unit or subunit of the development chain; and a

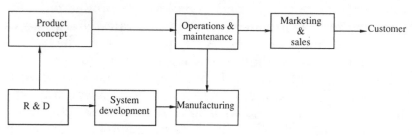

FIGURE 5.3 Product Development Cycle

unit cost element, $UC(i)$, based upon the cost to deliver a unit of each of the elements.

A simple example will help explain the makeup of these factors. Consider a sales force that is required to make $5 million per year in new revenue. This figure is the revenue driver. The productivity of the sales force is given by the new revenue per salesperson per year, or $500,000 per salesperson per year. The unit cost factor is the cost per salesperson, including all loaded factors—namely, $60,000 per year. Thus:

$RD = \$5,000,000$

$PF = 1/\$500,000$

$UC = \$60,000$

$E = RD*PF*UC = \$600,000$

A similar breakout can be performed for all functions. Thus, the profit of the company can be expressed as follows:

$$P = R - \sum_{i=1}^{n} E(i) = R - \sum_{i=1}^{n} RD(i)PF(i)UC(i)$$

This clearly states that the firm's profitability depends on the three elements that yield the expense. In Porter's terms, these are the value chain elements for the firm. By understanding what these elements are and how they compare to the competition, the firm can readily assess how it stacks up to its competitors.

For example, if the company is competing with a firm that has a lower unit cost per salesperson and higher productivity, then the competitor has a better margin on its sales effort, and can thus compete more effectively. A similar process can be followed on manufacturing, operations, and all development items.

The analysis of the value chain for any business starts with a recognition of the product development process and a detailed understanding of all of the elements in that process. (We provide considerably more detail in this area in Chapter 7.) Having that understanding, we can then perform:

1. *Element Costing.* For each element in the chain, determine the costs per element by revenue driver, productivity number, and unit cost. Note that competitors can compete on all three elements. The competitor can use a different revenue driver, more efficiently provide the element, or have lower unit costs.

2. *Competitive Assessment.* For all of the major competitors, determine their respective cost elements and element cost factors. Use this evaluation to determine where the competition is directly competing. This requires a much more comprehensive evaluation of the competition than is typically performed.

3. *Strategy Development.* Having assessed the areas where competition exists in the value chain, develop strategies to compete. For example, the firm may decide to compete on productivity and not on unit price. It may want to compete on revenue driver by segmenting the market differently, rather than any of the other two elements.

By thus determining the elements of the value chain the firm can determine the origin of its profit or value. In addition, if the profit is adequately high, the firm may lower costs and reduce prices to obtain increased market share. This type of strategy allows for controlled profitability in the short term, but for capture of significant market share during the business's more mature periods.

In later portions of this book, we return to the elements of the value chain and use them as key factors in developing company strategy.

CONCLUSION

Entrepreneurs often neglect the competitive section of the business plan. However, it is one of the more important ones, second only to the marketing section. The entrepreneur must understand the competition, realizing that the competition is not only those firms that directly compete, but also those who indirectly compete. The business's needs to succeed are critical. What are the success factors? If the new company has not satisfied them, it may be embarking on a fruitless journey.

6

THE DEVELOPMENT PLAN

The development plan presents the tasks a firm must accomplish in order to develop a finished product that can be sold to the end user. The development efforts include not only those of hardware and software development, but also of market and organization development. The development program encompasses efforts begun the time of plan funding and carried through until the firm produces revenue of a continuing nature. Thus, the development plan consists of the following elements:

Technical product development
Market development
Organizational development

The development plan must articulate the specifics of each of these areas as well as the overall goals and objectives of this phase, its budgetary limitations, and the most important factors contributing to the business's success or failure.

This chapter focuses on the structure and goals of the development plan, and indicates the elements and methods involved in developing the plan's details. The specific methods typically depend upon the type of business being developed, whereas the structure is consistent regardless of the type of business involved.

The major emphasis in the development plan is upon structure and goals. Development must be tightly focused; that focus is the product of a good business plan. The first step is defining the product and establishing the product development goal. If this goal is attained, the entrepreneur can assume a level of business success. However, if this goal is not attained, it is likely the firm will not succeed. In order to recognize the goal, the entrepreneur must articulate failure as well as success.

You defined the product in the market section of your plan; and in this section you will establish the goals and objectives of the development effort in both the technical and marketing areas. For example, the technical goals might be:

Development of the operating system

Prototype boards for the communications interface

500 Hour operations test with no failures

Acceptable beta test site acceptance by three companies

On the marketing side, the goals might be:

Letters of intent from 10 customers

Pre-development contracts from four customers

Co-marketing agreements with two OEM distributors

These goals are measurable and quantifiable, resulting in an increased valuation of the firm by reducing the risk to market. They are predicated upon determining the key uncertainties in the financial risks of the plan.

The goals you define for the development plan should have the following characteristics:

Quantifiable: Easily measured as to whether they have been achieved

Directed: Related to the success of the overall business

Impactable: Capable of being related to the set of business financials and shown to have an impact on the business

Achievable: A set of finite goals that relate to the business rather than some abstract notion of the business

The goal-setting process is a collaborative effort involving all the key principals of the business. If they disagree, it should be resolved by mutual acceptance by all parties, or by the elimination of the disagreeing party. Persistent disagreement in a start-up company will lead to short-term failure.

Once the goals of the development have been articulated and agreed upon, the tasks of the technical and marketing development plan are set forth. Each goal is stated, and tasks necessary to reach that goal are detailed. These goals are then reviewed by the firm's top management to assure that the firm achieves the overall goal of a successful business.

TECHNICAL PRODUCT DEVELOPMENT

The technical product development portion of the development plan is aimed at defining the steps needed to develop and field the product. The product development process is characterized by the following eight steps:

1. Goals: Establish a set of realistic goals for product development, including the performance and acceptance of the product.

2. Strengths: Characterize the strengths of the development team in attaining the established goals—for example, strengths in the area of software development, hardware integration, or other areas.

3. Process: Define and establish the process for product development, which may involve the software development process, its controls, and the implementation of development process details.

4. Steps: Detail all the steps to be taken in the actual development. These steps may include hardware development, packaging, and development of the manufacturing design model. Detail on each of the steps should be adequate to meet the specificity of the schedule and the budget.

5. Schedule: Create a detailed description of the time allocation and start of each of the steps that must be completed in the development plan.

6. Costs: Come up with detailed estimates of the expenses and the capital requirements for the development. The budget should be precise and should include the needs for labor expenses as well as capital elements.

7. Human Resources: Specify the people needed for the development process. Indicate where they are to come from, their talents, and when they are needed. The single most important ingredient of the development effort is the allocation of these human resources.

8. Risks and Risk Management: It will be essential to list the risks that are to be anticipated. In addition, these risks must be shown to be manageable; you must devise a plan to manage them.

These eight items are a necessary part of the product development plan. Let's examine these efforts in more detail.

Goals

The development process requires that a clear set of goals be established for the overall development. These goals should reflect the product needs in meeting the technical as well as marketing objectives. The goals should include the following (or similar) elements:

- Performance: How should the product perform? How many users should it support, how quickly should it respond, or how much data should it contain?
- Price: What is the price range of the product? How will we market it, and how will we price each of its elements?
- Interfaces: What are the interfaces to the end user? Will an open system allow for ease of expansion?

- Interoperability: Will the system have the ability to operate with other systems? If yes, is it to do so by means of standards or by means of a proprietary interface?
- Quality: What level of quality and customer satisfaction is required? Is this a part of a customer mission critical system?
- End user interface and support: Is the product designed to be serviced by the customer, or does the design require continued company contact?

These goals should be expressed in clear terms and should be transferred to all members of the development team with no ambiguity.

Strengths

The development team must contain strengths in many areas. Typically, the development team must be able to focus on the technical development and not the development of the customer base. However, the technical development team must communicate with the marketing side that is developing the customer.

The development team should have the following strengths:

Technical Depth and Experience

It is essential to identify the strengths needed for the development effort, and to assess the specific areas that will be required. For example, in one company, the development team was led by a technician from the company from which the founder came. The founder was a marketing person who was not capable of judging the competence of the technical person. The product was never completed, and the design had to be abandoned due to its inability to be manufactured.

Contacts

In a development team, the effort will, in many ways, be leveraged off of the sets of relationships and contacts of the development team members. So, it is essential to have a team that can draw on the resources of many people—those who can assist the PC layouts, provide parts distributor contacts, and have access to assembly shops. No team is a stand-alone team.

Cohesiveness

The team must be able to work together. Their strengths must complement each other, and they must not be put in a position of competing with each other.

In many development cases, other types of strengths are needed for the effort to succeed. The development team should evaluate these needs at the beginning, and the team should be complemented with those strengths that are lacking.

Process

A development process must be established that is understood by all of the development team players. Process establishes a means and a method to achieve the established goals. Process establishes the allocation of resources and identifies who does what, when—and how the individual parts interact.

Entrepreneurs often begin their effort with a general sense of direction and little else. They lack a plan, and are unaware of the need for process. In contrast, large corporations often possess an excess of process and lack individual creativity, which makes for successful innovation. The amount of process required in a start-up development effort must be balanced to provide direction and control, but at the same time ensure continued creativity and freedom.

In this section we develop a concept called the work breakdown structure (WBS) that provides the basis for the process. It establishes a set of steps that must be followed in the development and delivery of the product. The WBS alone is not sufficient. It states what has to be accomplished, but fails to address the issue of how it is to be accomplished. The "how" is the essence of the process.

The elements of the process are:

A WBS delineating the steps

The organization plan, mapping the WBS onto the organization, showing who is to accomplish the tasks

The review process to establish whether the firm is adhering to the success factors

The development of a detailed schedule that can be tracked by the management team

The clear assignment of tasks to the appropriate elements of the organization

Steps

We can consider the individual steps in the development cycle in an organized fashion. These steps are typical of the steps that must be followed in any development process. The developers of the prototypes must plan these steps in detail and execute them in accordance with the established process.

The steps include the following:

Individual Work Elements

The WBS provides the developers with module task elements, or partial lists of tasks that must be accomplished in order to deliver a successful prototype. The developers must address the total set of tasks and amend the work elements accordingly. One of the key tasks is the development and coordination of this list of work elements.

Entrepreneurs sometimes fail to take into account the individual work elements. In the process, they forget to include several of the critical path items associated with development. For example, in creating a new software network management product, the developers had done an exceptional job on the software and hardware requirements for the prototype. However, they failed to take into account the necessary changes to the power supplies in the development areas, thereby causing a three-month delay while they negotiated with the landlord on leasehold improvements. This simple work element should have been planned in the early development phases.

Deliverables

The deliverables must be clearly defined in terms of hardware and software as well as in terms of what they do. In many cases, Release Zero, which is delivered on the date the release was scheduled, does not function as required. If the process had developed a set of deliverables phased at intervals along the way, the developers could have predicted the release's delay as well as understanding the causes of the delay.

Testing

Quality is essential to the success of any business. The integral quality factor is meeting the customers needs and expectations. Failure to assure that this goal is accomplished is a sure means for business failure. Thus, it is essential that the product design undergo proper testing, which may mean assigning a separate quality assurance function to the development effort. In the current developments of new technology systems, one must also realize that hardware and software must receive the same care and attention. Too often careful attention is paid to the hardware elements, with major failures arising in the software—followed by new releases and versions of systems. Often these "improvements" do not represent new features and functions, but merely new releases with fewer errors in the software. So, testing should have its own plans and organization. A detailed test plan is the heart of a successful product development.

Interfaces and Integration

The larger the system, the more interfaces it will have. As systems are developed that fit into more complex environments, they are forced to interface with many more elements. As the development efforts progress, the sub-elements of the design must be integrated; finally, the entire design must be integrated with the external world. As with the test plan, the firm should also create a detailed integration plan.

Final Acceptance

The final delivery is the delivery of the prototype—or the beta test, pre-production unit—to the customer. Delivery should be done on time, and the unit should perform as expected. It is essential to create an internal final acceptance procedure for the release of the design. This acceptance procedure is the last of many steps; these steps are:

- Preliminary design review: Assuring the product's features, functions, and specifications
- Critical design review: Assuring all critical elements are satisfied and that schedules will be met.
- Final design review: Assuring design compliance and release for final implementation.
- Final acceptance

Delivery

The delivery of the product to the customer should be done in a timely and professional form. Delivery represents the end of the development cycle and the beginning of business operations.

Schedule

The development schedule should include all of the key elements of the WBS as well as all of the reviews that have been discussed. There are many techniques for scheduling, starting from the use of a Gantt chart detailing all of the tasks, to the more complex PERT and CPM scheduling methodologies. One of the most critical reasons for developing a schedule is not only to ascertain the time required, but to manage the process so as to have an adequate and reliable estimate of the time required to complete the project.

Scheduling is left to the entrepreneur, who may choose from

many software packages for support. However, the entrepreneur should ensure that the schedule include at least the following items:

Complete WBS Compliance

The schedule should include the WBS elements and should pay careful attention to software. Remember that software scheduling is still a black art; only through experience can a detailed schedule be developed. For example, one start-up company had to develop 10,000 lines of code. They felt that this could be done in three months by one person. After all, three months was almost 100 days, and a good programmer could do 100 lines of code a day. Wrong! Coding typically moves at five lines of code per day, and there are 200 effective workdays in a year. In other words, this was a 10-person, year-long effort. The company received quite a surprise.

Inclusion of All Reviews

The schedule should include all of the reviews that we have discussed, and show them on the development's critical path.

Estimates of Time to Complete

The time to complete is the key measure of success. If the actual time to complete is close to the amount budgeted, then development is on schedule. Remember, however, time to complete is not the difference between the total time and the time spent. It is a reflection of the productivity to date on existing efforts, and a projection forward on efforts to be done. For example, if the schedule assumed that the prior tasks were done at a certain rate, and they were accomplished at 25 percent over that rate, then this factor may be projected into future developments.

Integration into Budgeting and Actuals

Schedules should be integrated into the budget and tracking of the actual expenses.

Determining Critical Paths

All critical paths, or sequence of WBS elements and their dependencies, should be considered.

Costs

The costs associated with the development efforts are often considered in lesser detail than the costs of the ongoing business. This is a major problem, for funds are limited in the business's beginning. For example, a typical problem is the lack of funds due to misstatement of the business goals. An entrepreneur has decided to develop a prototype for the market to evaluate. He assumes that the prototype, if successful, can be modified—with minimal effort—for the production line. The staff developing the prototype, however, have never developed production hardware before. They have all come from a research lab environment. Therefore, the design has not been developed on a design-for-cost, design-for-manufacturability, or design-for-maintenance basis. The net result: a successful prototype, but a business failure. The production costs were three times the prototype development costs.

The entrepreneur should create a development budget that takes all of these items into account, remembering the established goals and process. The development budgets should contain the following elements, each of which should reflect the WBS elements plus overhead of the development effort:

1. *Direct Labor.* Direct labor includes the staff members working on the development team. Remember that the costs associated with the staff members should reflect competitive salaries; be sure not to underestimate the costs of acquiring the best people.

2. *Indirect Labor.* Labor elements not directly related to the WBS elements of the development program include the CEO, the finance staff, accountants, consultants, and oth-

ers. Typically, the indirect costs may be 25 percent to 75 percent of the direct labor costs.

3. *Overhead.* Overhead costs include taxes, benefits, deferred compensation, rent, office expenses, and other factors. It is in this area that the entrepreneur will often underestimate. For example, travel costs are often underestimated, as are costs associated with demonstrating the product at trade shows. Floor space at shows is quite costly, requiring the allocation of many technical staff members for periods of time, perhaps three to five times that of the show period.

4. *Other Related Costs.* Many other costs, such as leasing costs, are not directly related to staff.

5. *Capital Requirements.* Although capital is depreciated and not expensed, it is critical that a start-up company consider it as a cash requirement. The entrepreneur should make a detailed lease-or-buy decision on much of the equipment. In addition, the entrepreneur should carefully consider the use of outside contracting rather than internal efforts. For example, a company decided to develop a new computer terminal board, with the capability to perform the board layout, chip design, and the board stuffing and testing in-house. This required $4 million in capital, but they justified it in the long term. After one year the market changed, the cost of the equipment dropped, and the per unit costs of outside design, stuffing, and testing were reduced below the internal marginal costs. The company still carried the capital, depreciation, and interest. The firm was eventually sold. Remember, you cannot fire depreciation or interest; you must be very cautious with capital.

6. *Financing Costs.* Financing costs are sometimes ignored in the process of estimating the total development costs. Typically, these may include interest, attorney's fees, the costs associated with the venture capital placement, and other factors.

Human Resources

The human resource factors in the development plan are often the most crucial. As you staff the development effort, you will face three major barriers:

1. Acquisition of the proper personnel: Often a difficult task, first in identifying the key people and second in attracting them. The identification may be done through existing professional contacts or even through executive recruiters. The most important factor, though, is the selection of the correct person. Compromise at this point is deadly to the business. The second factor is the selection of all of the key people. Too often a technical start-up fails to obtain the proper marketing and financial person at the early stages, and this can readily lead to failure. The second part of staffing is acquisition, achieved by packaging an attractive success-directed package for the prospective candidate. It is essential to induce employees through proper compensation, including stock incentives.

2. Integration of personnel: Includes identifying the various positions and tasks, and integrating the individuals into a team. The most significant factor in team building is leadership, which is sadly lacking in American business today. Too often, management styles allow for consensus— an untenable situation in today's fast-moving management world. Leadership requires that the entrepreneur or the CEO become the leader, showing the direction and clearly articulating the vision of the company.

3. Management of the key personnel: Once the team is selected and integrated, it must be managed. In a start-up environment, a typical problem is the staff's attempt to take on the duties of the other staff members. Engineering starts to do a marketing job, the CEO starts to perform the sales role, and so on. Management's role is to focus the efforts, not to dampen enthusiasm. Engineering may effec-

tively support marketing and vice versa, but they should not supplant each other. Management should create a management chart and make some effort to keep it orderly.

Risks and Risk Management

During the development stage, businesses face many risks; a surprising number of these can be anticipated. An experienced team will have been exposed to risks in many other business environments; it should be possible to delineate the risks associated with the steps just discussed.

The development effort should then delineate the sets of risks in such areas as:

Technical development

Market development

Staff development

Financial support

Then, for each risk that has been identified, a risk management strategy should be articulated. The strategy should take into consideration how best to avoid the risk as well as what to do in the event that the problem does occur.

These eight items are necessary as part of the product development plan. Consider the following example of how this may be done for a typical start-up company.

Example

MiniSAT is a satellite communications company that has decided to develop a small satellite communications terminal for transmitting data between computers using a sophisticated communications protocol enhancement (e.g., IBM's SNA SDLC protocol). The company has decided to develop the earth terminal (the satellite transmitter and receiver) and the data interface unit for the terminal. The development effort encompasses four major areas:

Software
Hardware
Integration
Manufacturability

The eight-step development process is then applied to this effort. First the goals were established as follows:

Terminal price to customer of $7,500 per unit
Mean time to failure (MTTF) of 10,000 hours
Installation time of 4 hours
Mean time to repair (MTTR) of 2 hours
Support two major protocols: SDLC and BISYNC

These goals establish the overall baseline for the development effort. The company has as its sets of strengths a matured and established staff of software personnel. However, it does not have the radio frequency (RF) persons nor the manufacturing capability. So, the firm must include in the product development plan a strategy and action scheme to offset these weaknesses. In this case, the company has developed a strategic alliance with an RF manufacturing company in the Far East called Matsumani Electric. Matsumani has no software development capability, but it has manufacturing plants in Kyoto and Singapore. Thus, the company has avoided this development problem.

The process of product development focuses on the organization and development procedure. In this case, the organization in the development area will be as shown in Figure 6.1. A development director will manage a hardware development manager, a software (HW) development manager, an integration manager, a manufacturing interface manager, and a quality assurance (QA) manager.

The development process requires that the individuals in the organization have clearly defined goals and tasks. The tasks are the steps in the development process. We shall expand upon this

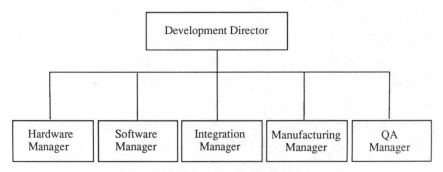

FIGURE 6.1   Development Organization

in detail later in this chapter, but let us now follow the example and develop the tasks.

Task development is performed in a very structured manner. The organization reflects the tasks to be performed. We break down the task into four areas:

Hardware development

Software development

Integration

Manufacturing

Table 6.1 details the next level of task breakdown. Again, we will discuss this later in detail. This approach is called the work breakdown structure (WBS) for the project.

From this table, you can see that the tasks are broken down into the smallest possible sub-tasks, which are the tasks that are scheduled. However, when presenting the plan in a formal setting, you will only need to present the high-level elements—typically, those top 10 to 25 tasks at the highest level. This is shown in Figure 6.2.

Once the tasks are defined, they are scheduled according to the start and finish dates. The schedule not only provides the details of the tasks, but also those of the key events in the development process. The key events are those elements that the investor will examine and may be the key factors in obtaining

TABLE 6.1 WBS for MiniSAT

1.0 Hardware development

   1.1 Antenna
      1.1.1 Definition
      1.1.2 Selection
      1.1.3 Test
      1.1.4 Interface

   1.2 RF components
   1.3 Modems
   1.4 Data interface unit

2.0 Software development

   2.1 Operating system
      2.1.1 Definition
      2.1.2 Design
      2.1.3 Coding
      2.1.4 Test
      2.1.5 Integration
      2.1.6 Documentation

   2.2 IO drivers
   2.3 Link protocol
   2.4 User protocol
   2.5 Multiple access protocol
   2.6 Diagnostics

3.0 Integration

   3.1 SubSystem tests
   3.2 System tests
   3.3 Alpha test
   3.4 Beta test
   3.5 Documentation

4.0 Manufacturing

   4.1 Design modification
   4.2 Preproduction run
   4.3 Cost minimization
   4.4 Manufacturing run

WBS No	Task Name	Duration (days)	Loading (md)	Start Date	Stop Date	Date 6/1 6/8 6/15
1.1.1	Antenna Define	23	45	6/1	6/24	+++++++++++++
1.1.2	Antenna Sel	21	22	6/24	7/20	
1.1.3	Antenna Test	34	34	7/21	8/30	
1.1.4	Antenna Integ	33	33	9/1	10/15	
1.2.1	Define	25	22	6/1	6/23	+++++++++++++
1.2.2	Sel	12	34	6/25	8/1	
1.2.3	Test	33	45	8/2	9/15	
1.2.4	Integ	45	22	9/16	10/15	
1.3.1	Define	21	12	6/1	6/13	+++++++++++++
1.3.2	Sel	22	34	6/14	7/17	
1.3.3	Test	13	45	7/18	9/1	
1.3.4	Integ	25	55	9/2	11/1	
.						
.						
.						
5.1	Alpha Test	5.1	24	3/1	1/13	
5.2	Beta Test	5.2	30	4/1	4/10	
5.3	Acct Test	5.3	45	5/1	5/15	

FIGURE 6.2 Schedule for MiniSAT

additional rounds of financing. For example, in this effort the key event may be the successful completion of the alpha test, a test of the entire system in a prototype stage. (The beta test is the test of the preproduction model.) Critical and final design reviews of software may also be key events.

For example, in a company called PicTel, the entrepreneurs were rewarded with additional stock if the image compression system met a set of standards by a given date. They were successful, and they got the additional equity.

Let us discuss the development schedule in further detail. Figure 6.2 lists the WBS tasks by number and by description, followed by the duration of the task and allocated responsibility. The responsibility may be by department or by person. Then we allocate the amount of effort required by the task in man-month loadings. Thus, task 1.1.1 takes twenty-three days and has a 2 man-day duration. We then indicate the start data as the date the task should start. We include the tasks upon which this effort depends—that is, the tasks that must be complete before starting the next task. Using this information, this program calculates the start and end dates for each WBS element. The interesting fact is that WBS element 4.4, the manufacturing run, starts on March 7, almost three months from the anticipated start date. As you can see, this method of estimating, by including dependent dates, shows inherent slippage in the system.

The effort's costs can be developed on a detailed basis. The costs provide detail of the expense and capital required as well as when they are required. The expenses are task-driven. Using the WBS, we estimate the duration and manpower required for each task. Then, using the rates per person, the expenses are obtained along with the timing. The capital procurement will be an additional itemized factor.

As we discussed, the people resources are the most difficult to obtain. Therefore, if the development requires significant resources, the description of where and when these are to be obtained is essential.

Finally, we need to address the risks and the management of the development risks. The developer must preempt his reader by detailing these along with ways to countervail them. The list below depicts risks and strategies for the MiniSat program:

- Multi-access protocol: Choose a protocol that best suits available RF equipment and user traffic.
- Software schedule: Develop detailed specs and use a structured methodology with frequent reviews.
- Delivery of prototype boards: Develop on commercially available boards, such as VME.
- Poor vendor integration: Maintain weekly vendor contact, and develop detailed spec and acceptance test.
- Loss of key personnel: Assign tasks to teams rather than individuals. Review documentation and train group as single team.

Product development must be succinct. However, it must also have detailed backup to sustain the results presented. In the plan itself, all that is necessary is a statement of the goals, the description of the tasks, the schedule, budget, and organization needed, and an assessment of the risks. The backup will be a detailed part of the development plan that must be prepared as part of the effort.

MARKET DEVELOPMENT

The market development portion of the development phase includes the efforts necessary to establish a presence with the customer and to position both the product and the company for success. As with the product development effort, you will need to describe the market development effort. Specifically, you must discuss the following items:

Goals

What is expected of the market development effort? What commitments are sought, and to what degree are we trying to determine the size and type of market?

Process

What specifically is to be done in the market development phase? What are the tasks? What are the milestones? What organization is needed to accomplish these goals?

Costs

This section describes the costs of the marketing side of the development effort, including all the manpower expenses, direct and indirect, as well as other ancillary marketing expenses. For example, it may be appropriate to hire a PR firm or an advertising agency. Be cautious in hiring such firms until a firm date on delivery can be established. Much of the frenzy in Silicon Valley was fed by PR firms, not by fact. A good PR firm can easily get the company's name in the trade press, such as *Forbes, Fortune,* or *Business Week,* but management must decide the timing and impact relative to the firm's ability to deliver.

Resources

As with product development, you must have a statement of needed human resources and how you will obtain them.

Risks and Risk Management

At what point do we pull the plug on the business? That is the issue of risks and risk management on the market side. We can always argue extending development of the new product, but if no market exists, there is no need to extend anything. Often called the "silver bullet" element of the plan, this is the statement of when to use the bullet to put the business out of its misery.

These steps follow those of the product development effort fairly closely. The major steps that must be accomplished on the market side, however, are generally more common and do not have as close a connection to the specific product. They are:

Identify the Target Market

This step includes the detailed work necessary to identify customers by name, and to identify the end user and the decision maker in the buyer company. This identification will require developing databases of customer contacts and a process whereby the sales force will be able to contact all key customers, tracking the blossoming of the customer relationship as the sales cycle develops.

Establish Distribution Channels

This is the most critical element of the market development phase and the one that is most often neglected. As we discussed before, distribution is the element of the business that gets the product from the factory to the customer. In many new companies, distribution occurs not only through direct sales forces.

These firms need to establish co-marketing efforts with existing distribution channels and to position the product so as to be complementary to those co-market products. In this phase, the negotiations for such an agreement should be made, and the costs of distribution clearly tied down through contractual commitments.

Establish Beta Test Customers

Beta testers should be friendly customers who are interested in assisting the company, partly out of their own interest, to evaluate the new product. In the market development phase, efforts should be focused on working with these customers, assuring them of what the product will and will not do. The product's success will depend on unambiguous expectations—that is, the customer should not assume one level of performance while the product delivers another.

Example

DSO is a business that will provide an on-line computer-based order entry service combined with a cash collection service through an automated clearinghouse. The firm's target market is distributed sales organizations, such as Mary Kay Cosmetics, Shaklee, Avon, and Tupperware. In targetting these companies, DSO has established the following goals:

- Obtain commitment from two DSOs prior to operation
- Sign up 2,000 of their sales representatives
- Obtain a fee of $10 per month for each representative

The effort is directed to the marketing and sales VP as well as the director of sales. Their efforts are tightly targeted. They must visit all the companies and make sales presentations. It was anticipated that they will have to take six to eight weeks to set up the meetings, two to three months to meet, and two months to close.

The major milestones are:

1. *Initial Customer Contact.* Includes contact with the top five DSO companies in the field. The contact must be at the highest level; start-ups should avoid the problem of dealing with too low a level of middle managers.

2. *Customer Presentations.* Requires the development of both a professional slide presentation, collateral sales material, and a demonstration of how the system and the service are envisioned to function. Care must be taken to anticipate customer-specific requirements that could turn into objections. In this case, objections might include needs to interface with their back office mainframe computers.

3. *Letter of Intent.* The targeted customers should be interested in providing a letter of intent, including a time schedule, for beta testing of the product.

4. *Test Trial.* A single customer should be targeted for a test trial to assure that the beta test with several customers will be successful.

5. *Start of Beta Test.* The beta test should commence on schedule. It should involve the marketing and sales team as the customer's eyes and ears on the project. Care should be taken to avoid too much exposure of the technical side, which could result in excessive delays in the product delivery.

6. *Customer Contract.* The major milestone in the market development phase is the customer contract. The customer should be prepared to sign a usage contract upon successful completion of the beta test.

This example shows how market development is more structured than product development. It may differ considerably in a consumer business, where there is a need for extensive distribution channel development. In this case, the business was terminated because the marketing team could not sign up two or more DSO companies. At the time the business began, significant change and turmoil brewed in these businesses. Specifically, Mary Kay was being brought private, Shaklee was retrenching,

Tupperware was being reorganized due to the breakup of Dart Kraft, and Avon had just installed a similar system.

ORGANIZATION DEVELOPMENT

The organizational development section of the business plan is straightforward. It addresses the need of the business to develop the key players for the development stage. For example, the key players may all be in place at the time of the plan. On the other hand, the manufacturing or marketing person may be absent. This part of the plan addresses the following elements:

Goals: What is needed and for what purpose?

Schedules: When are the key people needed?

Assets needed: What are the qualifications of the key people to accomplish their tasks? This portion is a statement of both the existing personnel and the people to be hired.

In addition to stating requirements for the business plan, however, the entrepreneur should develop a detailed organization plan that satisfies the development phase as well as the transition to the operations phase. The specific details that are needed for this plan, although not included in the business plan itself, are as follows:

1. *Organizational Charts.* As we have repeatedly stated, focus is the key element of success. Focus is attained through a clearly articulated statement of the goals and an organization that unambiguously attains those goals. Thus, the organization charts reflect this strategy for success. They must be clearly understood by all players in the organization.

2. *Position Description.* Most entrepreneurs will typically eschew the position description, which was one restricting element they fled from in the large, structured business world. However, just as we had to develop a

functional specification for the product, a detailed development plan for the product, and high quality customer contacts, we must do the same for the organizational side. Position descriptions state tasks to be accomplished and the ideal requirements for the person to fit that position.

Failure to obtain the right person leads to compromise at the most critical stage. Just because someone is a good friend who you may have worked with before is no reason to put that person as head of sales. Understand the requirements of the job, determine the background required, and then fill the position accordingly.

3. *Management Structure.* Recruit the most important people first. It is too easy to recruit the lower-level people, then find the right top management. The problem with that approach is twofold. First, the entrepreneur has significantly increased the management problem by putting in place less experienced staff. Second, the senior people have been preempted in their ability to search out the right people to work with them. A hidden third problem also exists: bringing in a person in the middle often breaks bonds between the CEO and the lower-level staff, leading to dissention and work problems. Thus, the sequencing of the management structure is critical.

4. *Recruiting.* Where to find the correct people? Recruiting can be a full-time job. If not done properly, it can all but destroy the start-up company. Therefore, the entrepreneur should consider other sources. First, the venture capitalists may be important sources of better people. Second, executive recruiters may also be ideal; they are often costly, but the better ones are clearly worth the cost. It is critical, however, to interview several recruiters before choosing.

Example

The management plan is presented as an integral part of the development plan. A typical management organization plan for a new business in the development mode appears in Figure 6.3.

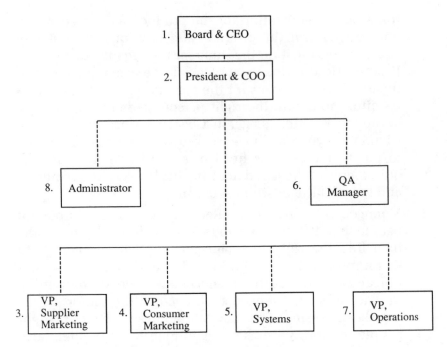

FIGURE 6.3 A Typical Development Organization

This plan is for a company that is interested in starting an interactive videotex shopping business. As such, the company needs extensive technical as well as marketing expertise.

While this organization is the same for the operations of the business (as we shall see in the next chapter), it may also serve as a basis for the development. The major factors associated with this effort are the key players and where they come from. In this plan, the players are:

President
VP, Supplier Marketing
VP, Consumer Marketing
VP, Systems
VP, Operations

VP, Administration

Director, Financial

Table 6.2 depicts the functions for such a set of positions and the experience required of the person filling the slot.

This plan should be detailed enough to assure the financial backers that the key people have been considered. In addition, you will need a description of those people who have filled the positions as well as a description of how the open positions are to be filled and when. This process may require a statement of staffing strategies, such as the following:

- Obtain the top people as quickly as possible. The president and marketing VP have been selected.
- Establish frequent board meetings to monitor the recruitment of key executives.
- Recognize the need for long lead times and adequate compensation packages for key personnel. Use the pool of available equity to attract management. Establish an equity allocation pool and seek board approval.
- Obtain good team players in management and use the strength of the president and the financial backers to assure early placement.

It is important to acquire the most competent people. They all must have an entrepreneurial capability and desire. Hiring people from large corporations may cause problems because the infrastructure that they expect is often lacking in start-up firms.

SCHEDULES, BUDGETS, AND CONTROLS

The development plan has a detailed set of schedules to meet the stated goals. We have spent some effort on the product development schedule and added the market and organizational development efforts. This section provides further detail on the

TABLE 6.2 Management Organization

Position	Function	Experience/Expertise
1. Board	• Provide overall strategic guidance and directions • Ensure financial requirements are met • Provide key industry contacts for supplier efforts	• Experienced in the business area
2. President	• Provide direct strategic goals • Develop and guide business strategies • Ensure careful financial controls (P&L) • Provide integration of marketing and operations	• Proven capabilities as General Manager of startup effort • Excellent technical and commercial or consumer marketing skills • Establish strategic and conceptual leader • Fifteen to twenty years experience
3. VP, Supplier Marketing	• Provide direct contact with suppliers and develop business relations • Develop supplier economics models for pricing strategies • Maintain continual supplier support	• Experience in commercial marketing for eight to ten years • Strong capability in formulating business deals with keen understanding of profit potential • Capability to express complex technical concepts to high level management
4. VP, Consumer Marketing	• Develop consumer marketing strategy • Develop sales strategy and sales force • Develop and implement promotional strategy • Develop and implement customer service strategy	• Strong background in consumer marketing (key purchased goods) • Experienced in developing and implementing strategies on tight budget controls • Established good working relationships and people skills • At ease with technology • Ten to fifteen years experience

TABLE 6.2 Management Organization (continued)

Position	Function	Experience/Expertise
5. VP, Systems	• Develop and evolve overall system architecture • Develop all computer software functions • Provide systems engineering function • Specify all hardware elements	• High-level technical expertise in communications and computers • Keen analytical capabilities • Experienced in management of large scale software developments • Ten to fifteen years experience
6. VP, Operations	• Test and integrate all hardware and software • Provide field installation and system operation • Develop all operational procedures	• Experienced in managing large-scale diverse operations of communications and computer systems • Strong track record of good cost control management • Fifteen to twenty years experience
7. Director, Financial	• Establish and maintain internal project management control system • Provide financial analysis support in modelling and planning • Provide DP support	• Experienced in budget control systems for high tech areas • Exposure to and experience with DP • Good finance knowledge • Ten years experience
8. VP, Administration	• Ensure day to day operations • Manage building services and procurement • Ensure adequate support staff	• Highly experienced administrators from high tech environment • Good people skills • Ten years experience

schedule and corresponding budget elements. The ultimate objective is to integrate these factors into a controlled environment for the development phase as a whole. To demonstrate to investors the business's viability, you will need not only a plan in place, but also a means to monitor and manage that plan.

Let us begin by an example that demonstrates how this process evolves. A start-up company wants to develop a service to assist the distributed sales organizations to more rapidly collect funds from their sales representatives and reduce their processing costs. The net result will be a reduction in overall operating costs and an increase in the profit margin. The goals for the development effort are as follows:

- Develop a transaction processing communications system to support two transactions per second.
- Interface with the regional automated clearinghouse to facilitate funds transfer.
- Secure the commitment from two DSO companies, such as Avon and Tupperware, to test the product. If successful, agree to participate for three years.
- Perform the test for a period of 10 months.

The business has three elements: technical, operations, and marketing. The development plan schedule builds upon these objectives, develops a detailed set of tasks, and outlines who will successfully complete these tasks.

We shall now develop the detailed infrastructure of the schedules, budgets, and controls as relates to a business of this type. This infrastructure can be extended to any other start-up business.

Schedule

The concept of a work breakdown structure (WBS) was introduced in the product development section. We can now expand upon that concept in detail. Any detailed plan contains the following elements:

1. *Tasks and subtasks.* List those tasks that must be completed to achieve the goals. They are hierarchically divided into three major areas: marketing, operations, and systems, and are subdivided into increasingly lower levels until specific tasks are defined.

2. *Organizations.* In order to assign and manage the tasks, an organization is developed. This organization has a functional characteristic that matches the task development.

3. *Schedule.* Each task is then assigned a timeframe for initiation and completion. The schedule shows the relationships among the tasks. As we shall discuss, the use of simple task schedules is appropriate; complex CPM or PERT charts are often unnecessary.

4. *Effort.* The effort in man-months is then allocated to each task and can be further subdivided into man-months per organizational element. Finally, the tasks can be costed out using the allocation of salaries per organizational unit.

5. *Capital Requirements.* Allocated to each task are the capital requirements. These represent the capital side of the cash flow requirements to support the new business.

Let us now return to the DSO business example. The WBS is a top-down determination of all tasks that must be performed in the development of the business. This business has three major task areas:

1.0 Systems: Includes the development of all software and hardware interfaces necessary for delivery of the system. It will also evolve into the ongoing product development functions of the business.

2.0 Operations: Includes the development of the business's operational infrastructure. It includes the development of communications, customer service, operations, and maintenance.

3.0 Marketing and Sales: Includes all of the elements associated with the development of the market, sales to new customers, management of the beta tests, and other elements.

Each of these areas can be further subdivided into a smaller set of tasks associated with the development effort. For example, we can further break down the Systems area as follows:

1.1   System Development: The general system concepts that manage the overall system from the point of view of architecture, interfaces, performance, and capacity.

1.2   Software Development: The set of overall elements that focus on development of all the software for the system.

1.3   Hardware Development: Focuses on the development and integration of all hardware elements for the system.

The areas can be further divided. Focusing on the software, we can go down another level. This will produce:

1.2.1   Operating Systems: All software elements that relate to the system's operation. This task may result in the selection and integration of an operating system. For example, the output of this task is the selection of UNIX.

1.2.2   Data Base: This task includes the definition of all system data elements as well as the selection of the system's database manager. It may also include the integration of the database into the system design.

1.2.3   Foreground Systems: This task is the development of all of the real-time software systems, those that perform real-time functions supporting the ongoing operation of the DSO network.

1.2.4   Background Systems: All of the non-real-time systems that support the DSO business and may also interface with the customers back office systems. These systems may be evolutionary in nature.

1.2.5   Test and Diagnostic Systems

We can still go further into the WBS diagram in the Foreground area. We have still not defined assignable tasks. To do so, we develop specific foreground modules, yielding:

1.2.3.1 Communications: This module handles all communications needs for the system. In some cases it may be necessary to further delimit the communications module, but for this example we assume that it can be adequately defined at this level.

1.2.3.2 Performance Monitor: This is a real-time process that collects data for the database. The data may pertain to customers or system performance.

1.2.3.3 DSO Process: This process sets up communications with the salesperson in the field. As with the communications process, it may be divided further into such tasks as presentation, input/output, setup, and other elements.

1.2.3.4 ACH Process: This process sets up communications with the automated clearing house for the purpose of establishing funds transfer. It is a critical process in that it is at the heart of the business, and has severe federal regulatory limitations placed upon its performance.

1.2.3.5 SR Process: This process allows for communications between the DSO system and the DSO company user. It provides for real-time management of funds transfers and transactions.

At this point we can introduce generic tasks required at the communications level. Let us assume that the communications element has been adequately defined so that it is a stand-alone module of work. Now we can develop the phases of the work in this module as follows:

1.2.3.1.1 Definition: The development of a detailed definition of all steps that have to be performed in the communications process.

1.2.3.1.2 Design: The design of all steps in such detail that the functions can be validated for meeting the design requirements.

1.2.3.1.3 Coding: The step that includes the physical writing of the code to perform the process.

1.2.3.1.4 Unit Test: This step performs tests on the code to ensure that it meets requirements.

1.2.3.1.5 Integration: This step integrates this module with all of the other modules in the system. At this point many inconsistencies may be discovered.

1.2.3.1.6 System Test: A full system test that integrates the system's hardware and software. It is the most critical test in system development.

1.2.3.1.7 Documentation: This task is often forgotten and poorly done. It documents what the code does. If done properly, documentation will often save the system as it evolves. Too many systems work on folklore rather than proper documentation.

At this point, the WBS will specify a task that can be assigned to a specific set of individuals. These tasks may be the above set of tasks for a specific module. For example, the coding of the communications system interface may take six man-months to perform, but it must be completed in three months. So, two people are required. If one looks at the above set of steps for the communications code, one can readily see how the set of code can have productivity rates of five lines of code per day per person, if one includes all of the steps.

The WBS is often a lengthy description of the tasks to be performed in the development. The tasks are specified to a level low enough to be assigned to a set of individuals and monitored at various management levels. WBS schedules typically go to the fifth or sixth level of depth. In this case the depth is five, as indicated by the number of subdivisions required to specify an executable task.

The procedure for developing a WBS is highly collaborative. It requires the support of the highest levels of management. The actual schedule is then a schedule of the final elements of the WBS, such as those shown above, for all the business areas.

We can relate the WBS concept to include the development organization, and relate WBS tasks to organizational elements and tasks. The business organization during the development phase has the following structure:

1.0 Systems

2.0 Operations

3.0 Marketing and Sales

Each of these separate organizational elements have departments and sections. In the systems organization are the following separate departments:

1.1 Development

1.2 Software

1.3 Hardware

In the software department, the software development engineers will be assigned the tasks described above in the WBS elements. In certain tasks, it will be necessary to get the support of the marketing as well as the operations staff. This will be the case in the sales rep interface, where the screens necessary to satisfy the DSO company and the end user are generated—really a marketing-driven parameter and not only a technical factor.

To complete the WBS approach, you will need to assign the WBS task modules to each organization. Some task modules may have the support of several organizational elements. Generally, however, try to keep the tasks confined to single organizational elements to ensure accountability.

The full WBS approach, then, consists of the following tasks:

1. Develop the program's detailed WBS, down to the individual task level.

2. Develop the organizational structure.

3. Correlate the tasks to the organization, assigning man-months of effort to each task and sub-allocating it by department.

4. Develop a schedule of the project, carefully laying out the WBS final elements. Then, using the level of efforts per task, determine the staffing needed to complete the tasks.

5. Assign direct salaries to each of the employees in each of the departments. Use these as the basis for the costing of each task.

6. Develop overhead numbers that are assignable to each task. Load the direct salaries accordingly.

7. Allocate capital, the date it is available, and the cost of the capital to each task.

Once all of these tasks are completed, you can then create the development expense budget, a budget that will be a controllable expense item in the business development process.

Budgets

The development budget results directly from the WBS structure, as we have just shown. The budget has three elements:

1. Revenue. That revenue expected from potential customers as a result of beta testing of the system or service on their premises.

2. Expenses. The total set of expenses that result from the WBS elements. The WBS has associated with it the cost per WBS task; this may or may not include the overhead element, which may be added on as a total overhead or individually. The choice depends on how the overhead will be managed.

3. Capital. The capital required for the development program includes any development systems, such as computers and manufacturing hardware, and any other items required for product development.

The revenue portion of the budget is usually the most at-risk factor unless a preagreed-to set of contracts exists for the development phase.

For example, in the development of a new service bureau company for the DSO case, the DSO companies have agreed to provide the start-up company with $250,000 each for the development of the test market evaluation. Using the three companies assumed by the developers of the plan, this results in $750,000 initial revenue.

The expense portion must also be allocated on a monthly basis, along with the number of staff members required to perform the tasks. Expenses will be broken down as follows:

Direct salaries

Direct overhead

Other direct expenses

For example, the direct overhead numbers should include the following:

Rent

Travel

Leases of equipment

Professional expenses

Employee overhead (Social Security, pension, health benefits, etc.)

Insurance

The other direct expenses are those related less directly to employees—for example, computer leases or telecommunications expenses for the telecommunications-intensive service company. The ratio of direct overhead to total salaries is the overhead ratio, which should not exceed 200 percent. In most start-up companies, it should be kept to 100 percent or slightly more.

Table 6.3 shows a typical budget for a one-year development. Also included are the capital requirements, the cash flow, and

TABLE 6.3 Budget ($000)

Item	Quarter 1	Quarter 2	Quarter 3	Quarter 4
Revenue	0	0	250	250
Expenses				
Salaries	350	350	450	450
Overhead	450	500	550	600
Other expenses	0	100	250	250
Total expenses	800	950	1,250	1,300
Net expenses	800	950	1,000	1,050
Capital	200	400	500	700
Cash flow	1,000	1,350	1,500	1,750
Cumulative CF	1,000	2,350	3,850	5,600

the cumulative cash flow. In this case, the estimated development costs are $5.6 million.

This table allows the investor to see the development costs and what the total exposure can be on the entire development program. Behind this overall budget, a detailed budget should be developed, item-by-item, based on the WBS.

Controls

The development process must have controls that carefully guide and monitor development. These controls have three key elements:

1. *Goals.* A set of well-defined goals must be established and adhered to. These goals are readily measurable and definable, and must be specified in a time context. Typical goals are the attainment of market distribution agreements, an available beta test software package, or the generation of revenue at a specified level.
2. *Tracking.* A process whereby the elements of the development process, such as the WBS tasks, are tracked and reported upon. Whereas the goals report on macro levels

of accomplishments, the tracking process will report on the micro level of progress in the development phase.

3. *Management.* The most intangible parts of the controls process are the management controls and policies and procedures to be followed.

The establishment of controls is best embodied in a Project Management Control System (PMCS). The PMCS has as its basis the elements of the WBS, the organization, the schedule, and the budget. A typical PMCS has the following elements:

1. *Planning.* Includes the development of the WBS, the allocation of manpower by organization, the scheduling of the WBS elements, and the development of a budget.

2. *Measurement.* To be successful, a PMCS must have a real-time measurement system that measures the expenditure of labor on a per-task basis, the receipt of capital equipment and the costs, the status of all work elements and the percentage completed, and a tracking of all expense elements.

3. *Monitor.* A PMCS must have a monitoring element that tracks manpower, tasks, capital equipment, and overall project status. Such measures as the budget and actual expenses—by task, department, month, and year to date—must be made available. In addition, the estimate of the cost to complete must be available. Table 6.4 depicts a typical project management schedule for a development project.

   In Table 6.4 the project is examined by total expenses on a task basis. Other breakdowns of the project may include more detail on expenses or more detail on organizations. The specific project usually dictates the approach taken. The key point, however, is that you must consider the need for the initial system, the need for the measurements, and the need for a tracking system.

4. *Control.* After the monitoring is performed, you must have a means for controlling the system. Control usually entails

TABLE 6.4 Project Management Schedule ($000)

	Week		YTD		Total		Etc	
	Budget	Actual	Budget	Actual	Budget	Actual	Budget	Actual
WBS No.								
1.1.1	23	27	135	142	144	172	31	45
1.1.2	22	24	122	123	132	144	22	23
1.1.3	12	10	109	210	222	234	78	99
1.2.1	3	0	3	0	3	0	99	99
1.2.2	5	9	5	9	5	9	134	134
2.1.1	0	0	0	0	0	0	150	150
2.1.2	0	0	0	0	0	0	225	225
3.1.1	24	33	223	224	300	334	0	35
3.1.2	33	55	250	220	250	220	0	0
Total	122	158	847	928	1,056	1,113	739	810

the implementation of work and materials order documents, which control the use of labor or capital on specific projects. It means that capital requires the approval of the proper person, usually the VP of finance and engineering. Also, in large development programs, each individual should be assigned a task. Those not assigned should be evaluated based on their direct contributions.

5. *Action.* Action elements of a PMCS usually entail reports, such as the yellow and red flag reports, on the status of specific elements of the project. The red flag report discusses the delay of a critical path element, such as a major piece of software or a major customer relationship. It should go directly to the CEO. It is key that management not be blindsided. An employee's failure to generate such a report should be grounds for immediate termination of employment. Yellow flag reports are reports that indicate the possible development of more serious difficulties in the near future. They, too, are of importance to the development effort.

Example

Consider a company developing a new software product that performs protocol conversion for a personal computer so that it may talk into a packet network at high data rates. The company has developed a detailed software development program and has targeted a direct sales approach for its product. It has defined the following set of goals:

Commitment from three companies for 100 units by month six

Beta test product available by month nine

The firm has established a detailed WBS and has introduced a PMCS. It has hired a controller, who has a Stanford MBA, to manage the program development.

The president is an aggressive, sales-oriented technical person, and is not a manager. She has hired a salesperson to work the sales area personally. The following things begin to happen:

- The president talks to several new potential customers and is so enthralled with a new product that she sells them on it.
- The president does not communicate this to the head of development, but talks directly to the software people. They begin a "small" project to test out her data. They assure her that it won't take long.
- The salesperson calls on the clients to close the deals. He finds that they are confused because he has not included the new products. The deals do not close.
- Engineering sees a slip in the development. The engineering head complains to his staff. A new engineer begins to play politics and goes around the department head directly to the president. A serious rift occurs. The engineering head now drops all interest in reaching target.
- Beta test units are three months late. The president fires the engineering head and takes on direct responsibility. The customers are concerned and never complete their offers.

- The company runs out of its first round of financing without product or customers. The venture capital board members believe the president has not acted wisely, and fire her.
- A new president is appointed from the board. The engineering staff members are disillusioned and quit.
- The company is dissolved and sold as a tax carry-forward to another company owned by one of the venture board members.

This is a true story; only some of the instances have been altered. It shows that, even with clearly defined goals and measurement systems, people management is the most critical link in the chain. The president must be up to the task of managing or be replaced quickly, either by termination or repositioning.

SUCCESS FACTORS

At the completion of the development, how do we know if we have a business? We may have reached our goals but we also need success as well as failure factors. One final element in the development plan is deciding on success and failure factors. Once we have established our goal, we must carefully and in a detailed fashion define success. In a similar fashion, we must have well-defined failure factors—those factors that we use to terminate the effort. They are critical to articulate to avoid a great deal of suffering and expense. Businesses often do not attain success, but they continue to bleed money for a long period. If they had created hard-and-fast failure factors, they could have saved themselves grief.

The success and failure factors are those elements of the business that, if measured at the end of the development cycle, will provide a yardstick of the business's future success (or lack thereof). These factors often relate to the financial viability of the business. The following are examples of businesses with appropriate success and failure factors.

Example

This business wants to develop a videotex service that uses a full-motion video approach. The company has a development program to test the service in 1,000 homes in two cities. The development program will last 18 months and the test market another year. The development effort will cost $16 million; the actual business will require $120 million for its total development.

The investors are willing to invest the development amount but they want to know what factors will reduce the risk in the long term. They also want to know what factors will show that there is no business, and that they should withdraw from the business and thus from the market opportunity.

The investors' concern is related to the capital required and the risk of not pursuing the business. In the event that the business is not pursued, a competitor may enter the market and dramatically reduce their market share.

Table 6.5 depicts the success and failures factors for this videotex business. If, at the end of the development effort, all the results are in the success column, a high reliability exists for a business. On the other hand, if the results are all in the failure column, there is a good chance that no such need exists. How-

TABLE 6.5 Success and Failure for a Consumer Business

Factor	Success	Failure
Customer sales (households)	>1,000	<500
Rate of penetration (subs/mo)	>100	<40
Subscriber usage (hrs/year)	>80	<60
Purchase volume ($/year)	>600	<300
Revenue per HH	>$250	<$100
Churn rate (%)	<30	>60
Supplier size (number)	>50	<10
Response time (sec)	<5	>15
Transaction errors (%)	<1	>4
Availability (%)	>98	<90
Terminal cost ($)	<200	>400

ever, there are uncertainties. Some results may appear as successes and others as failures; others may even lie in between. This is a management call. If there are five successes, three failures, and the rest undetermined, a high level of risk is implied with a possible positive outcome. At this point, high-level management must make the judgment.

Table 6.5 considers some of the entries in detail. The consumer sales factor states that, at the end of the trial, we would expect 1,000 households to be a success. If, on the other hand, we attain success on 500 or less, we have failed. This factor was developed on the basis of the market penetration necessary for the financial success of the business. Now consider the second factor. The sales rate of 100 subscribers per month meets that rate expected for a profitable business. The rate of 40 or fewer subscribers per month would result in a cash flow that would be too great and an IRR on the investment that would be too low.

Continue with each table entry, which relates back to a fundamental element of the profitability and viability of the business.

Example

A data radio network business was developed using radio modems in laptop computers. The business also provided full service and a backbone communications network. The success and failure factors are shown in Table 6.6. The business factors are similar to those shown in the consumer example. These factors

TABLE 6.6 Success and Failure for a Commercial Business

Factor	Success	Failure
Number of companies	>15	<5
Number of subs	>6,000	<1,000
Rate of sales (sub/month)	>700	<300
Churn rate (%)	<10	>20
Revenue ($000,000)	>3.2	<1
Availability (%)	>98	<90
Response time (sec)	<1	>10

are taken from a detailed analysis of the business financials, considering the key factors that would make or break the business.

We can analyze these success and failure factors in some detail. The first is the number of companies needed for a successful trial. In this case we assumed that 15 companies were appropriate. If it fell below eight, it was felt that the ultimate market penetration would be insufficient for success. Also, 6,000 subscribers were required for success; less than 3,000 was considered a failure. The churn rate is the rate in which subscribers leave the service on an annual basis. A churn of 15 percent was a success. If the churn reached 25 percent or greater, it was felt that the cost of gaining new sales made the business unprofitable. The system availability also determines how frequently the system operates. An availability of 98 percent was necessary for this vital business communications link. Since typical voice-grade data lines have an availability of 90 percent, it was felt that, if the availability dropped to that level, the effort was a failure.

Each of the entries in Table 6.6 depict critical elements of the business. It was essential that each of these elements be simply quantified and that they be highlighted at the beginning of the development effort.

Success/failure (S/F) factors are based upon the business and its financial models. The business factors relate to the revenue potential, the expense factors, its use of cash, its market penetration rate, and other factors that indicate how effectively the business can grow and prosper. The business plan must clearly state these factors and show how they relate to the success or failure. Thus designed, the business plan will include a silver bullet that allows all concerned to put the business out of its misery if it becomes clear that a failure is imminent.

CONCLUSION

The development plan describes the actual tasks necessary to develop the business to the point at which it is ongoing. It provides a set of actions to be followed and to be supported by the capital raised. The financing agents will assess the credibility of the plan in view of the funds available and the level of expertise of the people associated with the company.

The description of the development plan must be realistic. The WBS is the most important element of the development plan. It is key to do a top-down and bottom-up analysis of the tasks that must be performed, and to carefully allocate all costs and efforts.

7

OPERATIONS AND MANAGEMENT

The development portion of the business plan is specific and goal-oriented. In contrast, the operations plan describes how the business functions on an ongoing basis. The operations plan discusses both the organization and its responsibilities, who does what and why, the team used to accomplish the tasks and the capital, and expense factors related to business operations. The operations plan is the counterpart of the marketing plan. While the marketing plan focuses on the revenue side of the business equation, the operations plan focuses on the expense and capital side.

The operations plan is strategic; the development plan is tactical. The overall strategic intent of the operations plan is to effectively execute the business once it has become active.

In this chapter, we develop a very key concept used in the development of the expense, capital, and cost-of-goods models. The concept is that these functions are all influenced by the revenue model developed in Chapter 4. More specifically, the expenses, capital, and cost-of-goods models are directly driven by a set of parameters that are a direct part of the revenue model. We shall call these elements the revenue drivers. This chapter identifies these factors for all elements of the business. Once these have been identified, we can then use productivity ratios and unit cost factors to generate all of the operations plans.

ORGANIZATION

The organizational structure for the operation of the business is specified in the business plan, and is a key element for the financial analysis of the business. The organizational structure is the basis for the manpower requirements of the business. The choice of a specific organizational type will depend upon the type of business the company is in. The organization can be along product lines or along functional lines. The product line approach is usually more appropriate for more mature businesses with multiple products. An alternative to product line organization is to organize along market lines, an approach that aligns the organization to service the unique needs of differing market elements, such as direct sales versus OEM (e.g., indirect third-party vendors).

The methodology that we adopt in developing the organization plan will follow two paths. First, the organization must meet the overall objectives of the business. Second, the organization must be measurable in terms of meeting the stated goals. The second factor is missing in many organizations. The questions most often asked are, "Why are there so many people in the marketing organization? How effective is the sales force? Don't we need more staff in customer service?" In this chapter, we develop an organization that allows us to measure this effectiveness.

This methodology states that, once each element of the organization has been defined, the next step is to identify its relationship to the revenue stream through the revenue driver concept. Then each organizational element must have a defined productivity factor. This productivity factor determines how many staff are needed in that element to satisfy the need of the revenue driver. Finally, when we come to the expense side, we shall add a unit cost to each staff element.

Let us consider the sales organizational element. The revenue driver is readily understood to be the number of new customers. However, each new business may define customers in different terms. One must be certain to identify the sale to a company, an individual, a single buyer, or some other final purchaser of the product. Thus, if we define "customer" to mean the ultimate buyer, we know that, for the sales force, the revenue driver (RD) is:

RD (sales) = number of new customers

The productivity factor, PF, is a measure of how many staff are required to meet the revenue driver requirement. For example, in the sales force example, we may determine the sales cycle to be three months, the number of customers seen during that period to be 80, and the success to be one sale per ten customer visits. Thus, the salesperson will attain eight sales per quarter, or 32 per year. This means that the productivity ratio is one staff per 32 sales. The total staffing, TS, is then easily determined as follows:

TS (Sales) = RD (Sales) * PF(Sales)

where

PF(Sales) = Number of Staff/Sales = $\frac{1}{32}$

If the number of new sales are determined to be 3,200, then the number of sales staff is 100. We can also calculate the productivity in terms of dollars/sales staff/year, knowing dollars/customer/year. This is also a standard sales force productivity measure.

Thus, we consider it essential to know not only the organizational structure, but also the organizational drivers. In general, however, the best approach at the beginning is along functional lines. For example, the key functional areas of many organizations are developed below:

Marketing

This group defines the target market, develops the sales and promotional plan, establishes pricing, and manages ongoing product development programs.

The revenue drivers for the marketing function are generally the total number of customers, or the total number of companies that the marketing department is dealing with. For example, if a marketing department is developing software products for the financial services industry, then the size of the department is generally dependent upon the number of banks or other financial institutions that the company is dealing with. In a consumer business, however, the size of the marketing department may depend upon the total size of the company's consumer base. The productivity factor is generally the number of staff per total companies in the revenue driver.

Sales

The sales organization is directly related to the customer interface, the closure of the sale with the customer, and the ongoing maintenance of the customer's account.

The revenue drivers for the sales function are generally the most clear. They are driven by the number of new customers the company will obtain in the year. They may also depend on the total customer base, since some maintenance sales functions may be necessary. Generally, however, the sales force is directly related to the size of the new base generated.

The productivity factor is measured in terms of the number of staff per new customer. In many businesses, the productivity of the sales force is measured in terms of new revenue per sales person. It should be clear that this productivity measure is inversely related to our defined productivity factor.

Customer Service

Customer service is the essential element of any business that supports the product when it enters the customer's hands. Whereas the sales function is to get the product into the customer's hands, the customer service function is required to maintain the account. Depending on how service-intensive the business is, the customer service function may or may not be very manpower-intensive.

The revenue driver for the customer service function is the total number of users. This is not necessarily the total customer base; there may be many users per customer. Depending on the business, the customer service function may be labor-intensive or very lean. In a service business, customer service may often have the key operational role due to the ongoing relationship with the customer. The productivity factor is clearly the number of staff per user. We will show later how this productivity factor may be developed using more detailed performance factors, such as failures per customer per year, holding time per customer service call, and other detailed operational factors. These first three examples show how the productivity factors are developed.

Systems

The systems element of the organization develops the overall concepts of the technical side of the business. They may handle the sizing and performance factors for new customers, manage and operate the MIS center, and be the key players in the overall costing of the product. They are also the key managers of the technical sides of hardware and software development and the manufacturing processes.

The revenue drivers for this element are the total customer base. They not only have to deal with new customers, but also with supporting changes to the old customer base. Generally, the intensiveness of their efforts is shared equally among all customers.

Hardware Development

This element—the development arm of any company that produces hardware—defines, designs, and develops pre-production prototypes of the final product. Generally interested in only new products, it may also support the company's R&D functions. The revenue drivers typically are the new customers, although it also supports the existing customer base. This element generally is one of the fastest moving, and should be results-driven.

Software Development

This element, the counterpart of the hardware element, has as its major functions the development of new software and maintenance of existing software. This is a major difference between the two organizations. Whereas hardware is focused almost exclusively on new hardware, software is typically focused on existing product as well as new. In fact, many software organizations find the majority of their efforts focusing on the existing customers and older software products as the business matures. Thus, the revenue drivers are the new customers in the early stage and a weighted fraction of the total customers and new customers as the business matures.

Field Service

This element focuses on servicing the customer in the field. Computer companies depend on a strong field service organization that can install, test, and support the ongoing operations of the product on the customer's premises.

Clearly, the revenue driver for this function is the total number of user sites. This figure may exceed the number of companies but be less than the number of users.

Plant Installation

This function is a special element of what may appear under field service. It focuses on the specific installation of the equipment or software on the customer's premise. The major difference is that the plant installation may be more complex and require more specific expertise than that of normal field service. Clearly, the drivers are the same as for field service.

Network Installation

In many services it is necessary to establish a communications network. This work element represents the non-customer premise element of the installation part of the business. It also is driven by similar elements.

Operations and Maintenance

In certain service businesses, there is an ongoing need for operations and maintenance. This may include the staff that manages the network management and control facilities, operates the MIS facilities, or provides the ongoing equipment customization. Typically, this element has as a revenue driver the total number of users.

Manufacturing

Manufacturing is driven by the number of new users or products shipped. In many start-up companies, this function may be contracted out to third-party board-stuffing houses or special-purpose assembly shops. Generally, it requires special attention to develop a manufacturing strategy for the business.

Manufacturing Support

This function is required independent of whether the manufacturing is done in-house or at an outside facility. It is an extension of the hardware element of the operations, but it is the group that does the design for cost, manufacture, and maintainability as well as develops and supports all documentation. Generally, this element has as a revenue driver the number of new users.

Product Development

This work element is the most vital for the long-term development and survival of the business. A combination of both the technical and marketing sides of the business, it has the goal of developing all new products and enhancements to existing products. This element interfaces information provided by marketing with the systems organization, and provides for the new features and functions, as well as conceives prototypes of new products. It is generally driven by the total number of new customers required.

Billing

Billing is a customer-sensitive task. Many companies have lost customers or have had major cash flow problems because of poor billing operations. The most notable example of billing failure is that of U.S. Sprint and its major losses due to improper billing processes. Billing must ensure that cash is collected in a set number of days, and that customers who have questions regarding their bills are serviced politely, promptly, and properly. Customer service usually assists the customer when the product does not work; billing assists when the process does not work. Billing is driven by the total number of customers.

Testing and Evaluation

This element ensures that all tests are performed on the product prior to customer release. It has the line responsibility for product quality. Generally, it is driven by the total of new users to the business.

Quality Assurance

Quality assurance (QA) is an often-neglected but important element of the organization. QA's job is to ensure that all of the other elements perform their tasks properly. It should generally report to the CEO of the company, and should be staffed by the best possible individuals.

General and Administrative (G&A)

The G&A functions are those overhead functions that support business operations. They include financial, legal, personnel, senior management, and other functions not directly related to customers.

The G&A driver is the total number of employees in the organization. That is, G&A does not relate to the revenue elements directly, but supports those who do. The productivity factor is clearly the number of staff who support each employee. A measure of an efficient, productive organization is the relative small value to the productivity factor—that is, few staff in G&A per revenue-generating employee.

These are just a few of the overall functions that must be performed. Table 7.1 summarizes the elements of the organization, their functions, the respective revenue drivers, and productivity factors. In the next section this model helps us develop the ex-

TABLE 7.1 Organizational Elements and Characteristics

Element	Revenue Driver	Productivity
Marketing	Total customers	Staff/customer
Sales	New customers	Staff/new customer
Customer service	Total users	Staff/user
Systems	Total customers	Staff/customer
Hardware development	New customers & total customers	Staff/customer
Software development	New customers & total customers	Staff/customer
Field service	Total customers	Staff/customer
Plant ops	Total customers	Staff/customer
Network ops	Total users	Staff/user
Operations & maintenance	Total users	Staff/user
Manufacturing	Total new user	Staff/new user
Manufacturing support	Total new users	Staff/new user
Product development	New customer	Staff/new customer
Billing	Total customers	Staff/customer
Testing and evaluation	Total new user	Staff/new user
Quality assurance	Total ops empl.	Staff/total ops
G&A	Total employees	Staff/employees

pense model for the operations. In the operations of the business, however, this model also represents management's view toward the productivity of the organizational elements, and how best to set goals and measure performance.

Organizing the operations plan involves a four-step process:

1. Determine the tasks to be accomplished on the broadest levels. List these tasks and functions, and determine the functional cells.

2. Considering the nature of the business, cluster these tasks into organizational units. Try to eliminate as many levels of reporting structure as possible, and push the management responsibility down. Generally, we seek a flat management structure wherein the workers can have access to top management by, at most, three layers.

3. Evaluate the personnel who are going to perform these tasks. Look at talents and personalities, and realign the

tasks as necessary to keep the business functioning and the people happy. In the event of severe conflicts, consider eliminating the conflicting person before eliminating the conflicting task.

4. Determine the revenue drivers and the productivity factors for each of the organizational elements. Determine if the organization can achieve these levels of performance and if the staffing required is achievable.

Example

Consider a company that is in the business of developing and manufacturing a special-purpose telecommunications device to provide a switched data service to end users. The product may be integrated into a PBX or may be a stand-alone device. The company will manufacture the units in Singapore by means of a relationship with Liu-The Manufacturing. Continuing product enhancements are expected, and the company's long-term strategy is to develop vertical markets in the integrated data market for multi-media transmission (e.g., telephone wire, coaxial cable, fiber optics, and satellites).

Sales are made through direct channels as well as OEM, through distributors such as the PBX vendors as well as the local Bell operating companies (BOCs). The firm's president has worked in large structured companies and is a marketing-oriented person with limited sales and technical background. He recognizes that he has the following problems:

- The Singapore plant is new; he has never run a manufacturing operation like this before. Product quality and availability are important.

- Early sales are key. The direct sales approach is to large companies in the Fortune 500 and requires sophistication. On the other hand, the BOCs may represent a good OEM-type channel. They are different in character.

- Continued product enhancements are important. However, product ideas will come from the field where the customer will provide input as to specific needs. Development will be performed in-house, where the knowledge of the customer's requirements are not that clearly understood. The product will become more software-oriented in order to have the flexibility to modify its features and functions.

These factors lead to the following organization:

1. Direct sales
2. OEM sales
3. Marketing and product development
4. Manufacturing and operations
5. Engineering
6. Administration

This structure can be broken down into smaller units:

1.0 Direct Sales
   1.1 Sales force
   1.2 Sales support
   1.3 Customer service

2.0 OEM sales
   2.1 Sales force
   2.2 Sales support
   2.3 Customer service

3.0 Marketing
   3.1 Marketing
   3.2 Product development
   3.3 Advertising

4.0 Operations
   4.1 Foreign operations
   4.2 Manufacturing support
   4.3 Field service
   4.4 Quality assurance

5.0 Engineering
   5.1 Systems
   5.2 Hardware
   5.3 Software

6.0 Administration

The natural breakdown in terms of levels are divisions, departments, and sections. The major categories set forth in the previous example are the division levels, and the subcategories are the departments. Divisions are VP-level positions, and departments are director levels. We can further divide the engineering software department into sections:

5.3.1 Real-time section

5.3.2 Background section

5.3.3 Test section

The level of management at the section level is the standard manager. In order to establish the management personnel, it is important to start with the divisions and proceed to the working staff level. Remember that management personnel do more direct work the lower their the level in the organization. Thus, director or department level personnel are really workers as well as management.

The organization chart for this business is depicted in Figure 7.1. We shall use this format when we develop the expense format for the operations organization.

The operations plan must also discuss who is to fill the key positions in this organization, which is covered in detail in the latter chapters of this text. Identify the key positions and spell out the position requirements in detail. In turn, identify the key players in the business and indicate their roles.

OPERATIONS EXPENSES

The operations expenses are a direct consequence of the operations organization. We can size the organization using the revenue drivers and the productivity factors. This section uses unit cost factors to develop the overall operations expense model.

Simply put, in the previous subsection we found that the staffing requirement of an organizational element was given by the product of the revenue driver and the productivity factor. Thus,

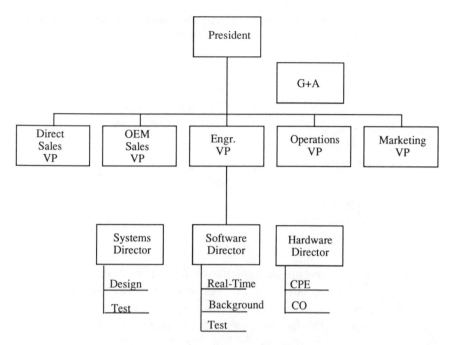

FIGURE 7.1 Organization Chart

if we use the average unit cost for employees in that organizational element, the unit element expense is the product of the staffing and the unit cost per staff. Specifically, let $E(i)$ be the expense in element i. Let $RD(i)$, $PF(i)$, and $UC(i)$ be the revenue driver, productivity factor, and unit cost in element i. Then:

$$E(i) = RD(i)^* PF(i)^* UC(i)$$

The operations expenses are driven by the operations organizational chart, which in turn looks to the revenue base for the business. Let us begin by considering a simple business example.

Example

The company, called DENTACOMP, makes a dental billing computer support package that it sells directly to dentists in a specific state. The package runs on an IBM computer and requires a modest level of customer service support. The organization is structured as follows:

1.0 Sales
    1.1 Sales force

2.0 Development
    2.1 Software
    2.2 Product

3.0 Operations
    3.1 Customer service
    3.2 Installation

4.0 Administrative

The sales are driven by the number of new dentists to whom the product can be sold. The development effort is ongoing at a fixed level, independent of the size of the customer base. Customer service depends upon the total number of dentists and the installation on the number of new dentists. The administrative expense depends upon the total number of employees.

Let *No Den* be the number of dentists and *No New Den* the number of new dentists. Then we have:

No Salespersons = No New Den / (No New Den/Salesper)

Let us say that a good salesperson can sell two dentists per week. Thus, on an annual basis (assuming 50 work weeks per year):

No Salespersons = No New Den / (2*50)

or

No Salespersons = No New Den / 100

If the direct salary of a sales person is $60,000 per year, then the cost per sale is $600.

In a similar fashion, we can say that the number of software people is:

No SW Persons = 5 + No Den / (No Den/SW Person)

This is a fixed plus variable amount. In this example, the ratios of No Den/SW are called the productivity factors. The total manpower loading is then the product of the revenue driver times the productivity factor. The revenue driver is obtained from the revenue statement, and the productivity factor from business experience in this type of business. One must be careful to validate the revenue driver.

Two factors must be kept in mind when developing the expenses for a new business:

1. Many functions have to be performed. The entrepreneur must not forget to include functions necessary for the survival of the business, such as quality assurance or an adequate billing or customer service organization.

2. Many proposed businesses have productivity factors that have no relationship to reality. The entrepreneur must investigate the typical productivity factors from his or her own experience as well as that of others. Can the entrepreneur improve on those factors, or may he be forced into less productive modes during start-up?

Therefore, the direct salary expense for each organizational element can be expressed as the product of the following factors:

RD : revenue driver
PF : productivity factor
UC : unit cost, or salary per employee

Thus, the expense per element is

$E = RD^*PF^*UC$

and the number of employees is

$$N = RD*PF$$

Non-direct employees, such as administrative personnel, are driven from the total direct employee base multiplied by their productivity factor. For example, there may be 10 direct employees per G&A employee.

The total employee base can be obtained via this process. The overhead is obtained in a similar way. The overhead elements, too, are driven by drivers, productivity numbers, and unit expenses. Let us take travel as an example. The travel expense is driven by the number of employees, and the productivity factor is the expense per employee. The product is the total travel expense.

A second example is rent. Rent is driven by the number of employees, the square feet per employee, the cost per square foot, and thus the total rent expense.

All other direct expenses can be determined in a similar fashion. These may be expenses that relate to business operations. For example, if the business operates a telecommunications network, this network's cost and its associated operations are a separate expense in terms of the fees paid to a third-party telecommunications carrier.

The following example details the expenses, both direct and indirect, for a business that runs a reservations service.

Example

This business operates a computer-based reservations service for bed-and-breakfast (B&B) inns and provides a real-time reservation capability. The company believes the B&B industry could effectively use its product to increase their level of reservations. The company intends to support this service with advertising and a full-service, toll-free telephone number to attract upscale customers to the affiliated B&B establishments. The company will place computer terminals that will assist in the reservations process at each of the B&B locations. In addition, the company will operate a national data communications network to confirm reservations and guarantee payment through a credit-card-clearing network interconnection.

Let us begin by considering Table 7.2, which depicts the firm's revenue drivers. The revenue is derived in the following fashion:

1. The primary driver for the revenue is the number of establishments, B&Bs, that the company sees in the market for each year of the business. These are not customer establishments, but represent the total market potential. Note that in the first year there are 4,000 establishments; by the tenth year this figure has grown to 9,432.

2. The second element is the number of rooms per establishment. In this example, it is fixed at eight rooms, on average, per establishment.

3. The third factor is the rate charged per room at the existing market establishment. Note in this example we anticipate a significantly increasing rate per room per night.

4. We then include the occupancy rate for each establishment.

5. The product of the above factors yields the total revenue in this present market, independent of this business. These numbers, based upon actual data, show a market of $500 million in 1986 and growing to $1.1 billion in 1990.

6. The total number of rooms in the target market can also be calculated.

7. The next factor, market penetration, is the most important. It says, for example, that the business anticipates capturing 10 percent of the total market in the first year. This means that it will capture 400 establishments. It is not yet clear in this model how many establishments have to be visited to get to that number, or how many people are required to attain it. Note that, in 1990, the firm anticipates 50 percent penetration; with the total market size in that year, we have 2,928 establishments.

TABLE 7.2 B&B Revenue

	Revenue Summary				
Year	1986	1987	1988	1989	1990
No of B&Bs	4,000	4,400	4,840	5,324	5,856
Rooms/B&B	8	8	8	8	8
Rate/room ($)	$50	$55	$61	$67	$73
Occupancy rate (%)	85	85	85	85	85
B&B revenue ($000,000)	$496	$601	$727	$879	$1,064
No rooms	32,000	35,200	38,720	42,592	46,851
% Penetration	10	20	30	40	50
No B&B sold	400	880	1,452	2,130	2,928
% BBI allocation	55	65	70	70	75
No rooms sold	1,760	4,576	8,131	11,926	17,569
Revenue base ($000)	27,302	78,084	152,624	246,233	399,029
Reservation fee %	12	12	12	12	12
Revenue ($000)	3,276	9,370	18,315	29,548	47, 883

8. The next factor depicts the total number of rooms sold.

9. The revenue base is the product of total rooms and average rate per room, including occupancy. This is the gross revenue base against which commissions are obtained.

10. The reservation fee is the fee that the company expects to attain as a result of providing the service. In this case it is 12 percent.

11. The total revenue is merely the total business base times the reservation fee. The business has a revenue of $3.3 million in its first year and will grow to $48 million in its fifth.

This revenue model describes the way revenue is generated in the business. It is driven by the acquisition of new B&B establishments. We can now use this information to determine, in detail, how revenue relates to the expenses of this business.

The expense side of this business is depicted in Table 7.3. The company has decided to divide itself into the following elements:

TABLE 7.3 Detailed B&B Expense Model

Year	Expense Model ($000)				
	1986	1987	1988	1989	1990
Mktg & Sales					
Mktg					
No. customers cum.	400	880	1,452	2,130	2,928
No. customers/Mktg	200	200	150	150	100
No. mktg	2	4	10	14	29
Sal/mktg	50	50	50	50	50
Mktg expense	$100	$220	$484	$710	$1,464
Sales					
No. new customers	400	520	660	823	1,012
No. new customers/sales	60	60	60	60	60
No. sales	7	9	11	14	17
Sal/sales	30	30	30	30	30
Sales expense	$200	$260	$330	$411	$506
Customer Service					
No. customers cum.	400	880	1,452	2,130	2,928
No. customers/cust svc	200	200	250	300	300
No. cust svc	2	4	6	7	10
Sal/cust svc	25	25	25	25	25
Cust svc exp	$50	$110	$145	$177	$244
Billing					
No. customer	400	880	1,452	2,130	2,928
No. cust/bill	200	200	200	150	150
No. bill emp	2	4	7	14	20
Sal/bill emp	25	25	25	25	25
Bill exp	$50	$110	$182	$355	$488
Advertising	$500	$500	$1,282	$2,068	$3,352
Mktg/sales exp	$900	$1,200	$2,423	$3,722	$6,054
No. mkt/sale emp	13	22	34	49	75
Development					
Systems					
No. customers cum.	400	880	1,452	2,130	2,928
No. customers/sys engr	100	100	75	75	75
No. sys engr	4	9	19	28	39
Sal/Sys Engr	45	45	45	45	45
Sys engr exp	$180	$396	$871	$1,278	$1,757
Software					
No. new customers	400	520	660	823	1,012

TABLE 7.3 Detailed B&B Expense Model (continued)

	Expense Model ($000)				
Year	1986	1987	1988	1989	1990
No. new customers/					
Software Engr	150	150	100	100	100
No. software engr	3	3	7	8	10
Sal/Software engr	45	45	45	45	45
Software engr exp	$120	$156	$297	$370	$455
Hardware					
No. new customers	400	520	660	823	1,012
No. customers/Hardware	400	400	400	400	400
No. hardware	1	1	2	2	3
Sal/hardware	40	40	40	40	40
Hardware exp	$40	$52	$66	$82	$101
Engr exp	$340	$604	$1,234	$1,730	$2,313
No. engr emp	8	14	28	39	52
Operations					
Training					
No. customers	400	880	1,452	2,130	2,928
No. customers/training	100	100	150	150	200
No. training	4	9	10	14	15
Sal/train	27	27	27	27	27
Train exp	$108	$238	$261	$383	$395
Customer Interface					
No. customers	400	880	1,452	2,130	2,928
No. customers/CI	150	150	150	150	200
No. CI	3	6	10	14	15
Sal/CI	25	25	25	25	25
CI exp	$67	$147	$242	$355	$366
Operations exp	$175	$384	$503	$738	$761
No ops emp	7	15	19	28	29
Field Service					
No. customers	400	880	1,452	2,130	2,928
No. cust/FS	50	50	35	35	30
No. FS Emp	8	18	41	61	98
Sal/FS	20	20	20	20	20
FS exp	$160	$352	$830	$1,217	$1,952
Field ser exp	$160	$352	$830	$1,217	$1,952
No. FS emp	8	18	41	61	98
G&A					
No. employees	35	68	122	177	254

TABLE 7.3 Detailed B&B Expense Model (continued)

	Expense Model ($000)				
Year	1986	1987	1988	1989	1990
No. employees/G&A	12	12	12	12	12
No. G&A	3	6	10	15	21
Sal/G&A	75	75	75	75	75
G&A exp	$219	$423	$764	$1,107	$1,587
Overhead					
Travel					
No. employees	47	80	134	189	266
Travel/employee	10	10	10	10	10
Travel exp	$470	$797	$1,342	$1,891	$2,660
Auto Rental					
No. employees	47	80	134	189	266
Exp/employee	1	1	1	1	1
Auto rental exp	$47	$80	$134	$189	$266
Spare Parts					
No modems	400	880	1,452	2,130	2,928
Exp/modem	0.50	0.50	0.50	0.50	0.50
Spare parts exp	$200	$440	$726	$1,065	$1,464
Equip Lease					
No. customers	400	880	1,452	2,130	2,928
Equip/customer	0.30	0.30	0.30	0.30	0.30
Equip lease exp	$120	$264	$436	$639	$878
Rent					
No. employees	47	80	134	189	266
Sq. Ft./employee	200	200	200	200	200
Exp/sq. ft.	20	20	20	20	20
Bldg exp	$188	$319	$537	$757	$1,064
Direct O/H					
Total salary	1,793	2,963	5,754	8,515	12,668
% DOH	24	24	24	24	24
Direct O/H exp	$430	$711	$1,381	$2,043	$3,040
Bad debt exp	$66	$187	$366	$591	$958
Profess exp					
Total salary	$1,793	$2,963	$5,754	$8,515	$12,668
% Prof exp	10	10	10	10	10
Prof exp	$179	$296	$575	$851	$1,267
Insurance					
Assets	420	840	1,273	1,730	2,222
% Assets	1	1	1	1	1

TABLE 7.3 Detailed B&B Expense Model (continued)

Year	Expense Model ($000)				
	1986	1987	1988	1989	1990
Insurance exp	$70	$196	$379	$608	$980
Total O/H exp	$1,770	$3,290	$5,876	$8,635	$12,577
Transmission Exp					
No. B&Bs	400	880	1,452	2,130	2,928
No. calls/day/B&B	5	5	5	5	5
Exp/call	0.60	0.60	0.60	0.60	0.60
Call exp	438	964	1,590	2,332	3,206
No. rooms sold	1,760	4,576	8,131	11,926	17,569
No. reserv/day/room	2	2	2	2	2
Time/reserv	0.20	0.20	0.20	0.20	0.20
Resv connect time	4,283	11,135	19,786	29,019	42,752
Exp/connect/hr	2.40	2.40	2.40	2.40	2.40
Connect exp	10	27	47	70	103
Telecom exp	$448	$990	$1,637	$2,402	$3,309
Net oper. exp	$4,012	$7,244	$13,267	$19,551	$28,554

- Marketing and Sales, composed of:

  Marketing
  Sales
  Customer service
  Billing
  Advertising

- Development, composed of:

  Systems
  Software
  Hardware

- Operations, composed of:

  Training
  Customer interface

- Field Service

- General and Administrative

The expense model follows the earlier model developed in this chapter. For example, in the marketing area we have, as the revenue driver, the number of cumulative customers. This is the total number of B&B establishments. In the sales area, we have the number of new customers or new B&B establishments. In this case we see that we expect the sales staff to generate 60 sales per year. This leads to a sales staff of 7 in the first year, growing to 17 in the fifth year. Advertising, contracted to an advertising agency, is entered as a fixed amount.

The G&A expenses are also fixed by the driver of total employees, and a productivity factor of 12 employees per G&A staff person. The sum of all of the salary expenses in this area yields the total salary. The overhead expenses, which must now be added onto this base, include:

- Travel: Driven by the number of employees and the cost per employee per year.
- Auto Rental: We allot a small amount per employee per year for auto rentals.
- Spare Parts: This business expenses the spare parts needed to maintain the terminals in the hands of the B&B operators.
- Equipment Leases: May include any office furniture and equipment.
- Rent: Typically, rent is based upon the cost per year per square foot. The square feet required is based on the amount per person; here it is 200 feet. The rent expense follows directly.
- Direct Overhead: This element includes Social Security, pensions, taxes, benefits, and other direct costs as a percent of base salary.
- Bad Debt: Revenue may be booked but the customer may never pay, so a bad debt expense is listed as an uncollectable.
- Professional Expenses: Expenses for accountants, attorneys, and other professionals.
- Insurance: Liability and property insurance.

In this example, the total salary expense is $1.793 million in the first year; the overhead is $1.770 million. The total expense is $4.012 million. The overhead expenses usually are equal to or exceed the amount of direct salaries.

This example clearly indicates how expenses directly relate to the revenue plan, and that the overhead expenses are also related to revenue through the direct salary and staffing plan. This is typical of many businesses, especially those in the start-up mode.

Example

Consider the case of a distributed sales organization (DSO) business, wherein the sales companies, such as Avon and others, have field salespersons who need to communicate with a central location for the purpose of inventory management and funds transfer. One of the factors that must be present in the operations section of the plan is the introduction of the employee ratios. These ratios allow the business developer to determine how effective the overall plan will be in meeting the competition and in making its overall corporate goals. We shall use the DSO business as a base to develop these ratios.

The four following employee ratios are typically calculated. They are:

1. *Revenue/Employee.* Measure of how effectively the company generates revenue. A company with high revenue per employee is one that highly leverages its employees and is probably using high value-added or is a strong user of technology.

2. *Expense/Employee.* This measure will allow the analyst to determine factors attributed to the employees. A low cost per employee may mean tight controls on overhead or a low-paid workforce. A low-paid workforce may be a short-term advantage, but in the long term, cost cutting may lead to the loss of key personnel.

3. *Net Operating Income/Employee.* This measure is the difference between the total income and the net expenses, on a per employee basis. It is a natural outcome of the first two ratios. It shows how profitable each employee can be.

4. *Capital/Employee.* A measure of how capital-intensive the business is. We consider this ratio in more detail later in this chapter.

These ratios are depicted in Figure 7.2 for the DSO business. Using this as an example, we can state a great deal about the nature of this business.

1. *Revenue/Employee.* This ratio varies from $130,000 to $170,000 per employee per year. As discussed in the first part of the book, this generally is a labor intensive business. We can compare this ratio to the salary per employee to get an additional measure of the revenue to direct salary dollar.

2. *Expense/Employee.* This ratio initially exceeds the revenue indicating a business loss. It fluctuates for this business due to the nature of the sales effort required for the continued introduction of the product.

3. *NOI/Employee.* Initially, this figure is negative but begins to grow more positively. Note that it also fluctuates. The analysis of this number will be important in the labor-intensive business, as discussed before.

4. *Capital/Employee.* Note that this is not a capital-intensive business. The capital per employee is very small, thus resulting in a small capital per revenue or large revenue per capital dollar.

These ratios should be developed for all possible business plans. They are usually calculated by the investors and will be compared to ratios that are typical in similar industries. As you progress through the financial parts of the business plan, you will find that there are many simple ratio checks such as these that experienced investors use in determining the viability of the business. It is important that the entrepreneur develop an intuitive feeling for these checks so as to defend the plan. In later stages of the business, they will return as measures of ongoing operational effectiveness.

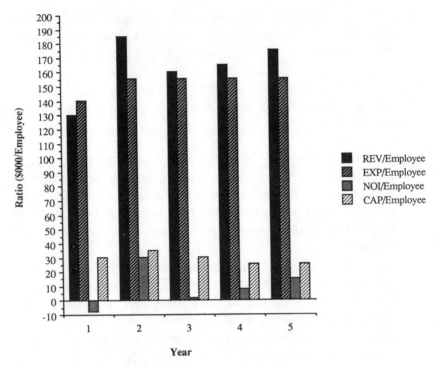

FIGURE 7.2   DSO Revenue Ratios

Example

Consider the case of a computer terminal manufacturer, Digital Transport Inc. The company is developing a device that will allow simultaneous use of voice and data over the same telepone line. The company needs to market this product to the end user, such as a bank, as well as to the telephone companies. The company has decided to also manufacture, install, and support operations of the product. The company has been organized with the following elements:

- Marketing and Sales: Providing the standard functions.
- Telco Interface: Providing the special interface support needed to ensure that the product is sold to and serviced to the local telephone companies. Failure to succeed in this area will cause a failure in the business.

- Engineering: Performs the standard engineering functions.
- Manufacturing: The company has decided to manufacture the product through internal board assembly and testing to ensure product quality and to demonstrate that quality to the telephone companies, who are concerned about that issue.
- Operations: This function supports the product at the company's premises after it has been shipped. It will control new software releases.
- Field Service: Performs the standard field service functions.

Figure 7.3 depicts the salary expenses for each of these segments over the first five years of the business. Note that the marketing and sales element is the largest of all the business operations, indicating that this is really a marketing-driven business. The second element of the expenses is the engineering. Be careful here with the manufacturing element; they are not expensed because they are part of the cost of goods and not part of the operating expense. The next section discusses this concept in more detail.

This analysis helps the planner better understand the major emphasis of the business. In this case, we have found that it is marketing- and sales-driven. At this point, we could look at the operations and field service elements and see that they are quite

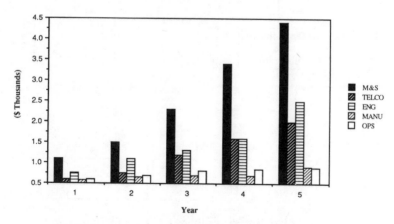

FIGURE 7.3 Digital Transport Expense Roll-Out

small. This perception may cause some concern, since it assumes that the product will be of such a high quality that it will require little support once it is sold. This observation may send the planner back to evaluate the quality assurance program to see if it meets the standards required in the operating expense assumptions.

This form of analysis should be performed by the planner in conjunction with ratio analyses. By performing both of these analyses, the planner can better understand the business and how it positions itself with its competition.

Now consider an example that contains all three of the elements we have developed. In this example, we demonstrate the organization, the relationship of the key ratios, and the actual comparison of the specific organizational expenses. Recall that,

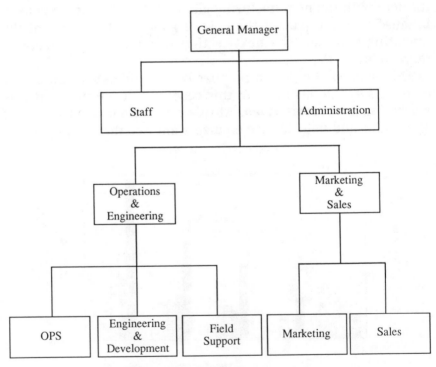

FIGURE 7.4   MiniSAT Organization

when looking at the organization, we can develop the overall expenses model. When we look at the ratios, we can better understand the productivity and effectiveness of the business. Finally, when evaluating the expenses, by category, we can determine what type of business we are actually operating.

Example

MiniSAT was a business that developed a small satellite terminal and also operated the satellite system that provided a communications service to users of IBM terminals. Figure 7.4 represents the operations organization for the business. It follows the lines that we have developed for the other businesses.

Figure 7.5 depicts the key ratios for this business for three of the operating years: Years 1, 5, and 7. Note that, for this business, the revenue per asset dollar is only $0.41 in Year 1, growing to $1.99 in Year Seven. This is a capital-intensive business. The revenue per employee grows from $148,000 to $298,000; it develops from a labor-intensive to a non-labor intensive business. What is important with this example is that a business may grow from one extreme to another. The management must recognize this and manage the development of the operations organization accordingly.

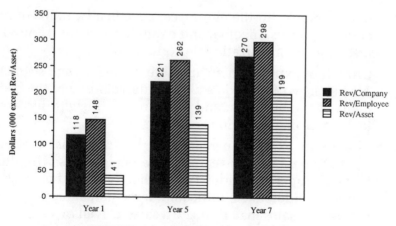

FIGURE 7.5   MiniSAT Revenue Ratios

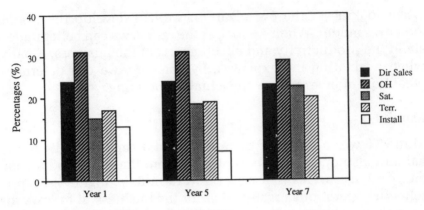

FIGURE 7.6   MiniSAT Expense Percentages

For this same example, Figure 7.6 shows the ratios in percent of the expenses. The key point is that the figure shows the expenses as percentages. Also note that the percentages change from year to year. By looking at the expense as percentages of the total, we get a better perspective on the change in the business mix.

From these examples, you can see that it is important not only to develop the organization and the expense model, but to analyze the expenses relative to each other and to the business. Specifically, the following three charts should be available:

1. Ratios relative to the employee; specifically, ratios of revenue, expenses, income, and capital. These ratios provide measures of organizational productivity.

2. Growth of expense in an absolute value for each segment. This chart will provide a clear understanding of the major focus of the business, and may provide insight into areas lacking proper attention.

3. Change in expense percentages, by functional area, for each segment in key years. These percentages will allow the developer to understand what type of business is being considered. As indicated, large percentages in marketing and sales may indicate a sales-driven business, creating a long-term problem if the business witnesses strong technical innovation and competition.

The operations expense section should thus detail an understanding of the business, how it changes in form as it develops, the management strategy to handle that change, and the set of absolute dollar numbers.

CAPITAL REQUIREMENTS

As with the expenses, capital is also driven by the revenue from the business. In this section we briefly describe the capital model. It follows directly from the expense model. A similar approach is taken in the development of the cost of goods model, which is discussed in the next section.

The capital is broken down into its separate elements. For example, if the business is computer driven, then the three capital elements are CPUs, communications equipment, and memory. If the business is manufacturing, it requires test, assembly, and packaging machines. The capital elements are given in terms of:

RD: Revenue driver

PF: Productivity number

UC: Unit capital of the cost per capital element

Thus we can divide the capital into its basic set of elements (e.g., computers, modems, fiber links, and others). Then we can determine the size of these individual capital elements. For example, if i represents miles of installed fiber, then $RD(i)$ is the revenue driver in terms of the number of customers, $PF(i)$ the productivity factor in miles of fiber per customer, and $UC(i)$ the unit capital in capital per fiber mile, we can develop the total capital required to meet the revenue model as:

$$C = \sum_{i=1}^{N} RD(i)*PF(i)*UC(i)$$

which is identical in form to the expense model. This equation can then be utilized for all of the individual capital elements.

Example

A business provides computer services on a time-sharing basis. Each user has a need for 1 MIP (millions of instructions per second) of capacity. The cost per MIP is $50,000. Thus, for 100 users on the system,

$$C = 100*1*\$50,000$$

or

$$C = \$5,000,000$$

As the user base grows, so too does the capital requirement. The following example depicts the capital for a service bureau business.

Example

The DSO service bureau services several companies; each company has several thousand sales representatives (SRs). The SRs present a computer and communications traffic load onto the system. To meet this load, the system must have the CPU, memory, and communications capacity.

Begin by considering the revenue model for this business, shown in Table 7.4.

- The first element is the total number of companies that have been signed onto the service. In this case, it is two in the first year, growing to 12 in the fifth year.
- Each company has SRs who visit homes and sell their company's products. We assume that each representative sells products in groups, starting with 80 sessions per SR per year in the first year, and decreasing to 45 per year in the fifth year. For example, this may be 45 Tupperware parties per year per SR.
- The next factor is the number of sales representatives per company. In the first year, it is 200,000 on average. As the

TABLE 7.4 DSO Revenue

Year	Revenue Summary ($000)				
	1	2	3	4	5
No. companies	2	5	8	10	12
No. trans/CR/year	80	70	60	50	45
No. SR/co (000)	200	170	120	90	75
% Penetration	5%	8%	10%	15%	20%
No. trans (000)	1,600	4,760	5,760	6,750	8,100
Gross rev/trans	$400	$400	$300	$300	$300
No. SR (000)	20	68	96	135	180
Yearly fee/SR ($)	$120	$120	$120	$120	$120
Fee rev	$2,400	$8,160	$11,520	$16,200	$21,600
No. trans (000)	1,600	4,760	5,760	6,750	8,100
Rev/trans ($)	$2	$2	$2	$2	$2
Process rev	$3,200	$9,520	$11,520	$13,500	$16,200
Revenue	$5,600	$17,680	$23,040	$29,700	$37,800

business expands, it addresses the smaller companies so that by the tenth year it drops to 60,000 SRs on average.

- We assume that this service is not for all the SRs. Thus we begin with only 5 percent penetration and increase to 20 percent.
- We then can determine the total number of transactions per year, directly from the number of SRs and the transactions per SR.
- This also allows for the calculation of the number of active SRs;
- then, the assumption of an annual fee of $400 per year per SR;
- and a total number of transactions, 1.6 million growing to 8.1 million;
- charging $2 per transaction for the service;
- showing the total revenue being the sum of the fee revenue and the process revenue. It should be clear that this is a process revenue-based business.

This analysis of the business's revenue allows the entrepreneur to understand the revenue sources and the positioning of the business as being service oriented. We can now use this revenue model to develop the capital model for the business. As shown in the capital model in Table 7.5, we have three capital elements in this business:

- CPU or computer capacity: We assume that we can modularly expand the computer capacity as the customer base grows. This is possible today with the use of such machines as Digital Equipment Corporation's VAX family of computers.
- Memory: More memory is needed as we expand due to the need to store more data.

TABLE 7.5 DSO Capital Model

	Capital Summary ($000)				
Year	1	2	3	4	5
Initial capital	$0	$0	$0	$0	$0
Net capital	$0	$1,140	$3,127	$3,400	$3,839
No. trans/min	27	79	96	113	135
CPU capital/TPM	15	12	10	10	10
New CPU capital	$400	$552	$8	$165	$225
CPU capital	$400	$952	$960	$1,125	$1,350
No. SR (000)	20	68	96	135	180
Mem/SR (MByte)	1	1	1	1	1
Cost/mem ($000/MB)	$10	$10	$10	$10	$10
Mem capital	$200	$680	$960	$1,350	$1,800
New mem capital	$200	$480	$280	$390	$450
No. trans/min	27	79	96	113	135
Hold-time/trans	5	5	5	5	5
No. comm inter	13	40	48	56	68
Capital/CI	$50	$50	$50	$50	$50
Comm Capital	$667	$1,983	$2,400	$2,813	$3,375
New comm cap	$667	$1,317	$417	$413	$563
Total new capital	$1,267	$2,349	$705	$968	$1,238
Total capital	$1,267	$3,489	$3,832	$4,367	$5,076
Depreciation	$127	$362	$432	$529	$653

- Modems: As we add on new customers, we need modems to communicate with them over the phone lines.

Using this structure, we can now consider each of the capital elements and determine the amount needed and the new amount required in each year. Note that we start the top of the capital model with initial capital and net capital. Initial capital is that capital that the company has prior to this operation plan. Throughout this book we shall assume that it is zero. The net capital is the capital that the company has at the end of the previous year, and that is used as the base for the new year.

Now examine the CPU requirements. The revenue driver here is the number of transactions per minute, a figure we found on the revenue model. The productivity factor is the CPU capacity in MIPs per transaction per minute. In Year 1 we see that the system has 27 transactions per minute. The CPU requires 7 MIPs per transaction per minute to handle that rate of transactions. The unit capital cost is $100,000 per MIP. Thus, the total capital for the CPU in the first year is $400,000. We can perform the same analysis, as is indicated in the table, for the other two elements.

This leads us to the lines at the end of the capital model. These are:

1. *Total New Capital.* The capital required in the year indicated to support the added business. It may also include new capital to support retired capital plant, especially true in the outer years of the plan.

2. *Total Capital.* The total capital on the books of the company. In the first year it is the new capital. In later years it is the sum of the new capital plus the capital from the past year, less the depreciation. It should be noted that the net capital of the next year is the total capital less the depreciation.

3. *Depreciation.* Represents the allocation of a depreciation expense on the capital model. Depreciation is a measure of the reduction in the effective use of capital in its capa-

bility to support revenue generation. There are many ways to develop a depreciation schedule, but for simple purposes, we shall assume a fixed lifetime—in this case 10 years—and use one-tenth per year of the capital value at the time of purchase as the capital depreciation. So, in this example, we see that in the first year we purchased $1.267 million and depreciation was $126,700, or one-tenth the amount.

4. *ITC or Investment Tax Credits.* Allowed until 1987, they were credits towards taxes as an incentive for capital investment and no longer apply.

Note that on the capital model we obtain total capital and total new capital. The new capital is that capital added in the present year. The model may be made more precise by incrementing the capital in amounts typical for the capital addition. For example, we may have to buy computers in large segments of $500,000 rather than in $5,000 amounts. This detail factor associated with the actual purchasing policy may be added to the capital model after the fact.

You can calculate depreciation in many ways; see the works of Glenn Welsch and Robert Anthony for some of those ways. Throughout this book, we assume a straight-line depreciation over the life of the equipment, with no accelerated depreciation schedule. Therefore, if the capital invested in year n is $C(n)$ and it has a life of M years, the annual depreciation for each of the M years is $C(n)/M$.

COST-OF-GOODS MODEL

In those businesses where manufactured items are placed into inventory, it is necessary to develop a cost-of-goods model. This model expenses those manufactured goods that are sold in what is termed the cost of goods, and places the items that are not sold into inventory. The operations of the business must take this fact into account as both an expense as well as a cash-flow item.

Many hardware businesses find that a great deal of their cash goes into financing the inventory of unsold goods.

This section does not go into a great deal of detail; more detail appears in the chapter on financial analysis. Let's begin with some overall concepts. To manufacture an item, you need two elements: labor and materials. For example, to develop a modem board, we need chips and board materials, and labor to assemble and test the board. Let us take a single board and examine it in some detail.

On the material side, the board requires:

1. *A CPU Chip.* The master processor chip, which controls all of the signals on the board.

2. *A UART Chip.* A communications controller chip that allows the board to talk to electronic devices, such as printers.

3. *A ROM Chip.* This chip contains non-destroyable memory. It usually is the chip that contains the programming for the board's special functions.

4. *A RAM Chip.* This chip, which contains destroyable memory, stores temporary data.

5. *A Clock.* Keeps all of the signals in synchronization.

6. *Gates.* Special-purpose chips that allow interfacing of all other chips.

7. *A Board.* The physical board itself.

8. *Board Assembly Hardware.* May include connectors, mounting devices, and power interfaces.

On the labor side, the board requires the following efforts:

1. *Incoming Inspection.* Inspecting all of the new parts to ensure that there are no errors or defects.

2. *Purchasing.* Preparing purchase orders and managing the vendors to ensure on-time delivery.

3. *Inventory Support.* Managing the inventory to keep parts available and secure.

4. *Board Stuffing.* Inserting parts into each of the boards.

5. *Board Soldering.* Soldering all of the inserted elements.

6. *Board Inspection and Test.* Testing boards on a static basis to ensure that all connections are correct, and on a dynamic basis to ensure logical performance of the board.

7. *Board Burn-in and Acceptance.* Stress-testing of each board to ensure that it meets all of the quality standards.

8. *Packaging.* Assembling the boards into their respective packages.

9. *Warehousing.* Storing the boards as they await shipping to the customer.

Thus, a single board requires $125 in parts and an allocation of $75 in labor. The labor estimate is based on the productivity of the employees and the layout of the manufacturing system.

During the flow of manufacturing, the product may be in one of four states:

- Unassembled: The parts-and-materials-only stage.
- Partially assembled: The work-in-process (WIP) stage. In the WIP stage, the board has all its parts allocated, but only part of the labor.
- Finished goods: The board is fully assembled but has not been sold.
- Sold goods: The board has been sold and is booked to sales.

In the flow of business, the entrepreneur will want to expense the last stage but to recognize that the other stages still represent assets to the company.

Example

Let us consider the case of the company that makes the modem replacement devices and develop the issues that emerge in the cost-of-goods model. At the beginning of its existence, the company has no product and an empty warehouse. It will follow these steps:

1. The company will purchase raw materials. It knows that each finished product will require $100 in raw materials.
2. The company will assemble the units. It knows that it will cost $75 per unit in direct labor and $45 in an allocated manufacturing overhead.
3. It will require inventory of raw materials, work in process (board assembled but only partially complete), and finished goods.
4. It will sell a fixed number of units in a year.

Table 7.6 depicts the evaluation of the cost of goods and unit cost of goods for this product. Begin at the top and move down the analysis to understand the total.

- Units sold: The total sold in the year.
- Finished goods (FG): Units in inventory but not sold.
  Start year with 0
  End year with 30 percent of 2,000, or 600.
- Work in Process (WIP): Units partially assembled.
  Start with 0
  End year with 35 percent of 2,000, or 700 partials.
- Raw materials (RM): Parts per assembled unit.
  Start with 0
  End year with 40 percent of 2,000, or 800 units' worth of RM.
- Labor and materials per unit:
  Raw material (RM) of $100
  Direct labor (DL) of $75
  Manufacturing overhead (MOH) of $45
- Total raw materials purchased equals:
  Units sold, plus
  Units to finished goods, plus
  Units to WIP, plus
  Units to increase raw materials inventory.

TABLE 7.6 Cost-of-Goods Model

Key Inputs	
FG %	30
WIP %	35
RM %	40
RM/Unit	100
DL/Unit	75
MOH/Unit	45

Key Outputs	
COGS/Unit	220
Turn	4.07

Cost of Goods

Year	1	2	3	4	5
Units Sold	2000	3500	6000	7400	10000
Begin FG	0	600	1050	1800	2220
FG % sales (units)	30	30	30	30	30
End FG	600	1050	1800	2220	3000
Change in FG (units)	600	450	750	420	780
Begin WIP	0	700	1225	2100	2590
WIP % sales (units)	35	35	35	35	35
End WIP	700	1225	2100	2590	3500
Change in WIP (units)	700	525	875	490	910
Begin RM	0	800	1400	2400	2960
RM % sales (units)	40	40	40	40	40
End RM	800	1400	2400	2960	4000
Change in RM (units)	800	600	1000	560	1040
RM/unit	100	100	100	100	100
Direct labor/unit	75	75	75	75	75
Man OH/Unit	45	45	45	45	45

No. units sold	2000	3500	6000	7400	10000
No. units to FGI	600	450	750	420	780
No. units to WIPI	700	525	875	490	910
No. units to RMI	800	600	1000	560	1040
Total RM units	4100	5075	8625	8870	12730
RM (&)/unit	$100	$100	$100	$100	$100
RM costs ($)	$410,000	$507,500	$862,500	$887,000	$1,273,000
Labor/WIP unit	50%	50%	50%	50%	50%
No. units sold	2000	3500	6000	7400	10000
No. units FGI	600	450	750	420	780
No. units WIPI	700	525	875	490	910
Total DL& MOH units	3300	4475	7625	8310	11690
DL/unit	75	75	75	75	75
MOH/unit ($)	$45	$45	$45	$45	$45
DL costs ($)	$221,250	$315,938	$539,063	$604,875	$842,625
MOH costs ($)	$132,750	$189,563	$323,438	$362,925	$505,575
Total labor ($)	$354,000	$505,500	$862,500	$967,800	$1,348,200
Change in RMI ($)	$80,000	$60,000	$100,000	$56,000	$104,000
Cost to manufacture ($)	$684,000	$953,000	$1,625,000	$1,798,800	$2,517,200
Chg in WIPI ($)	$112,000	$84,000	$140,000	$78,400	$145,600
Cost of goods manufactured ($)	$572,000	$869,000	$1,485,000	$1,720,400	$2,371,600
Chg in FGI ($)	$132,000	$99,000	$165,000	$92,400	$171,600
Cost of goods sold ($)	$440,000	$770,000	$1,320,000	$1,628,000	$2,200,000
COGS/Unit ($)	$220	$220	$220	$220	$220

TABLE 7.6 Cost-of-Goods Model (continued)

Year	Cost of Goods				
	1	2	3	4	5
INVENTORY VALUES					
Begin RMI	$0	$80,000	$140,000	$240,000	$296,000
Change RMI	$80,000	$60,000	$100,000	$56,000	$104,000
End RMI	$80,000	$140,000	$240,000	$296,000	$400,000
Begin WIPI	$0	$112,000	$196,000	$336,000	$414,400
Change WIPI	$112,000	$84,000	$140,000	$78,400	$145,600
End WIPI	$112,000	$196,000	$336,000	$414,400	$560,000
Begin FGI	$0	$132,000	$231,000	$396,000	$488,400
Change FGI	$132,000	$99,000	$165,000	$92,400	$171,600
End FGI	$132,000	$231,000	$396,000	$488,400	$660,000
Begin inventory	$0	$324,000	$567,000	$972,000	$1,198,800
Change inventory	$324,000	$243,000	$405,000	$226,800	$421,200
End inventory	$324,000	$567,000	$972,000	$1,198,800	$1,620,000
SALES FACTORS					
Number of units	2,000	3,500	6,000	7,400	10,000
Revenue/unit ($)	660	$660	$660	$660	$660
Revenue ($)	$1,320,000	$2,310,000	$3,960,000	$4,884,000	$6,600,000
Inventory turn	4.07	4.07	4.07	4.07	4.07

- Total labor is:

  Labor percent for WIP times DL and Manufacturing OH
  Labor for FG (in units) times DL and MOH
  Labor for sold units times DL and MOH

- Cost to manufacture equals all cash flow items:

  Total raw materials purchased
  Total labor

- Costs of goods manufactured equals costs allocated to finished goods and units sold; it is cost to manufacture less increase in WIP.

- Cost of goods sold equals cost of goods actually manufactured less the cost of goods increased in finished goods inventory.

The cost-of-goods model is probably the most complex statement in the business plan, as you can see by perusing Table 7.6. It represents a flow of funds into the company, and the management of those funds through goods sold and those kept in inventory. Note that the percent of units in inventory is a key factor in governing the cost of goods. By keeping more inventory each year, we effectively raise the cost of goods per unit. Thus, the operations plan must articulate how the inventory is to be managed.

The inventory management problem is driven by such factors as the lead time on hardware components, the need to provide units into the distribution pipeline, and other factors. The measure of the business is the turn on inventory. As we shall see in the next chapter, inventory is an asset not yet converted into cash. Thus it has to be financed with debt or equity. This fact implies that inventory must be managed. Turns of inventory of four or five are not uncommon.

So, we can assign inventory values to raw materials, work in process, and finished goods to find the expense of the cost of goods sold. We shall detail this process in the next chapter, which requires that we develop the balance sheet concept for the new company.

CONCLUSION

The operations and management section of the plan focuses on the business's operations as it progresses. The section stresses the ongoing functions and the organizational needs of the business as it evolves. The net result is the organizational chart and the evolution of the expenses, capital, and cost-of-goods model for the business. These can then be combined with the revenue numbers generated in the marketing chapter and used for the financial analysis of the business.

The reader is cautioned on developing an operations plan for too short or too long a time span. The examples in this book cover 5 years, which may or may not be correct for all businesses. For example, in a business with a short product life cycle, such as a consumer product business, 10 years may be excessively long. It may be impossible to predict the evolution of the business beyond five years, at most. In large capital-based service businesses, such as the fiber optic business, you may need to use fifteen years to average the lifetime of the capital asset. We shall discuss these factors in further detail as we delve into the financial modeling of the business.

8

FINANCIAL STATEMENTS

The financial statements embody the business in a structured form, permitting the financing entity as well as the entrepreneur to determine its strengths and weaknesses. In many cases, these statements represent a level of expertise that frightens away the business plan writer. In this chapter, we develop a framework that will allow the technically trained entrepreneur to readily develop a set of useful and presentable financials. Once the product and market are defined, the financials act as the backbone of the business plan.

This chapter focuses on the following set of financial statements:

1. *Revenue Statement.* Forms the basis of the business and builds upon the concepts presented in Chapters 4 and 7. The reader should remember that the revenue statement is the driver of all other business statements developed in this book.

2. *Capital Statements.* These follow from the business structure and the revenue drivers. The capital statement reflects the way in which capital and depreciable assets are deployed. We shall treat the capital assets from a business perspective and leave tax variations to a separate section.

3. *Cost of Goods.* This statement provides a measure of the cost asssociated with the manufacture of the goods sold. It does not appear in a service business, but it is the key ingredient of a hardware business. It also accounts for the

      unsold good in terms of the carried-forward inventory, which is important since it is necessary to fund inventory through working capital.

4. *Expense Statements.* Includes the cost of operations.

5. *Income Statements.* These represent the revenue and expense items, and include the flow of cash. The cash flow statement is a separate statement and is frequently the basis of the business evaluation, as is discussed in Chapter 9.

6. *Balance Sheet.* The balance sheet is the basis for the business assets and its health. A good income statement only reflects a single year. The balance sheet will reflect how well the company can grow.

7. *Financing Statement.* This statement acts as the basis of funding the business, ensuring that it can meet its working capital requirements as well as its growth requirements.

8. *Sources and Uses.* This statement describes where the money comes from and where it goes. This statement's key point is that sources must always balance uses. These sources may be from the business, from debt, or from equity.

9. *Cash Flow.* The cash flow portion describes the workings of the business exclusive of external financing. It is a measure of how well the business can generate cash by itself. The cash flow statement tells the reader how well the business can support itself or how much money is needed.

Figures 8.1 and 8.2 depict the interrelationship between these statements and the key variables that are part of them. Figure 8.1 maps the individual statements and their interrelationships. Figure 8.2 details the elements of each statement. Again, the reader should note that the revenue statement is a driver for all other financial statements—a continuing statement that the business should be marketing-driven.

Our approach in this chapter is analytical and is directed at users who will place these statements on computers for the eval-

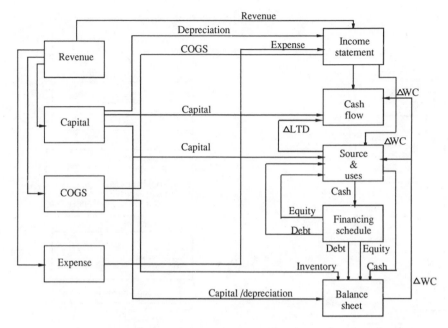

FIGURE 8.1   Financial Interrelationships

uation of various scenarios. With the advent of the personal computer and spreadsheet software, financial analyses are even more critical to the business plan and should be done with considerable detail and precision. The accuracy of the financials will usually depend most on the revenue and market projections.

REVENUE STATEMENT

The revenue statement will be the driver to all other statements. It must reflect not only the sources of income but the factors that influence those sources. The basic divisions should be along market segment and product segment lines, accounting for differences in the driving factors of business development. In the prior chapters we developed revenue statements to determine the total detail in the development of the revenue from the market data. In this chapter we focus upon the key elements that will

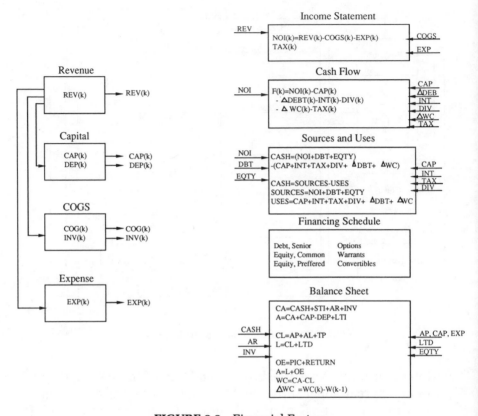

FIGURE 8.2 Financial Factors

appear in the financial portion of the business plan. In essence, we present a slightly abridged version of the revenue model that was developed previously.

This chapter develops these concepts using two businesses, a service business and a hardware business. These business are briefly described below.

Business 1: Infotel (Manufacturer)

The first is a manufacturing company called Infotel, which manufactures two major products and sells them in two channels. The first product is a low-end communications controller, which allows the user to interconnect PCs to local area networks. The second product is a high-end micro-message switch, which allows arbitrary connection to any channel.

One of the two market channels is an OEM channel, wherein the company sells to a value-added reseller who integrates the product into its own package. The second channel is a direct distribution channel, wherein the company sells the product directly to the end user.

The revenue drivers are the number of companies, the price per unit, the number of units, and the growth in each segment. The churn factor represents the number of new companies that must be reached each year in addition to those that are needed for growth. (Churn represents the number or percent of old customers that are lost due to migration to competitors or to newer products.) It is important to include the churn factor since the numbers of companies as well as number of new companies drive the marketing and sales expense. That is, it is cheaper to market to an old buyer than to find and market to a new one, assuming that the product is good.

Business 2: OpTel (Service)

OpTel, a fiber optic network communications supplier, is capital-intensive and provides a bypass communications service to the user. It differs from a manufacturer in that it sells no goods, only a service. However, to sell the service, it must provide for a large plant and service infrastructure to support the customer. In addition, its sales are for longer periods, typically a five-year service contract. These contracts have a certain value to the business even if they include a cancellation clause.

The revenue drivers in this business are:

Number of miles of fiber
Number of customers
Number of locations
Number of new customers
Number of new locations

Number of T1 or data channels per customer

Revenue per T1 or data channel per month

New service revenue

The more fiber, the greater the number of locations, the higher the possibility of getting business. Yet there is a point of diminishing returns. If the customer base is concentrated, then the business has no reason to expand to areas of low concentration. In addition, if there are few T1s per building, the firm has little incentive to enter that building.

Now we can develop the revenue model for these two businesses. Tables 8.1 and 8.2 depict the revenue models for the businesses. In both cases, the revenue model starts with a logical expression of the revenue developed from the main revenue drivers. Segments and product lines are differentiated since they will later have an impact on the business base. Then, there is a rollout of five years. The choice of the number of years is not arbitrary. Many of the plans that we have reviewed have only five years. That may be too short to truly evaluate the potential. On the other hand, in a product business, the product life cycle is often too short to allow for more than five years. So, a compromise must be met. A five to ten-year period allows the investor to view the business from a long-term perspective, and it forces the planner to envision follow-on products. This model then provides the basis of a growth strategy.

Now consider each of these two businesses in terms of their revenue statements and identify the key revenue drivers for each.

Business 1: Infotel

In the Infotel case (Table 8.1), the revenue summary is provided along segments and then subdivided along product lines. Infotel has three segments: the asynchronous market, the IBM reseller market, and the DEC-(Digital Equipment Corporation) compatible market.

For each of these markets, the plan determines the total market

TABLE 8.1 Revenue for Infotel

Year	Revenue Summary ($000)				
	1	2	3	4	5
Segment 1	$2,009	$9,502	$28,045	$57,318	$73,332
Segment 2	$112	$410	$664	$1,449	$2,583
Segment 3	$847	$4,852	$13,448	$25,219	$36,859
Total Revenue	$2,968	$14,765	$42,157	$83,987	$112,774

TABLE 8.2 Revenue for OpTel

				Revenue Summary ($000)		
Year	1986	1987	1988	1989	1990	
No. miles (trunk)	35	35	35	35	35	
No. customers	4	21	48	97	157	
No. locations (sites)	41	182	211	264	330	
No. new bldg entries	30	95	10	17	21	
No. bldg entries cum.	30	125	135	151	172	
No. sites/entry	1.38	1.46	1.57	1.74	1.91	
No. new customers	4	17	28	48	60	
No. entry/customer	7.50	5.98	2.78	1.57	1.10	
No. T1/customer	75	66	34	22	18	
No. T1	300	1369	1654	2156	2788	
No. bldg entries	30	125	135	151	172	
Rev/T1/mo	500	543	594	650	692	
Transmission rev	$1,800	$8,924	$11,790	$16,822	$23,143	
No. new customers	4	17	30	53	70	
Chg/NewCo/T1	3	3	3	3	3	
Sign-up rev	$900	$3,207	$855	$1,505	$1,896	
No. new drop	30	95	10	17	21	
Cost/drop/T1	0	0	0	0	0	
New drop rev	$0	$0	$0	$0	$0	
Up-front payment	$0	$0	$0	$0	$0	
TOTAL REVENUE	$2,700	$12,131	$12,645	$18,327	$25,039	

size based on an estimate of the total installed base of terminals. Then it delimits the market by those terminals that will have the proper access to telephone lines. Note that, in the early years, it is a small number. Then the market is further delimited by the users for whom it is appropriate. Then the penetration rates are applied, and finally a market share is determined. Using all of these delimiting factors for each of the segments, the revenue plan further assigns amounts to the two distribution channel alternatives: direct and VAR (e.g., OEM). The net result is the total revenue per segment.

In each segment, the number of companies, the units per company, and the price per unit are given. Here the number of companies must track back to the market plan, and must be achievable. The same is the case for the number of units. The price per unit is based on the market pricing strategy. It is clear that the primary revenue drivers will be the number of customers to be sold in each of the three segments.

The revenue model develops the segment revenues and combines them to the total business revenue. This approach is identical to the approach developed in Chapter 4. The exact process of determining the numbers for penetration and appropriateness, as well as the installed base, require the application of the market research methods of Chapter 4.

A summary chart at the bottom of the revenue model frequently allows for the key expense drivers to be summarized. These include the number of companies, the number of new companies, and the number of products.

Business 2: OpTel

OpTel's is a more complex model of a revenue stream since factors influence the business in many dimensions. In the InfoTel model, the key drivers were the number of units and the number of customers. OpTel has several drivers. In Table 8.2, the revenue model uses these drivers to develop the base; then they are used in the other financial elements. Here it is important to obtain the number of new drops in a building and the number of new T1s since they will affect the capital and the expenses. The number of new companies will also directly affect the marketing and sales expenses.

Detailed backup should exist for the revenue model in the marketing section of the plan. As discussed in Chapter 4, the details will be based upon some form of direct contact with the target customer base.

The revenue portion of the plan should focus on such issues as sensitivity to key assumptions, the breakout of the sources of revenue, and the summary of pricing factors that are key to the success of the business. The market section has developed the revenue model in considerable detail. The revenue presented in the financial section should merely summarize material developed in the market section. Therefore, the financial section of the plan should focus on these factors:

Scenario or Sensitivity Analysis

A discussion of the impact to the business if the market does not develop quickly, if the pricing cannot be attained, or if the market share is not great. The entrepreneur should attempt to factor into the revenue analysis the sensitivity of the business to the key assumptions made in the development of the marketing plan.

Summary of Price Factors

The price factors assume a reasonable and rational customer, with a similar type of competitor. In addition, the pricing includes costs for distribution associated with the mark-up of the price. The financial section should expand on what the impact will be on the business if the competition fights heavily on price and the business is forced to reduce the price by 20 percent to 50 percent. Can the business survive? Can the business reduce the price to gain early market share? How quickly must it gain that share?

Revenue by Business Segment or Element

The plan should summarize the revenue ratios by such elements as segment or product element. For example, if there is a great effort to obtain revenue from a small segment that may be of strategic importance, this should be known. In addition, each product offering should be marginally profitable, at the least. If each segment and element are not profitable, the concept of loss leaders may be employed, but the entrepreneur should remember that the firm may not be able to make up the loss in volume.

Key Revenue Ratios

Should include the revenue per company, revenue per segment, revenue per end user, or any of the many ratios already discussed. These ratios provide the investor with early warning signs of areas in which the business is likely to find trouble.

The revenue section of the plan should carefully summarize the revenue and succinctly present the key factors relating to the revenue that will encourage investor confidence.

CAPITAL MODEL

Capital includes all those elements that are purchased by the company and have a lifetime that exceeds one year. They are the elements that are "capitalized," then depreciated over time. In a highly capital-intensive business, the capital is dedicated in the early phases when the expenses are small as compared to depreciation. One other element is the replacement costs of the capital base. The equipment has a lifetime; at its end, it must be replaced. The capital model must take this replacement into account by providing the following factors:

- Business drivers from the revenue model that impact the need for capital equipment
- Capital drivers that reflect how much of a per unit capital equipment is needed for each of the business drivers
- Capital per unit costs, or how much each unit of new capital will cost
- Lifetimes of the capital equipment and replacement schedules

- Depreciation and investment tax credits
- Total new capital and total capital

Example

In OpTel's Year 1, the initial capital—the capital the company may have on its books at commencement—is zero, as in most start-ups. The net capital is the amount carried over from the previous year, less depreciation. In this case there is none. Table 8.3 shows the resulting capital model.

- Revenue Driver: A need for 35 miles of fiber.
- Capital Driver: The cost per mile of new fiber is $150,000.
- Capital: The revenue driver times the capital driver, or $5,250,000.
- The fiber is assumed to have a fifteen-year life, so no replacement is needed.
- Adding the other factors yields a total capital of $7.2 million, which is also
- The total new capital.
- Depreciation is over 10 years since the company argues that fiber in this city has a significant chance of being broken or destroyed.
- For the second year, the net capital is not the total capital, less the depreciation for that year.
- The process continues for the second and other years of the business.

When the same process is followed for InfoTel, the capital is allocated to the manufacturing plant.

The key observations to be made in the plan concern the capital elements, including the need for capital, the revenue per asset dollar number to determine the capital-intensity of the business, and the depreciation effects.

The business may also want to determine the benefit of leasing the capital through a capitalized lease or through a third-party

TABLE 8.3 Capital Model for OpTel ($000)

Year	1986	1987	1988	1989	1990
Initial capital	$0	$0	$0	$0	$0
Net capital	$0	$6,552	$11,525	$10,684	$10,175
No. new miles	35	0	0	0	0
Cap cost/mile	150	150	150	150	150
Fiber cap	$5,250	$0	$0	$0	$0
No. new bldg entry	30	95	10	17	21
Cost/entry	68	67	60	60	60
Bldg entry cap costs	$2,030	$6,335	$578	$1,011	$1,264
No. new NCC	1	0	0	1	0
Cap/NCC	0	0	0	0	0
NCC cap	$0	$0	$0	$0	$0
No. miles	35	35	35	35	35
No. miles/switch	50	50	50	50	50
No. switch	1	1	1	1	1
No. new switch	1	0	0	0	0
Cap/switch	0	0	0	0	0
Switch cap	$0	$0	$0	$0	$0
No. new miles	35	0	0	0	0
No. miles/hub	25	25	25	25	25
No. new hub	1	0	0	0	0
Cap/hub	0	0	0	0	0
Hub cap	$0	$0	$0	$0	$0
Total new capital	$7,280	$6,335	$578	$1,011	$1,264
Total capital	$7,280	$12,887	$12,103	$11,695	$11,439
Depreciation	$728	$1,361	$1,419	$1,520	$1,647

lease. The use of a lease reduces the capital required as well as making an impact on the negative cash flow. This reduction of the cash flow will show itself in a reduction of the capital required through debt or equity.

The capital observations to be made are as follows:

- Capital intensiveness through revenue per asset dollar should be measured at this point. Investors are typically concerned by businesses that are highly capital-intensive. Rarely do such businesses obtain financing. One major exception is Federal Express, for which Fred Smith obtained in excess of $50 million for the financing of the Memphis hub operation.

- Lease versus buy alternatives and the impact on financing should be considered in detail. All too often, the company wants to own everything. This may not be necessary and, in fact, may negatively impact early capital-raising efforts.

- Depreciation life versus asset true life. This requires asset replacement after its true life. Be certain to include this factor. Many capital-intensive plans fail to address the replacement of the capital plant.

- Capital required per year and the total capital required. The plan should carefully allocate the capital acquisition on the basis of when it is needed and not when it is wanted. The entrepreneur should view capital as if it were an expense. It is part of the cash flow, and thus must be accompanied by a source. That source of cash could be quite costly.

The plan should contain some reference to each of these items, which flow directly from the financials developed.

COST OF GOODS

Two major expense items are usually considered in determining the performance of a business. The first is the cost-of-goods item, which represents the results of converting raw materials into product, which is in turn sold to the customer. The second is the set of operating expenses of the company, sometimes called selling and administrative expenses.

Let's focus on these two elements: cost-of-goods and operating expenses. For non-product companies, there are generally no cost-of-goods expenses. Operating expenses exist for all types of companies. This section concentrates on the cost-of-goods model associated with product manufacture. The key insight to be gained is that, unlike capital or operating expenses, cost-of-goods is reflected equally on the income statement and on the balance sheet. On the income statement the impact will be the cost of goods element; on the balance sheet it will be the inventory element.

In developing the cost-of-goods (COGs) model, we focus on how capital resources and labor are transformed into finished product, how the costs are allocated, how the residual assets are assigned to an inventory account, and how these elements are managed and evaluated.

Let's return to Infotel, which makes telecommunications products. We examine the manufacturing process and the disposition of the product in some detail:

Step 1: Raw materials are purchased to be used in the manufacture of the goods. These materials may be composed of resistors, circuit boards, chips, and enclosures for the units. For the most part the raw materials are listed as items that could be resold because a market generally exists for these items.

Step 2: The raw materials are processed by placing the resistors and chips on the circuit boards and loading the software into the ROM. These items are then called work-in-process (WIP). They are not yet ready to ship, but are no longer easily sold to a third party. In addition, value has been added as a result of the assembly labor and the manufacturing overhead.

Step 3: The boxes are tested and fine-tuned. They are now called finished goods. At this point, they have a great deal of added value; they cannot be sold piecemeal

Step 4: as resistors and chips, but they could possibly be sold as a working product.

Step 4: At the beginning of the first year, Infotel had no products. As the products are manufactured, they are sold. However, at the end of the year, a collection of product is still raw material, and WIP and finished goods are accumulated. These have some value, which must be recognized in the inventory.

Step 5: Cost of goods (COG) is that allocation of the manufacturing process that is the cost to manufacture all the goods, less the changes in the raw materials, WIP, and finished goods inventory. For example, if the company buys $500 in raw materials, uses $500 in labor, and makes 100 units, then the cost to manufacture is $1,000. If at the end of the year it has 20 units left, then the COG is the allocation of that cost to 80 units. Table 8.4 provides the detail in that process.

Number of Units Sold

Represents the total product sold in a set year—for example, 4,280, as is the case for the Infotel product in Year 1.

Change in Units

Three elements will be viewed during the year: finished goods (FG), work in process (WIP), and raw materials (RM). These will be viewed as the amount in terms of units at the beginning of the year and the amount in units at the end of the year. We shall use units of RM, WIP, and FG as the base measure because it will allow for easier calculation of inventory. We now must make a management decision on how much of our annual sales, in percent, we want to have in inventory at the end of the year in each of these areas to assure that we can meet our customers' needs. Note that too little inventory may result in long delays to the customer and a loss in business. Too great an inventory may result in excessively high carrying costs and the risk of not selling the items.

TABLE 8.4 Cost-of-Goods Analysis for Infotel

Year	1	2	3	4	5
Units sold (000)	4.28	22.94	68.01	145.67	177.90
Begin FG	0.00	0.43	2.29	6.80	14.57
FG % sales (units)	10%	10%	10%	10%	10%
End FG	0.43	2.29	6.80	14.57	17.79
Change FG (units)	0.43	1.87	4.51	7.77	3.22
Begin WIP	0.00	0.34	1.84	5.44	11.65
WIP % sales (units)	8%	8%	8%	8%	8%
End WIP	0.34	1.84	5.44	11.65	14.23
Change WIP (units)	0.34	1.49	3.61	6.21	2.58
Begin RM	0.00	0.26	1.38	4.08	8.74
RM % sales	6%	6%	6%	6%	6%
End RM	0.26	1.38	4.08	8.74	10.67
Change in RM (units)	0.26	1.12	2.70	4.66	1.93
RM/unit	190	190	190	190	190
DL/unit	60	60	60	60	60
MOH/unit	50	50	50	50	50
No. units sold	4.28	22.94	68.01	145.67	177.90
No. units to FGI	0.43	1.87	4.51	7.77	3.22
No. units to WIPI	0.34	1.49	3.61	6.21	2.58
No. units to RMI	0.26	1.12	2.70	4.66	1.93
Total RM units	5.31	27.42	78.83	164.31	185.64
RM ($)/unit	$190	$190	$190	$190	$190
RM costs ($000)	$1,009	$5,210	$14,977	$31,219	$35,272
% Labor/WIP unit	35%	35%	35%	35%	35%
No. units sold	4.28	22.94	68.01	145.67	177.90
No. units FGI	0.43	1.87	4.51	7.77	3.22
No. units WIPI	0.34	1.49	3.61	6.21	2.58
Total DL&MOH Units	4.83	25.33	73.78	155.61	182.03
DL/unit	$60	$60	$60	$60	$60
MOH/unit	$50	$50	$50	$50	$50
DL costs	$290	$1,520	$4,427	$9,337	$10,922
MOH costs	$241	$1,267	$3,689	$7,781	$9,102
Total labor	$531	$2,786	$8,116	$17,117	$20,023
Total costs ($000)	$1,540	$7,997	$23,093	$48,336	$55,295
Change in RMI	$49	$213	$514	$885	$367
Cost to manufacture	$1,491	$7,784	$22,580	$47,451	$54,927
Change in WIPI	$78	$341	$824	$1,420	$589

TABLE 8.4 Cost-of-Goods Analysis for Infotel (continued)

Year	1	2	3	4	5
COG manufactured	$1,413	$7,443	$21,756	$46,031	$54,338
Change in FGI	$128	$560	$1,352	$2,330	$967
Cost of goods sold	$1,284	$6,883	$20,404	$43,702	$53,371
COGS/unit	$300	$300	$300	$300	$300
INVENTORY VALUES					
Begin RMI	$0	$49	$262	$775	$1,661
Change RMI	$49	$213	$514	$885	$367
End RMI	$49	$262	$775	$1,661	$2,028
Begin WIPI	$0	$78	$419	$1,243	$2,663
Change WIPI	$78	$341	$824	$1,420	$589
End WIPI	$78	$419	$1,243	$2,663	$3,252
Begin FGI	$0	$128	$688	$2,040	$4,370
Change FGI	$128	$560	$1,352	$2,330	$967
End FGI	$128	$688	$2,040	$4,370	$5,337
Begin inventory	$0	$256	$1,369	$4,059	$8,694
Change inventory	$256	$1,114	$2,690	$4,635	$1,924
End inventory	$256	$1,369	$4,059	$8,694	$10,617
SALES FACTORS					
Number of units (000)	4.28	22.94	68.01	145.67	177.90
Revenue/unit	$693	$644	$620	$577	$634
Revenue ($000)	$2,968	$14,765	$42,157	$83,987	$112,774
Inventory turn	11.62	10.78	10.39	9.66	10.62

In the model we show the beginning inventory, and for each of the three elements provide a percentage needed at the end of the year. Management must decide on that percentage. This model then gives the end-of-year number of units of RM, WIP, and FG.

Inventory Units

We can now determine the units sold and those that go to the three types of inventory: raw materials inventory (RMI), work-in-process inventory (WIPI), and finished goods inventory (FGI).

Unit Costs

We can now determine the costs of each unit of product manufactured and those sent to inventory. To do so, we must allocate three costs:

- Raw material cost per unit: The cost of the parts and purchased elements for each unit.
- Average labor per WIP unit: Consists of direct labor and manufacturing overhead. Since WIP is not completed, we must assign a fraction of the completed costs to this unit. In this example, we assign 35 percent of the total to the average WIP unit.
- Average labor per FG unit: Includes the total direct labor per unit and the total per unit manufacturing overhead.

Total Costs

The total costs are the cost of all raw materials for sold goods and all elements that go into increasing the inventory, plus all direct labor and manufacturing overhead costs for sold units and inventory units. In the example, we see that the calculations are on all units sold and into inventory. Note that the total cost is the cash flow that goes into the manufacturing process. From this we will now assign costs to the product sold and also assign an inventory number to the products that we anticipate selling. Inventory will not appear as an expense, but will be a transaction on the balance sheet.

Cost to Manufacture

This cost is the total cost less the cost that resulted from increasing the raw materials. It is a measure of all costs that go into the process of creating a product in the manufacturing process. It includes not only sold goods, but also WIP and FG.

Cost of Goods Manufactured

The total cost to manufacture finished and sellable goods. It is the cost to manufacture, less the increase in WIPI. Note that the

WIPI does not have sellable units, but the units have had a manufacturing allocation. Thus, the cost of goods manufactured reflects the cost of units that are finished.

Cost of Goods Sold

The essential number that reflects the allocation of costs to the sale of the items actually transferred to a customer in return for revenue. It is the cost of goods manufactured, less the change in FGI.

Inventory Values

We can not take the above elements and determine the inventory's value. Using the units and unit costs, the table shows the beginning and ending inventory values for RMI, WIPI and FGI.

Sales Factors

Include the revenue per unit and the inventory turn numbers. In this example, we see variation in the revenue per unit and in the inventory turn. Note that, in this case, the turn is quite high. Some businesses have a lower turn and thus a higher inventory.

The business strategy can be influenced by the type of manufacturing needed—on shore (e.g., in the United States) or off shore (i.e., in the Far East)—the impact in inventory needs, the response time of a third party manufacturer, or other such factors. Inventory is carried on the balance sheet and does not appear as an expense. However, as we shall see, carrying excess inventory will impact the working capital needs, which in turn will impact the return to the investor. Excess inventory is a poor way to operate; it must be carefully controlled.

In the financial section of the business plan, the discussion on the cost of goods typically focuses on the issue of achievability and comparability to other, similar businesses. As is typically found, the sales price is 2.0 to 3.5 times the cost of goods. Thus, the COG number is used as a benchmark. As discussed in Chapter 7, we need to have an operational justification of the COG number.

In this section of the plan, the focus on the COG is financial. The facts to be highlighted are:

Sensitivity to inventory turn—how many days inventory is necessary?

Risks to overstock and understock of inventory

Impact of labor prices as well as the availability and price stability of key items

The ability to ramp up or expand the production line

The ability to get customer financing of inventory through factoring the receivable accounts

OPERATING EXPENSES

Chapter 7 developed the operating expense model in significant detail, and emphasized the importance of revenue drivers and productivity factors. This section puts a new slant on the expense model as it appears in the financial section of the business plan. Note that its major impact will be on assuring the investor that the income statements reflect the total set of true costs.

The operating expenses reflect several factors about the way the business is operated:

Organization

First, the operating expenses reflect the organization of the business. They should be broken down into functions as they would appear in the business operations. That is, they should include such major functions as:

Marketing and sales

Engineering

Operations and maintenance

Network operations

General and administrative (G&A)

For example, Table 8.5 indicates OpTel's major areas, which are subdivided into functional areas. In this case, we have the following elements:

- Marketing and Sales: These areas are divided into the elements necessary to support these functions.
- Engineering: Supports the ongoing development support for the business.
- Operations and Maintenance: This element provides for the installation of the equipment.
- Network Operations: Provides for network management and customer support.
- General and Administrative: General management and support services.
- Overhead: All of the expenses necessary to support the daily operations of the business.

We can further detail these elements of the organization as follows:

1.0 Marketing and Sales
    1.1 Marketing
    1.2 Sales
    1.3 Customer Service
    1.4 Billing
    1.5 Advertising

TABLE 8.5 Expenses for OpTel

| | Expense Summary ($000) | | | | |
Year	1	2	3	4	5
M&S exp	$680	$1,053	$1,703	$2,661	$3,738
Engr exp	$95	$673	$794	$1,008	$1,279
Net O&M exp	$239	$239	$239	$239	$239
Plant O&M exp	$379	$589	$377	$439	$505
G&A exp	$189	$369	$414	$539	$704
OH exp	$2,407	$5,393	$5,835	$7,355	$9,399
NOE	$3,990	$8,316	$9,362	$12,242	$15,863

2.0 Engineering
    2.1 Systems
    2.2 Software
    2.3 Hardware

3.0 Network Operations and Maintenance
    3.1 Operations
    3.2 Maintenance

4.0 Plant Operations and Maintenance
    4.1 Operations
    4.2 Maintenance
    4.3 Construction management
    4.4 Construction engineering

5.0 General and Administrative

Each of these organizations is broken down into specific functional blocks, onto which detailed specifications will be made. It is critical to perform this step; unfortunately, most plans provide these numbers on a percentage basis only, and fail to make the investor understand how the business works.

Revenue Drivers

The next step is the development of the revenue drivers. As discussed in Chapter 7, these drivers impact the revenue requirements. This approach also reflects the market-driven viewpoint of the business plan.

In each functional area, drivers fuel the need for personnel. In the sales area, for example, the driver is the number of new companies. In the construction blocks, the driver is the amount of new capital. In the network operations area, the driver is the total number of customers; in the plant area, it is the total number of drops.

Productivity Factors

We now know who does what, but not how well they do it. For example, how many new customers can a salesperson sell in a year? In the case of OpTel, it starts with only one new sale per year and grows to four. These numbers should be judged against industry standards; for OpTel, 20 sales per year would be highly unrealistic.

Cost Factors

The final element: How much does each unit cost in terms of the direct salaries per staff person. Again, these figures must reflect realistic base salaries. Overhead is included in a different element.

Overhead

Once the people-dependent base expenses are developed, the overhead expenses are added. These expenses relate to the people and the items necessary to support the people. For example, Table 8.6 shows that Infotel has the following overhead expenses:

Travel

Auto rental

Rent

Direct overhead (FICA, taxes, health care, etc.)

Bad debt

Professional expense (legal fees, etc.)

Insurance

These items add up to the total operating expense. As shown in Tables 8.5 and 8.6, it is essential to see the allocation of these expenses and compare them to the expenses for a similar operation. Perhaps it is possible to compete on a cost basis if the costs of the product can be reduced by improving efficiency or productivity, or by structuring the business differently.

Expenses are typically detailed in the operations section of the plan. In the financial section, they may be presented in the context of the differing revenue scenarios, as well as indicating the labor-intensiveness of the business.

TABLE 8.6 Expenses for Infotel

Year	Expenses ($000)				
	1	2	3	4	5
M&S exp	$623	$1,421	$3,046	$5,302	$7,041
Telco suppt exp	$143	$470	$1,307	$2,439	$2,909
Engr exp	$280	$594	$853	$1,141	$1,907
Manuf suppt exp	$80	$160	$200	$200	$400
Operations	$106	$204	$292	$328	$390
Field service	$180	$230	$248	$278	$330
G&A exp	$181	$361	$594	$863	$1,147
OH exp	$1,815	$4,111	$8,043	$13,453	$17,727
Net operating expense	$3,408	$7,550	$14,582	$24,003	$31,851

Generally, operating expenses are summarized in simple tabular form in the financial section of the plan. The detailed breakout presented in Table 8.5 is not required for the plan, but is essential for the development of the operating expense figures. In evaluating the validity of the plan, however, it is essential that the validation of the expenses be available in the operations section of the plan.

INCOME STATEMENT

The income statement is straightforward and contains the elements of the business's cash-generating capacity. The income statement is the first statement that combines the revenue, cost-of-goods, capital (via depreciation), and operating expense models. The income statement consists of the following items:

1. *Revenue.* The gross revenue of the business, generally given for a minimum of five years and a maximum of ten.
2. *Cost of Goods.* Relevant only in a manufacturing business. As we have discussed, the cost of goods reflects the costs associated with the manufacture of the products that are sold. It does not reflect the total cost to manufacture.

3. *Gross Margin.* The cost of goods subtracted from the revenue gives the gross margin. In most manufacturing businesses, the gross margin must be fairly high, ranging from 50 percent up to 80 percent. This is true because the remaining portions of the revenue must go to the operating expenses and to profit.

4. *Net Operating Expenses.* Represent the costs of all salaries and indirect costs associated with business operations.

5. *Net Operating Income (NOI).* The most important variable, it represents the free cash flow generated from the business, and is a measure of debt and capital carrying capacity. The NOI is the difference between the gross margin and the operating expenses.

6. *Depreciation.* Depreciation is an expense element on the income statement. Although it does not represent the flow of cash from the business, it does reflect the impact on the value of the assets used in generating revenue. The reader is cautioned in selecting the appropriate schedule. Depreciation also helps generate a tax reduction and provides a measure of the flow of funds to new capital.

7. *Profit Before Interest.* The NOI less the depreciation costs. It may also be called the gross profit.

8. *Interest.* In most cases some form of interest is needed for the business due to the carrying of debt. The amount of interest and its form will depend on the nature of the investment in the business.

9. *Profit Before Tax.* The profit before interest, less the interest. It is also called the pre-tax profit.

10. *Taxes.* The taxes on the business. There may be a difference in taxes that are actually filed from those in the plan. Care must be taken to seek professional guidance on the actual tax filing.

11. *Dividends.* Paid in after-tax dollars, dividends can be significant, as Chapter 9 discusses in greater detail.

12. *Profit After Tax.* The ultimate bottom line of the business, it is the actual funds paid into the business and that finance the business growth.

Table 8.7 and 8.8 depict the Income statements for our two businesses. We examine each in detail to discover differences in the operations of the two businesses.

Business 1: Infotel

The gross margin in this business starts at 57 percent—not uncommon in a start-up of this type. It is reduced to 52 percent as the business matures. The gross margin must be comparable to industry standards, which it is in this case.

The largest expense element is the set of operating expenses that leaves a NOI margin of (58) percent for the first year and up to 24 percent for later years. The problem is that the NOI margin

TABLE 8.7 Income Statement for Infotel ($000)

Year	1986	1987	1988	1989	1990
Revenue	$2,968	$14,765	$42,157	$83,987	$112,774
Cost of goods	$1,284	$6,883	$20,404	$43,702	$53,371
Gross margin	$1,684	$7,882	$21,753	$40,285	$59,403
Margin %	57%	53%	52%	48%	53%
Expenses	$3,408	$7,550	$14,582	$24,003	$31,851
NOI	($1,724)	$331	$7,171	$16,282	$27,551
Margin %	−58%	2%	17%	19%	24%
Depreciation	$87	$138	$198	$264	$349
Profit before int	($1,811)	$194	$6,974	$16,019	$27,202
Margin %	−61%	1%	17%	19%	24%
Interest	$0	$0	$0	$0	$0
Profit before tax	($1,811)	$194	$6,974	$16,019	$27,202
Margin %	−61%	1%	17%	19%	24%
Taxes	$0	$0	$2,624	$7,849	$13,329
Dividends	$0	$0	$0	$0	$0
Profit after tax	($1,811)	$194	$4,349	$8,169	$13,873
Margin %	−61%	1%	10%	10%	12%

TABLE 8.8 Income Statement for Optel

	Income Statement ($000)				
Year	1986	1987	1988	1989	1990
Revenue	$2,700	$12,131	$12,645	$18,327	$25,039
Expense	$3,990	$8,316	$9,362	$12,242	$15,863
Net oper income	($1,290)	$3,815	$3,283	$6,085	$9,175
Margin %	−48%	31%	26%	33%	37%
Depreciation	$728	$1,361	$1,419	$1,520	$1,647
Profit before int	($2,018)	$2,453	$1,864	$4,565	$7,529
Margin %	−75%	20%	15%	25%	30%
Interest	$480	$720	$720	$240	$0
Profit before tax	($2,498)	$1,733	$1,144	$4,325	$7,529
Margin %	−93%	14%	9%	24%	30%
Taxes	$0	$0	$0	$1,089	$3,588
Dividends	$0	$0	$0	$0	$0
Profit after tax	($2,498)	$1,733	$1,144	$3,236	$3,941
Margin %	−93%	14%	9%	18%	16%

does drop to 19 percent in the fourth year as the business starts to ramp itself up. The business planner must carefully account for this phenomenon. (Note that this effect would not have been observed if the analyst had used margins rather than the more detailed approach that we have developed for the set of operating expenses.)

Infotel has no debt, only non-dividend-bearing equity. Note also that depreciation is small because the business does not require excessive capital plant.

The after-tax profit margins are from (61) percent to 12 percent. The latter margin for profit is optimistic. The margins in this business are more likely to be between six and nine percent, roughly half those projected in this model. The reason for this is that, as competition enters the industry, the prices per unit sold are reduced. This fact hits the bottom line directly.

The planner should be certain that the income statement reflects the true expenses for the early years and the impact of competition on the revenue in later years.

Business 2: OpTel

In this case, the business is service-oriented and so has no cost of goods. The first difference is the large negative NOI for the first year, which is a direct result of two factors. First, the customer is paying a fixed amount for a long period, so the revenue stream is paced over several years. Second, in order to get a service business started, significant up-front expenses are accrued in securing the customer base. Unfortunately, many venture capitalists do not understand these fundamental differences in these two business forms. Thus, the venture capital community does not invest heavily in service businesses.

However, the NOI margin grows to 37 percent, a dramatically different number from that of the hardware business. Depreciation is greater, especially as a percentage during the early years.

In this case, an interest rate applies due to the method of financing the business. We shall discuss that in detail later. The tax situation is different. Here we have a negative income, and thus establish a tax credit. That credit can be applied against later taxes of the business. As the business matures, the after-tax profits rise to 16 percent, a higher number. The problem of price is not as significant in a service business because the switching costs are much higher.

CASH FLOW

The cash flow profile starts with the income statement and addresses the issue of how much cash is needed to run the business. Table 8.9 depicts the cash flow for the two businesses. The elements of the cash flows are:

1. *NOI.* The major positive source of cash from the business. It may be negative during the early years; it will be this factor that will result in large negative cash flows in the early years.

2. *Interest.* A use of cash. The interest will pay off debt from loans made to finance the growth of the business.

TABLE 8.9 Cash Flow for Infotel and OpTel

	Cash Flow Analysis: Infotel ($000)				
Year	1986	1987	1988	1989	1990
NOI	($1,724)	$331	$7,171	$16,282	$27,551
Interest	$0	$0	$0	$0	$0
Taxes	$0	$0	$2,624	$7,849	$13,329
Dividends	$0	$0	$0	$0	$0
Capital	$874	$503	$598	$661	$853
LTD Reduction	$0	$0	$0	$0	$0
Chg WC	($503)	$1,555	$3,644	$6,220	$2,237
Cash Flow	($2,096)	($1,727)	$305	$1,552	$11,132
Cum CF	($2,096)	($3,823)	($3,518)	($1,966)	$9,166

3. *Taxes.* The taxes are those that are actually paid to the appropriate government institutions.

4. *Dividends.* Dividend payments to preferred shareholders, or actual dividends issued to shareholders of record.

5. *Capital.* Unlike depreciation, capital is a negative cash flow to the business. In the cash flow statement, capital is included at its total amount, and not just the depreciation.

6. *Long-Term Debt (LTD) Reduction.* A payment to reduce the long-term debt. It does not appear on the income statement, but is a real outflow of cash to the company. As we shall see, it does appear on the balance sheet.

7. *Change in Working Capital (WC).* The concept of working capital is simple but plays an important role in the cash needs of the business. WC is defined as current assets less current liabilities. For example, one current asset is the accounts receivable; a current liability is the accounts payable. Thus, the working capital on these two items is the difference in the receivables and payables. If the receivables can be kept small and the payables stretched out, the business generates cash on this working capital float. Unfortunately for new businesses, payables are kept short due to lack of credit, and receivables are long due to poor customer leverage.

	Cash Flow Analysis: OpTel ($000)				
Year	1986	1987	1988	1989	1990
NOI	($1,290)	$3,815	$3,283	$6,085	$9,175
Interest	$480	$720	$720	$240	$0
Taxes	$0	$0	$0	$1,089	$3,588
Dividends	$0	$0	$0	$0	$0
Capital	$7,280	$6,335	$578	$1,011	$1,264
LTD Reduction	$0	$0	$0	$0	$0
Chg WC	($2,584)	($177)	$1,411	($375)	($399)
Cash Flow	($6,466)	($3,063)	$575	$4,120	$4,722
Cum CF	($6,466)	($9,530)	($8,955)	($4,835)	($113)

Let's examine the cash flow in a typical business. The revenue in year $k+1$ is represented by $R(k+1)$, and is defined as the revenue booked in that year. Remember that we can book revenue but not receive it as cash, since the revenue may still reside as a receivable. The receivables are accounts that represent money due but not received.

Define $AR(k+1)$ as the accounts receivable at the end of the year $k+1$. These are the amounts that are booked as revenue in that year, but not yet converted to cash. Let $AR(k)$ be the accounts receivable at the year k; assume that they are converted into cash in year $k+1$. Therefore, we can say that the cash inflow in year $k+1$ is $CI(k+1)$ and is given by the equation:

$$CI(k+1) = R(k+1) - AR(k+1) + AR(k)$$

That is, the cash in is the revenue booked, less the revenue not yet converted to cash in that year, plus the revenue converted to cash from the previous year.

Now look at the cash outflow in year $k+1$, represented by $CO(k+1)$. It is the sum of all expenses in that year, $E(k+1)$, plus the capital in that year, $C(k+1)$. As with the revenue, we do not pay all the expenses in cash flow since some of them may still reside in accounts payable. Thus, at the end of the year, we may still owe an amount $AP(k+1)$. This reduces the cash flow. However, the accounts payable from the preceding year, $AP(k)$, are due payable as cash in that year; these are cash outflows. We have:

$$CO(k+1) = E(k+1) + C(k+1) - AP(k+1) + AP(k)$$

The cash flow then becomes $CF(k+1)$, which is $CI(k+1)$ less $CO(k+1)$:

$$CF(k+1) = R(k+1) - E(k+1) - C(k+1) - \{ [AR(k+1) - AP(k+1)] - [AR(k) - AP(k)] \}$$

where we define the working capital as $WC(k+1)$:

$$WC(k+1) = AR(k+1) - AP(k+1)$$

Then we can write the cash flow as:

$$CF(k+1) = R(k+1) - E(k+1) - C(k+1) - [WC(k+1) - WC(k)]$$

This simple example can then be expanded to include all the expense elements as well as other non-cash current assets and liabilities. This process will lead to an expression for the cash flow from the business. The cash flow, CF, is then defined as follows:

$$CF(k+1) = NOI(k+1) - INT(k+1) - TAX(k+1) - DIV(k+1) - CAP(k+1) - LTD(k+1) - (WC(k+1) - WC(k))$$

The cumulative cash flow is the sum of the CF, called CCF. Several cash flow measures relate to the performance of the business. They are:

1. *PNCCF.* The peak negative cumulative cash flow. It says how deep the business will go into debt and also how much financing will be needed for the business.

2. *NPV.* The net present value. It is a discounted version of the CF, where the discounting is done at some cost of money. It represents the present value of the business, as-

suming some cost of capital. This concept is developed in more detail in the next chapter. The NPV for a cost of money of COM is given by:

$$NPV = \sum_{i=1}^{N} \frac{CF(i)}{(1+COM)^i}$$

3. *IRR*. The internal rate of return. It is the cost of money that makes the NPV equation equal 0. It is a measure of the potential return expected on the investment each year. For venture capitalists, an IRR of 50 percent is typical. For a large corporation, an IRR of 20 percent is acceptable. Thus it is essential to understand the investor's needs and the operations of the business.

It is important to perform the NPV and IRR calculations in the absence of any debt financing, dividends, or prior sunk costs. The evaluation of these items is done in the absence of any financing alternatives or their impact on the tax situation. They are all done under 100 percent equity financing. (See the books by Fred J. Weston and Thomas Copeland or Richard Brealey and Stewart Myers for a more detailed description of the calculations of NPV and IRR.)

We can now consider each of the businesses in terms of the cash flow analyses. Table 8.9 presents the cash flows for the two businesses. Infotel has no significant capital; it takes three years for the business to have a positive operating income. The management of the working capital has added a positive cash flow for the first three years due to collecting the receivables in a short period and extending long-term credit on the payables. It is also a reflection of the management of the inventory of the cost of goods model. This results in, a ten year period, an NPV of $4.7 million and an IRR of 43 percent—quite an attractive IRR for the business.

Example

As shown in Table 8.9, OpTel is the extreme of a capital-intensive business. The first year alone requires $7.2 million.

Again, the management of the working capital allows a $2.5 million credit. This business, over ten years, has an IRR of 39 percent and an NPV of $7 million. The peak cumulative cash flow is $8.9 million. From this cash flow profile, we can understand certain key facts about capital-intensive businesses:

- Initial Large Losses: The first years are typically the most dangerous. They are the years that have the largest losses due to reduced revenue and large amounts of capital required.
- Working Capital Management Can Generate Cash: We see that the change in working capital allows for a positive cash flow—so the change in working capital is negative. This is a result of paying bills after we collect receipts for service. Generally, this may be a positive cash flow item if the business is well-managed. However, the vendors may want upfront payments, thus reversing the situation. The entrepreneur should be very wary of this element of the cash flow.
- Capital is the Greatest Element: The company may want to perform a lease-back analysis to determine if the IRR can be improved with better cash flow management through a lease program. The lease will improve the cash flow, but will not impact the balance sheet.

Example

Table 8.9 shows that, in contrast to the capital-intensive service business, Infotel is inventory-intensive and product-oriented. Its cash flow statement highlights the differences. These are:

- Cash Flow is Generally Positive Earlier: This is particularly true for the business where it peaks in the second year, and goes positive on a cash flow basis in the third year and on a cumulative basis in the fifth year.
- Working Capital is Harder to Manage: A direct result of the inventory requirements. In the OpTel example, we noted that the business could actually obtain cash from working capital management. At Infotel, the inventory eliminates that oppor-

tunity. In fact, remember that the inventory turn in this business was about 10. If we find that the turn is less—say, five—we can have a significant working capital management problem.

In summary, the cash flow analysis should contain the following information:

The IRR of the investment

The NPV of the investment

The peak cumulative negative cash flow

The turnaround year

A discussion of the working capital management

Generally the presentation of the cash flow is in chart form, as demonstrated in Table 8.9.

BALANCE SHEET

The balance sheet represents the worth of the company in terms of its assets and liabilities. The balance sheet is divided into three areas. The first is the set of assets, both short-term or current and long-term. The second part is the set of liabilities—in other words, what the company owes. These are also divided into short-term and long-term categories. The difference between the assets and liabilities is the net worth, or owners' equity. We shall see in Chapter 9 how this owners' equity plays an important role in valuating the company.

This section develops the balance sheet and relates it to the sources and uses statements. In many start-up ventures, the balance sheet is neglected; all that is shown is the income statement. It is the balance sheet that shows how well the company can survive in the long-term, and what borrowing power it may have from more standard financing sources.

Let's begin by considering the balance sheet for the manufacturing business, Infotel, shown in Table 8.10.

TABLE 8.10 Balance Sheet for Infotel ($000)

Year	1986	1987	1988	1989	1990
Assets					
Current Assets					
Cash	$904	$1,677	$1,982	$3,534	$14,666
Sht-term invest	$0	$0	$0	$0	$0
Accts receivable	$366	$1,820	$5,197	$10,355	$13,904
Inventory	$256	$1,369	$4,059	$8,694	$10,617
Tot cur assets	$1,526	$4,867	$11,238	$22,583	$39,187
Capital plant-dep	$787	$1,152	$1,553	$1,950	$2,454
LT invest	$0	$0	$0	$0	$0
Sundry assets	$0	$0	$0	$0	$0
Total assets	$2,312	$6,019	$12,791	$24,532	$41,641
Liabilities					
Current Liab					
Accts payable	$1,056	$1,986	$3,743	$6,081	$8,064
Accrued liab	$68	$151	$292	$480	$637
Taxes payable	$0	$0	$525	$1,570	$2,666
Tot cur liab	$1,124	$2,137	$4,559	$8,131	$11,367
Long-term debt	$0	$0	$0	$0	$0
Other noncur liab	$0	$0	$0	$0	$0
Total liabilities	$1,124	$2,137	$4,559	$8,131	$11,367
Owners' Equity					
Shares @ par	$0	$0	$0	$0	$0
Adtl paid-in cap	$3,000	$5,500	$5,500	$5,500	$5,500
Retain earnings	($1,811)	($1,618)	$2,731	$10,901	$24,774
Tot owner equity	$1,189	$3,882	$8,231	$16,401	$30,274
Tot liab/own equity	$2,312	$6,019	$12,791	$24,532	$41,641

Current Assets

The current assets of the business are divided as follows:

1. *Cash.* This is cash on hand at the end of the fiscal year. Remember, the balance sheet is for a particular date in time, unlike the income statement, which represents the events between two dates in time. Cash may be in a non-

interest-bearing account, such as the company checking account.

2. *Short-Term Investments.* These are cash assets that may be in treasury notes or certificates of deposit that are readily accessible. At Infotel, the company has put $904,000 in its checking account and nothing in short-term instruments, giving them instant liquidity. However, this is not good business practice. Expect the treasury function to keep 80 percent or more in a short-term investment.

3. *Accounts Receivable.* These are assets that relate to revenue not yet received. The receivables are usually measured in days, with the base being the revenue. For example, if the annual revenue is $36 million and there are 90-day receivables, this represents $9 million in receivables. We have booked the revenue and reflected it in the income statement, but it exists only as a receivable. This is one of the most important factors in the financial management of the business. An investor will typically look at the revenue and the receivables to determine the business's credibility. If the receivables are a large percentage of the revenue, they may suspect mismanagement.

4. *Inventory.* We discussed this item before in connection with the cost-of-goods model. Inventory represents the materials that are manufactured but not yet sold. They have value, but this value has not yet been converted into cash income.

   The sum of these values represents the current assets of the business. These assets could hypothetically be rendered into cash at some factored amount. For example, one could "factor" the receivables to raise cash by selling the receivables to a third party at a reduced rate, and letting the third party worry about collecting. Typical factoring results in 40 percent to 60 percent of the balance sheet value being reduced to cash. The same could be done with the inventory. Cash, however, is cash at full value. Thus, the strength of the balance sheet is represented on the current assets side by the ratio of cash to other current assets.

5. *Capital Plant Less Depreciation.* A long-term asset that lists all the plant and property at book value, less all accumulated depreciation. In some companies, the property (including plant and real property) may actually have appreciated. However, for the sake of the balance sheet, it has depreciated.

6. *Long-Term Investments.* These are cash or cash type investments that cannot be reduced to cash in less than a year. For example, they may be long-term notes or other such instruments. For the most part, start-up companies do not have such assets.

7. *Sundry Assets.* Other long-term assets that fit in no other category.

8. *Total Assets.* The sum of the above represent total assets of the company.

Liabilities

The liabilities follow the assets first by current liabilities, then long-term liabilities. The current liabilities are:

1. *Accounts Payable.* The payments due vendors or suppliers. They have been accounted for on the net operating expense line, but have not really been accounted for in a cash flow. As with the receivables, they result in a days-payable number, which is the ratio of total payables to total third-party expenses (both expenses and capital).

2. *Accrued Liabilities.* These may represent salaries or other expenses that are due but not yet paid. For example, employees may be paid monthly, and although expensed on NOE, the paycheck may not yet be issued.

3. *Taxes Payable.* This area accounts for expensed taxes not yet paid. For example, taxes are paid quarterly, so that the fourth-quarter taxes, although not yet paid, are reflected as due.

The current liabilities are the sum of these items. The ratio of current assets to current liabilities is called the current ratio, and it represents how well the current debts can be paid out of readily available cash. In year 5 at Infotel, we have a current asset of $39 million and a current liability of $11 million. This is a current ratio of 3.6, which is very comfortable, even if factoring is necessary.

The other liabililties are non-current and composed of two elements:

Long-Term Debt: The long-term debt of the company.

Other: Any other long-term liability, even pension or lease liabilities.

As before, the total liabilities are the sum of these numbers.

Owners' Equity

Essentially, owners' equity is the difference between the assets and the liabilities.

1. *Shares at Par.* When issued, the stock may have a par or nominal value, such as $1 per share. However, this is no longer necessary in most states.

2. *Additional Paid-In Capital.* The capital paid for stock in excess of par. For zero par, this is the money raised from stock offerings. In this example, Infotel raised $3 million in Year 1 and $2.5 million in Year 2. Thus, the additional paid-in capital $5.5 million.

3. *Retained Earnings.* The earnings that are retained. If we reexamine the income statement, we find that the business had an after tax-profit, which is added to the retained earnings for the year. That amount becomes the retained earnings.

The assets equal the liabilities plus the owners' equity, and should balance. Let us examine why this should be so true looking at the payables and receivables. If we do not get the receivables for 150 days, this reduces the cash pool because we must still pay our debts even if others do not pay theirs. However, if we have no receivables and large payables, we have a large cash reserve to offset the future debt. This process continuously balances out the business operation.

This discussion leads to the concept of working capital. Working capital is defined as current assets less current liabilities. Companies with large working capital look like good companies. However, a closer look may alter that interpretation.

Example

In Year 5 at Infotel, current assets are $39.2 million and current liabilities are $11.4 million. The working capital is $27.8 million. However, $13.9 million is in receivables, and $10.6 million in inventory. If all goes badly, the firm may only collect 20 percent of the receivables ($4.8 million), and the product may die, leaving a useless inventory. However, the liabilities are still due. So, the nature of the working capital is important. The working capital also represents what the company needs to satisfy its operations. The change in working capital represents how much additional free cash is needed to manage the company. This cash does not come from the net income; it must come from somewhere else.

The change in working capital is the working capital of this year less the working capital of last year. If we focus on that change less cash, then that number represents the additional cash the company needs to fund its growth. We used that number in the cash flow expression of the last section. For example, at Infotel, the change in WC, less cash, for Year 5 is $6 million. That means that the company needs that much money to support the receivables and inventory.

Example

If we look at Table 8.11 for OpTel, we see a different situation. The WC, less cash, is negative, which means that there is a real cash flow because the company pays late and collects early. In this case, the company manages its working capital in a much better fashion.

TABLE 8.11 Balance Sheet for OpTel ($000)

Year	1986	1987	1988	1989	1990
Assets					
Current Assets					
Cash	$534	$970	$1,545	$1,665	$4,387
Sht-term invest	$0	$0	$0	$0	$0
Accts receivable	$222	$1,100	$1,454	$2,074	$2,853
Inventory	$36	$64	$61	$58	$57
Tot cur assets	$792	$2,135	$3,059	$3,797	$7,297
Capital plant-dep	$6,552	$11,525	$10,684	$10,175	$9,792
LT invest	$0	$0	$0	$0	$0
Sundry assets	$0	$0	$0	$0	$0
Total assets	$7,344	$13,661	$13,743	$13,972	$17,089
Liabilities					
Current Liab					
Accts payable	$2,779	$3,613	$2,451	$3,268	$4,223
Accrued liab	$36	$178	$236	$336	$463
Taxes payable	$27	$134	$177	$252	$347
Tot cur liab	$2,842	$3,925	$2,864	$3,857	$5,033
Long-term debt	$4,000	$6,000	$6,000	$2,000	$0
Other noncur liab	$0	$0	$0	$0	$0
Total liabilities	$6,842	$9,925	$8,864	$5,857	$5,033
Owners' Equity					
Shares @ par	$0	$0	$0	$0	$0
Adtl paid-in cap	$3,000	$4,500	$4,500	$4,500	$4,500
Retain earnings	($2,498)	($764)	$379	$3,615	$7,556
Tot owner equity	$502	$3,736	$4,879	$8,115	$12,056
Tot liab/own equity	$7,344	$13,661	$13,743	$13,972	$17,089

As you can see, the strategic issue on working capital is that there must be a good control of current asset growth, less cash; otherwise, it has to be financed by the company.

SOURCES AND USES

The final financial statement is that of the sources and uses (S&U). This statement provides a view of the money's origin and destination. Table 8.12 depicts the S&U statement for Infotel.

TABLE 8.12 Sources and Uses for Infotel ($000)

Year	1986	1987	1988	1989	1990
Sources					
Beginning cash	$0	$904	$1,677	$1,982	$3,534
NOI	($1,724)	$331	$7,171	$16,282	$27,551
Senior debt	$0	$0	$0	$0	$0
Junior debt	$0	$0	$0	$0	$0
Equity (common)	$3,000	$2,500	$0	$0	$0
Equity (prefrd)	$0	$0	$0	$0	$0
Total sources	$1,276	$3,735	$8,848	$18,264	$31,086
Uses					
Purchase	$0	$0	$0	$0	$0
Capital reg	$874	$503	$598	$661	$853
Int senior debt	$0	$0	$0	$0	$0
Int junior debt	$0	$0	$0	$0	$0
Taxes	$0	$0	$2,624	$7,849	$13,329
Dividends (com)	$0	$0	$0	$0	$0
Dividends (pref)	$0	$0	$0	$0	$0
Chg in junior debt	$0	$0	$0	$0	$0
Chng work Cap	($503)	$1,555	$3,644	$6,220	$2,237
Chng in LTD	$0	$0	$0	$0	$0
Total uses	$372	$2,058	$6,866	$14,730	$16,419
Net cash	$904	$1,677	$1,982	$3,534	$14,666

The sources are as follows:

1. *Beginning Cash.* In the first year, the business has no cash in its internal coffers; it has to raise all the cash externally. In later years, the business must find other sources in order to keep the beginning cash in the positive range.

2. *NOI.* The net operating income—the cash that the business generates. In this example, the NOI is negative, and is thus a negative source or use.

3. *Senior Debt.* The senior debt acquired in that year, not the accumulated debt. In this business, there is no senior or secured debt.

4. *Junior Debt.* Unsecured junior debt may involve debentures; more will be said on this topic in Chapter 9.

5. *Equity (Common).* The cash generated from the common debt in that year.

6. *Equity (Preferred).* The preferred equity capital raised.

The uses are:

1. *Purchase.* Applies if the business is purchased in a year. It generally does not apply to a start-up unless it buys a new business. It does apply if the business is bought from an existing company.

2. *Capital.* The capital required in the year.

3. *Interest.* Interest on both senior and junior debt.

4. *Taxes.* All taxes.

5. *Dividends.* All dividends on common and preferred stock.

6. *Change in Debt.* Includes the payment of both junior and senior debt. Note that the debt repayment plans may be fixed or variable. In a variable plan, the company has a fixed number of years to repay debt; the annual amounts may vary.

7. *Change in Working Capital.* The additional amount of money needed to support the working capital needs.

The total sources must equal or exceed the uses. The excess of sources over uses is placed into the cash for next year. If we compare Infotel to OpTel, we see that OpTel's WC needs actually generate cash, reducing the need for additional capital and cutting interest payments, thereby increasing the value of the company.

It is important to note that the sources and uses are similar to cash flow, but they include details on where the money is coming from. Typically, the business plan does not have a sources and uses statement, since that is a negotiating position to be taken during financing. However, it must be worked out to develop the financing strategy.

KEY FACTORS

The financial section summary should include a review of the key financial factors. The list developed in this section shows the potential investor the snapshot view of the total business outlook. The factors are as follows:

Internal Rate of Return

The IRR provides the analyst of the business with a measure of the business investment. Remember that the IRR is a measure of the effective interest rate that the investment will provide, averaged over its lifetime. Implicit in the determination of the IRR is the size of the investment necessary to support the business. The IRR is also calculated on the after-tax cash flow from the business, and not the before-tax figure. For instance, an IRR of 8 percent is an after-tax number; if it were a secure investment it would represent an excellent return. However, in a start-up company, the investors are typically looking for IRRs that exceed 25 percent because of the significant risk associated with any new venture.

Net Present Value

The NPV represents the increase in the firm's value that will occur if this investment is made. In simplistic terms, if the NPV is $12 million and we act on the business opportunity now, we could arguably increase our wealth by that amount. However, the investor will always use a significant discount factor in the NPV calculation, thus reducing the NPV a great deal. We shall see in Chapter 10 that the NPV is one of several measures used for the valuation of the business.

Profit After Tax in Final Year

The after-tax profit provides a measure of the size or scale of the business. Using the revenue for the appropriate year, it also yields the profit margin. Care must be taken to ensure that the profit is not too small or too large. Too small a profit may mean that no room exists for error; too large a profit means that the prices are too high or that the expenses have been underestimated.

The after-tax profits provide a critical measure of success. The market value of the firm can also be determined from the after-tax profits, based upon a price-to-earnings ratio approach. Specifically, if the price-to-earnings (P/E) is 20 and the after-tax profits are $10 million, the market value of the firm is $200 million. It is for this reason that the after-tax profits are so critical.

Revenue in Final Year

The typical venture capital-funded deal is one in which the investor would like to see $100 million in the fifth year. However, such opportunities are rare. The revenue in a target year is a critical measure of the business. First, the choice of the target year is critical. Most investors do not want to see their investment wait 20 years; however, it is unrealistic to get a return in two years. A balance must be met. The result: the target year is typically five to seven years. In addition, the target revenue should be appreciable to match the interests of the investor.

Book Value in Final Year

The book value is the result of the assets less the liabilities. Typically, the book value is a conservative measure of the value of the firm. Another ratio that is important and can be calculated directly is the ratio of the market to book value. As we discussed, the market value is based on the after-tax profits and the P/E. The ratio of the market to book values is a measure of the future expectations in the business.

Peak Negative Cumulative Cash Flow

The PNCCF is a measure of the total investment to be made in the business. It gives the investor a quick look at the amount of capital required.

Peak NCCF Year

This is the year at which the PNCCF occurs, a measure of how long investments are to be made in the business. Typically, this does not exceed 3 years.

Turnaround Year

The turnaround is the year in which the CCF (cumulative cash flow) is positive for the first time. In effect, it is a measure of how long the investor will have to wait until the business, by itself, will flow cash outwards.

Total Cumulative Capital

This figure represents the total amount of money required over the investment period for the business. It is a measure of the capital-intensiveness of the business.

Revenue/Asset First and Last Year

The revenue per asset dollar is another measure of the capital-intensiveness of the business. As discussed in Chapter 2, this ratio describes the nature of the business and is a measure of the need for future financing to replace capital.

Revenue/Employee

This ratio is a measure of how effectively the employees generate revenue, and how people-intensive the business is.

NOI/Employee

This is the most critical employee-related ratio. It depicts the ability of a single employee to generate profit for the company.

Capital/Employee

This figure measures how heavily each employee is leveraged by capital. It should be remembered that, for each dollar of capital, there will be an associated depreciation dollar eventually. Also remember that we can cut back on people, but that a company cannot fire depreciation or interest.

Inventory Turn

For hardware-related businesses, the inventory turn is a critical measure of the business's vitality and management effectiveness. As we have stated, the inventory turn will impact the working capital requirements as well as the need for financing.

Current Ratio

As we have already discussed, the current ratio is the ratio of current assets to current liabilities. It reflects the vitality of the company as well as a measure of the working capital.

Table 8.13 summarizes these key factors, their meaning, and their uses.

TABLE 8.13 Summary of Key Factors

Factor	Meaning	Use
IRR	Annualized return	Acceptable range
NPV	Net value to firm	Valuation
PAT%	Profitability	Reasonable
Revenue final year	Size of business	Investment
Book value	Value of business	Investment
PNCF	Capital required	Safety of investment
PNCF year	Length of investment	Time before return
Turn around year	Time before self-supporting	Risk exposure
Cumulative capital	Capital intensity	Investment intensiveness
Rev/asset	Capital intensity	Return potential
Rev/employee	Labor intensity	Growth potential
NOI/employee	Profitability	Rate of return
Cap/employee	Capital intensity	Leverage
Inventory turn	Ratio of sale/inventory	Risk of leverage
Current ratio	Current assets/current liabilities	Ability to pay debt

CONCLUSION

In this chapter we developed the basic concepts of the business plan financials. The financials are the foundation for evaluating the total business opportunity. As we have seen, the financials require first an understanding of the business and detailed knowledge of its operations.

PART III

9

FINANCING THE VENTURE

So far we have seen what is needed to develop a business. This chapter expands on a strategy to finance the new venture. The entrepreneur must develop that strategy before dealing with the venture capitalist or other sources of capital. In addition, the entrepreneur must have alternatives to the plan and be prepared to say no to offers that will leave him or her with too little of the business. The entrepreneur must also consider when and how to cash in his chips in the business to reap the rewards of his investments. This chapter attempts to do just that.

We start with the valuation of the entrepreneur's contribution to the source of the capital. The venture capitalist wants to get as great a portion of the business as possible; the entrepreneur wants to give away as little as possible. Valuation is a logical process that allows the entrepreneur to deal effectively with the source of capital.

Then follows the process of how the capital is raised, and from whom. Sources may include the venture capitalist, private placements, secured debt, or licensing.

The financing alternatives vary from debt to common or preferred stock. These alternatives are tied directly into the business plan financials. The focus is always toward what the entrepreneur will get at the end of his or her involvement.

VALUATION

For well-developed companies, a standard method of evaluation depends on the book or the market value of the company. The

281

book value is defined as the value of the company, as recorded on its balance sheet, in terms of assets less liabilities. Its market value is defined as the stock price times the number of shares outstanding.

In valuing a new company, these simple means are not readily available. No stock exists to tell the firm's market value, nor is there a solid asset base against which to judge the company. For the most part the firm consists of an idea, a business plan, and possibly a small amount of revenue and a large need for capital.

However, five methods prove useful for valuing a start-up company.

Reproduction Value

This method, the simplest, is the one many venture capitalists use in their first cut at valuation. They look at the venture, estimate how many man-months have been spent in writing the business plan, and multiply that figure by a weighted cost per man-month.

As an example, six people in a small company wanting to build a fiber optic business had spent a year investigating the business and preparing the plan. Estimating the reproduction cost at $15,000 per man-month and totaling the number of months at 72, you reach an evaluation of $1,080,000. If the venture capitalist gives the company $500,000 to start, they want 50 percent.

This method ignores the assets that may have been developed in the process. It ignores the business potential. It even ignores the risk of that potential. It also gives the company away before it gets out of the starting gate.

Present Asset Value

This method looks a little bit deeper into the business, asking what the assets of the start-up venture are. It includes not only the business plan, but the following items:

1. *Patents.* These may be granted or filed for. They represent what the principals can do, and also present a possible barrier to entry for the competition.

2. *Prototypes.* Prototypes may be in hardware or software, and demonstrate that the item could work. They also represent a selling tool to talk to the customer and assess the market potential.

3. *Profits/Revenues.* These show that a market exists for the service, and that the entrepreneur has gotten to the first step of delivering the product. In most cases the profit may not exist and the revenue may be minuscule. Nevertheless, this is the most important element of the present asset value.

4. *Clients.* These are potential customers. This asset may be demonstrated in binding letters of intent, non-binding letters of intent, or even contingent purchase orders, showing that the entrepreneur has contacted a customer and the customer has been willing to commit in writing to the product.

5. *Contracts.* Actual contracts to purchase the product represent possible revenue streams.

6. *Business Plan.* The plan as we have developed it.

7. *Contingent Capital Commitment.* In this case, the entrepreneur may have found some source of capital contingent upon getting a large capital supplier.

We can now value the fiber optic company using this method. The following are available to the company:

- A business plan valued at $1 million.
- Letters of intent for five-year revenue of $20 million. At an after-tax profit margin of 10 percent, these letters are valued at $2 million.
- Rights of way at a 50 percent discount and on an exclusive basis. The rights of way would normally be worth $4 million per year but are available at $2 million.

• Agreements with a construction company to get access to buildings at a guaranteed rate. This is valued at $500,000.

These items then lead to a valuation of assets of $5.5 million— dramatically larger than the first approach. It leaves the company with over 90 percent of the equity for the $500,000 financing first proposed.

Net Present Value Basis

This method is based solely upon the business plan. It assumes that the business is financed solely by debt. It then calculates the net present value (NPV) at a discount rate that contains a risk factor. Recall that the NPV is given by the following:

$$NPV = \sum_{i=1}^{N} \frac{CF(i)}{(1+k)^i}$$

where $CF(i)$ is the cash flow from the business in year i, and where the cost of capital, k, is a sum of risk-free values, typically 14 percent plus a risk premium. The risk premium must reflect the risk of revenue, capital, and operating expense. If the revenue can be assured by agreements, if the capital estimate can be assured by prior experience in both the industry and by the experience of the entrepreneurs, and if the operating expense can be assured in a similar fashion, then the risk may be estimated. The k value can be given as:

$$k = k_0 + k_{rev} + k_{cap} + k_{exp}$$

In the above example, we can estimate the k values as follows:

k_0 is a risk-free rate of 14 percent.

k_{rev} is the revenue risk rate, estimated at 10 percent due to the presence of agreements.

k_{cap} is the capital risk rate, estimated at 5 percent due to the known base in the industry.

k_{exp} is the expense risk rate, estimated at 6 percent due to the fact that the entrepreneurs have been through this process before.

Using these four factors for total risk, the sum is the total risk for a resulting k of 35 percent. The NPV is calculated to be $4.2 million.

We now have three estimates. The first is $1 million, the second $5.5 million, and the third $4.2 million. The entrepreneur now has a basis to estimate his company's worth.

Return on Investment Valuation

This valuation method is based upon the projected financials but includes the impact of the initial investment made by the venture firm or other entity. The initial investment of I is made for S per share. Although this results in $P\%$ of the company, that value is irrelevant at this point.

Using the after-tax cash flow and the other investment dilutions, an EPS (earnings per share) is determined for each year of the business. Using examples of similar businesses, the P/E (price-to-earnings) ratio is estimated for the cash flow and a market value is determined for each year k. The value of the equity on a per-share basis in year k is $E(k)$. The investor then sets a return on his investment, annualized so that, in year k for a return of $R\%$ annually, the per-share value S is given by:

$$\$S = \sum_{i=1}^{N} \frac{\$E(i)}{(1+R\%)^i}$$

where the discount factor is the denominator.

As an example, say an investor makes a $500,000 initial investment and wants a 50 percent annualized return, with a payout in Year 5. Then the discount factor is $1/(1.5)^5$, or $1/7.59$, or 0.13 times the selling price in Year 5. In our previous example, the selling price is estimated to be $7.31. Thus, the value per share is $0.96, assuming 14,000,000 shares outstanding. Thus, the venture capitalist gets 520,000 shares, or 4 percent, of the company. This values the company at $13,400,000.

As the return rate increases, however, the value of the company decreases. Consider a 100 percent return giving a per-share value of $0.23, or a valuation of $3,154. The latter is probably the better value, given the desire of the investor to include a hefty risk premium.

Book Value Valuation

This last valuation method works under the concept that the company can be sold at a multiple of the book value, and that the investor still wants to get the return on the sale as in the previous method.

Consider the investment discussed above. The company in Year 5 has a book value of $31 million. If the multiples for companies in this range at that time is 1.5 times book, this gives a book-based value of $46.5 million. The investor places $500,000 in the company and expects a 100 percent return so that, by Year 5, the investment is worth $16 million. This represents 34 percent of the company. Projecting backwards, the company is worth three times the investment, or $1.5 million. It is important to note that the driving factors here are the expected rate of return and the multiple of book value.

To summarize the valuation methods for this example, we have:

Reproduction valuation: $1.1 million

Present asset valuation: $5.5 million

NPV valuation: $4.2 million

Return-on-investment valuation: $3.2 million

Book value valuation: $1.5 million

These results indicate that the easiest method is the reproduction method, the one usually used by venture capitalists. It also consistently gives the lowest value to a business. The present asset method often overvalues the assets with no accounting for risk. The NPV method accounts for the business and the risk, but does not give a market premium. The market premium is usually given in the ROI method, but it may be discounted by the excessive risk premium of the investor. Table 9.1 presents the advantages and disadvantages for each of the schemes.

SOURCES OF FINANCING

The entrepreneur will be interested in obtaining financing from alternate sources at different times in the venture's development. This section discusses the several sources of available financing and the advantages and disadvantages of each. Later in this chapter we discuss the sequencing of the financing that is appropriate at the different stages of the venture.

TABLE 9.1 Comparison of Valuation Methods

Advantages	Disadvantages
Reproduction Value	
• Easy to calculate	• Does not count assets
• Measures current expenditures	• Does not include business value
• Good for investor	• Gives lowest value
Present Asset Value	
• Counts intangible assets	• Does not reflect business
• Values revenue potential	• Does not count risk
NPV Value	
• Based upon business potential	• Does not count market value
• Factors on risks	• May overvalue certain risks
• Quantitative	
ROI Value	
• Based on business concept	• Requires high risk premium
• Factors in market premium	• Targets IPO liquidation
• Uses controllable factors	• May give away too much
Book Value	
• Uses business concept	• Requires high risk premium
• Conservative method	• Does not factor in market factors
• Lower risk	• Assumes a buyout to liquidate

Determining the Financing Phase

The first step in deciding on a source of financing is to see what phase the company is in. Four general rounds of financing are defined by the phase that the business is in.

First Round

This is the seed money financing stage. During this phase, the entrepreneur might only have the draft business plan and may need up to $200,000 in capital to get the key ingredients together. This is the riskiest stage, and the one in which the majority of the equity is lost. Some venture firms are willing to invest in this phase due to an interest in the business area or due to a belief in the principals that make up the venture firm.

In one case, a large and reputable venture firm invested $1 million for 50 percent of a firm that had no business plan, no operational management, no marketing or sales skills—just what appeared to be the right technical people to generate the right product. This form of financing is rare and depends upon a blend of chemistry and luck.

In another case, a small company used its personal funds to generate the business plan, create the first product, and get its first contract. The net result: they avoided the first round of financing and held onto 100 percent of the company. In addition, the company was valued at more than $5 million by the time it needed real expansion financing. As you can see, the choice of first round financing depends upon the ability of the entrepreneurs to finance their own venture.

Second Round

This round finds a plan and a potential market, but no developed product. The financing is needed to develop the product to the stage where it could be marketed. Typically, it is a complicated product that requires a manufacturing skill, software that requires significant development, or a service that requires an infrastructure.

In this round, the entrepreneur has the capability of identifying and even working with the end user customer in developing the product. Typical among these efforts is the beta site testing of a new software product. Consider a software company that developed a new financial analysis package with an artificial intelligence approach to expert systems. The product was very user friendly and satisfied an important need. It was developed by internal financing. To test it before financing, the firm went to several large accounting firms and investment bank houses. Three agreed to beta test the product if they could subsequently purchase it for a 25 percent discount. The firm agreed and not only had a tested product, but letters of recommendation and three orders. However, they needed a round of financing to maintain the company and hire the additional software personnel that were needed.

Third Round

A firm approaching this round has a product, a well thought out business plan, and even some customers. It may even have a revenue stream and some profit. At this point, the entrepreneur may need capital to expand, capture, and secure market share.

For example, a small computer terminal company had manufactured and beta tested a product for use with distributed sales organizations. These DSO companies now wanted to purchase 20,000 units if they could be purchased for $150 per unit in volume. The company needed special assembly equipment for final assembly. They had developed a relationship with a Korean company to do off-shore manufacturing of the product. They needed $4 million for the new equipment and for working capital. At this point the company was valued at $16 million, so it was possible to get the $4 million with, at most, 25 percent dilution and the issuance of warrants.

Fourth Round

A company at this point is established, may have $2 to $5 million in revenues, and may even have a strong profit position—yet it is not generating adequate internal funds for growth. It may need considerable capital to maintain market share in a growing industry.

In this fourth round, the company can go public with its IPO (initial public offering). The company has high growth, rising profits, is in a growth industry, and can demand a large multiple. As an example, the telecommunications switching market for PBXs saw great activity in the late 1970s and early 1980s with large demand and high market interest.

Finding the Financing

We've looked at four phases of financing. Now let's examine the possible sources.

Private Placement

In the venture business, the entrepreneur will attempt to raise capital from individual investors directly or through some intermediary. He or she must put together a package for the total amount and sell interests in that package to interested parties. The person or firm doing the placement must be aware of the SEC requirements that limit what can be done under such a placement.

Basically, the limits that the SEC places are along two lines:

1. *Rule 504 Regulation D.* This line is for offering up to $500,000. It requires a filing of the Regulation D form and has the following major constraints:

    No more than 35 non-accredited investors
    Restricted stock to be held two years
    No general solicitation
    Follow standards of full disclosure
    Adhere to Blue Sky State rules

2. *Rule 505 Regulation D.* This line is for offerings up to $5,000,000. The requirements are as above, but expand to a larger base of investors. Rule 505 is typically used by investment houses or venture capital firms.

With a good lawyer and the right support it is possible to raise seed money under Rule 504. The restrictions need some explanation. First, a non-accredited investor is anyone who does not have $1,000,000 in assets. It may be friends or family who believe in you. Restricted stock, a common form of stock, cannot be traded in any form for two years. It is typical that venture entrepreneurs get restricted shares. When they go public this may still be the case.

The Blue Sky laws are state laws that require a review by a state committee to assure buyers that there is no overt fraud or unstated risk. Some states do not have such laws; we suggest that the entrepreneur check with attorneys to determine the present status in his or her states.

Private Corporate Placement

In this case the entrepreneur can go to a large company or set of companies who may have a strategic interest in the product area and provide the company with funds. This plan works well where the corporate funds provider has an interest in a new product area and desires to take a position in the company as a means for guaranteeing a source of technical information and supply of product.

Funding levels in a private corporate placement are varied, and may be able to meet the entrepreneur's requirements. The problem is that many times the interest on the part of the larger company may be too intense and can result in overmanagement. A typical example is the set of companies funded by Exxon Enterprises. Prime amongst them was Intecom, a very successful switch manufacturer, which was almost managed out of existence by the overreaching of the corporate founders.

Venture Capital

This source is the most widely known. Such books as those by A. D. Silver, D. J. Gladstone, and Joseph O'Flaherty can give the reader a better understanding of the workings of the venture capital firm. These firms generally have a fund that they apportion accordingly. Their objective may be to get a 50 percent or greater annual return on their investments.

The advantage for many a start-up is that a good firm may bring some management support. The bad part of that is that it may not want the present management to stay around too long. The venture capital firm has an interest in getting out of the investment in, at most, five years—sooner if possible. The venture agreement is often very restrictive and may require the entrepreneur to accept personal responsibility for the debt of the company.

Limited Partnerships

In certain investments where there are large tax losses in the early years, entrepreneurs may have an interest in setting up a limited partnership to fund the venture. In this case the assets may be transferred to the partnership, then leased to the company. The partnership then can allocate the depreciation and tax losses as tax benefits to the limited partners. This source of funding requires a syndication of a partnership, and generally does not work unless there are appreciable up-front losses and the at-risk rules of the IRS are adhered to.

R&D Tax Shelters

This form of financing has developed as a result of IRS tax codes that allow for rapid tax write-offs on R&D efforts. They are usually used for large corporations, but can also be applied to ventures. Tax considerations require a high level of sophistication, and may also need an oral reading from the IRS to assure investors that their investment is eligible for the tax credit. This process also requires that a syndication be performed.

Public Offering

Public offerings may be done in a variety of ways. The IPO, or initial public offering, is usually handled by the venture firm or the investment banker. These offerings are passed by all states on the Blue Sky basis.

A second form of public offering is the so called "Denver deal"—penny stock deals that are done in states that do not have Blue Sky laws, such as Colorado. They are usually done for highly speculative companies with little if any assets and one to five employees. They are done by regional investment houses.

A typical Denver deal was for a company with one employee, a business plan, and raising $1,500,00, of which $750,000 went immediately to pay debts that were 180 days in arrears. The stock sold for $0.10 per share; 15 million were shares issued in the offering, with 30 million outstanding. The company had no revenue.

Debt

This is the simplest but possibly the hardest form of financing to obtain. It requires an asset base to secure the debt and results in a freezing of those assets against the security. The debt can be obtained from banks or other financial institutions.

Other Forms

Still other creative forms of financing, such as licensing agreements, prepayments on contracts, leasing, and prepayment combined with R&D contracts relate to the specific business. The entrepreneur should have a hold on several of these alternatives, especially in meeting with a venture capitalist.

FINANCING ALTERNATIVES

The previous section discussed the phases of financing and the sourcing. This section focuses on the type of financing that could be obtained in any one of these phases or through any one of the sources. The financing alternatives discussed below can be used separately or in conjunction with one another. The next section goes into detail as to the impact that these will have on the business.

The alternatives that are available are as follows:

Common stock
Preferred stock
Warrants
Options
Convertible debentures
Secured debt

Each of these have different effects on the cash flows, profitability and book values of the company.

Common Stock

Common stock is the simplest form of financing. The company has shares issued at various times. These shares can be authorized or outstanding. Shares are authorized by the board for subsequent issuing. They may or may not be issued or held by a person. Outstanding shares are issued. Treasury shares are shares that were once outstanding but have been repurchased by the firm.

A third type of common stock is founders' shares, which are obtained by the founders at inception of the business. If shares are issued beyond the founders' shares for some value, it will be for the per-share value or greater of the stock at the time of offering. This then establishes a market value for the company—the product of the total shares outstanding times the price per share.

For example, a company has a million founders' shares and no other stock. It has a book value of $2 million. It sells one million shares of stock at $5 dollars per share. The company now has a market value of $10 million, and the entrepreneurs now own 50 percent of the company.

Common stock may also issue dividends at a fixed rate of dollars per quarter. This dividend is purely optional. There are various theories as to how best to deal with dividend policy, but that is beyond the scope of this text.

Preferred Stock

Preferred stock generally has no voting rights for the holders. However, it does have a guaranteed dividend payout, assuming the company can afford the cash flow. Many times the dividend may follow as a percent of the purchase price of the share of preferred, and remain fixed.

Preferred holders have recourse above common holders in the event the company goes into bankruptcy. Preferred stock is not reflected in the ownership of the company in shares outstanding. If there is no par value, it appears only as value in excess of par in the balance sheet.

Warrants

Warrants are options to purchase stock for a fixed period of time. They allow the holder to exercise the warrant and pay the company the agreed price, thus gaining common shares in the company. The disadvantage of warrants is that they are usually issued in conjunction with some other form of financing and are structured to provide to the purchaser a capital gains exclusion on the gains, but also dilute the earnings per share of the stock of the firm. The exercise of warrants can cause a dilution at the wrong time. However, they are used as incentives to the financing entity.

Options

Options are typically granted as options to the employees or others in the firm. They are like warrants in that they give the holder the right to purchase stock in a certain time period for a given price. However, employee warrants are generally priced higher and are employee incentives.

Convertible Debentures

Convertible debentures are junior debt notes that carry an interest payment, but which are subordinated to secured debt. For the most part, convertible debentures are unsecured debt. They have a provision, however, that allows the holder to convert them to common stock at a fixed conversion price for a fixed period. A non-dilution clause typically accompanies them so that the conversion is kept at the rate in place at the time of issue. The advantage of convertibles is that the interest is lower and they do not encumber senior or secured debt. However, the conversion clause can have the same effect as warrants with no additional cash flow. What is allowed is the forgiveness of the remaining convertible debt. The result is lower earnings per share.

Secured Debt

Secured or senior debt is a loan that is secured by the firm's assets. It generally carries the highest interest rate and may be required to be amortized over a fixed period. This form of financing is usually obtained from banks or financial institutions. Table 9.2 shows the advantages and disadvantages of these various forms of financing.

We can expand upon the details that we have presented for the financing schemes in the financing schedule (see Table 9.3). The table begins with common equity and 1,000,000 shares to the

TABLE 9.2 Financing Alternatives

Type	Advantages	Disadvantages
Common stock	• No interest	• Dilutes ownership
Preferred stock	• No liability	• Dilutes ownership • Requires dividends
Warrants	• No liability	• Dilution • Loss of conversion control
Options	• No liability	• Dilutes ownership • Poor conversion timing
Convertible debentures	• Less dilution	• Liability • Reduces ownership • High total cost
Secured debt	• No dilution • Early repayment	• Fixed debt payment • Negative cash flow impact

TABLE 9.3 Financing Schedule ($000)

	COMMON EQUITY					
Year	1986	1987	1988	1989	1990	1991
No. ownrs shrs (000)	1000	1000	1000	1000	1000	1000
No. new common shares	2000	1000	500	0	0	0
New common cap	$2,000	$2,000	$2,000	$0	$0	$0
No. shares out	3000	4000	4500	4500	4500	4500
Purchase/share	$1	$2	$4	$4	$4	$4
Dividend rate (%)	0%	0%	0%	0%	0%	0%
EPS ($.00)	($27)	($22)	($9)	$24	$59	$77
P/E	15	15	15	15	15	15
Val/Share ($.00)	($400)	($326)	($132)	$361	$880	$1,152
Mkt Value	($12,000)	($13,050)	($5,940)	$16,248	$39,610	$51,854
Mkt/Book Val (%)	($1,000)	($560)	($151)	$324	$517	$467
Owners Eqty %	33%	25%	22%	22%	22%	22%

	PREFERRED EQUITY					
Year	1986	1987	1988	1989	1990	1991
No. new preferred	0	0	0	0	0	0
No. shares preferred	0	0	0	0	0	0
No. common/pref	1	1	1	1	1	1
No. equiv. common	0	0	0	0	0	0
Dividend rate (%)	12%	12%	12%	12%	12%	12%
Dividends	$0	$0	$0	$0	$0	$0
Price/share	$2	$3	$4	$4	$4	$4
New preferred cap	$0	$0	$0	$0	$0	$0
Total preferred	$0	$0	$0	$0	$0	$0

	WARRANTS					
Year	1986	1987	1988	1989	1990	1991
No. new warrants	0	0	0	0	0	0
Total warrants	0	0	0	0	0	0
Common warrants	1	1	1	1	1	1
No. equiv. common	0	0	0	0	0	0
No. warrants exer	0	0	0	0	0	0
Warrants cap	$0	$0	$0	$0	$0	$0
No. warrants	0	0	0	0	0	0
Price/warrant	$2	$2	$2	$2	$2	$2

TABLE 9.3 Financing Schedule ($000) (continued)

OPTIONS						
Year	1986	1987	1988	1989	1990	1991
No. new options	0	0	0	0	0	0
No. opt exer	0	0	0	0	0	0
Option cap	$0	$0	$0	$0	$0	$0
No. options	$0	$0	$0	$0	$0	$0
Price/option	$2	$2	$2	$2	$2	$2

CONVERTIBLES						
Year	1986	1987	1988	1989	1990	1991
No. new convertible	0	0	0	0	0	0
Total convertible	0	0	0	0	0	0
No. convertible exer	0	0	0	0	0	0
Conversion cap	$0	$0	$0	$0	$0	$0
No. conversions	0	0	0	0	0	0
Conversion price	$2	$2	$2	$2	$2	$2
New jun debt	$0	$0	$0	$0	$0	$0
Junior debt	$0	$0	$0	$0	$0	$0
Interest JD (%)	10%	10%	10%	10%	10%	10%
No. eqv shrs (000)	3000	4000	4500	4500	4500	4500
Fuly dilEPS ($0.00)	($27)	($22)	($9)	$24	$59	$77

SENIOR DEBT						
Year	1986	1987	1988	1989	1990	1991
New senior debt	$0	$0	$0	$0	$0	$0
Total senior debt	$0	$0	$0	$0	$0	$0
Interest SD (%)	15%	15%	15%	15%	15%	15%

PURCHASE CAPITAL						
Year	1986	1987	1988	1989	1990	1991
Purchase	$0	$0	$0	$0	$0	$0

owners in founders' shares. The company then issues new common shares at a per-share value, providing cash to the sources statement of the business. The increase in the shares dilutes the owners' equity percent of the company. In this example, we have included the earnings per share (EPS) and the price-to-earnings (P/E) ratio so as to determine an effective market value. Here we see that the market value of the firm increases.

The second element of the financing schedule is the preferred equity. As with common stock, the number of new shares and the price per share are essential values. However, preferred stock does not dilute the owners' equity directly. The issue with preferred, however, is the need to frequently issue dividends on the stock. In addition, many preferred shares may come with a conversion clause.

The third element of the financing schedule is the warrants. Warrants can be issued at any time and by themselves do not generate cash to the uses statement. They also come with a conversion factor: how many shares of common each warrant will buy, at what price. When a warrant is exercised, it generates cash and an increase in the common shares outstanding. Thus, in the financing schedule, we start with the issuance of warrants, and terminate them when they are converted to common. In some cases, warrants are never exercised because the exercise price may be too high.

Options provide the next entry on the financing schedule. Like warrants, options generate cash only when exercised. The result is cash and the increase in common shares outstanding.

Convertibles are also called junior debt. In the convertible element of the financing schedule, we typically issue junior debt, a debt that generates an interest requirement. The debt has associated with it a conversion clause that says that it can convert the debt to common shares at a conversion price per share. For example, if the debt is $1,000,000 and the conversion price is $1 per share, the debt is eliminated at conversion and the balance sheet reflects a reduction in debt but an increase in the owners' equity. The debt is converted to cash in excess of par. The advantage of conversion is evident if, and only if, the stock price is well above the conversion price.

The final elements of the financing schedule are the senior debt and the purchase price elements. These do not impact the equity values of the company.

IMPACTS OF FINANCING

We have discussed the various times, types, and sources of financing of the new venture. This section demonstrates the effects and impacts of using the different types of financing.

The entrepreneur should focus on certain areas of impact when evaluating the impact of financing. They are:

- Impact on the equity of the firm
- Risk to the firm in cash exposure
- Impact on the value of the firm
- Return of cash from the investment
- Impact on breakeven year and CCF peak negative year

All types of financing are burdens, albeit necessary ones, on the firm. Therefore, they should be evaluated from the firm's perspective. The venture capitalist will evaluate them from his or her perspective.

Let's look at an example of a company whose revenue, new capital, and expenses are shown in Table 9.4. The company grows from a $1 million-per-year company to over $22 million in five years. It does not require a great deal of capital overall, but it does require up-front capital to get going.

The company has a net operating income margin of 35 percent by Year 5, as such, it can be highly profitable. The business needs financing to get it over the first three to four years. With the types of numbers shown, it could be a very healthy investment.

Let's now consider six types of financing for this company. For each of the cases we shall look at the income statement, the financing schedule, and the balance sheet. We shall also summarize the results in terms of the key factors. The cases are detailed in the tables that follow and the subtle differences require a care-

TABLE 9.4 Company Financials (Revenue, Capital, Expenses) ($000)

	Revenue Summary					
Year	1986	1987	1988	1989	1990	1991
Revenue	$1,000	$2,500	$5,000	$9,500	$14,250	$21,375
	Capital Model					
Year	1986	1987	1988	1989	1990	1991
Initial capital	$0	$0	$0	$0	$0	$0
Net capital	$0	$1,600	$2,480	$3,584	$3,267	$3,014
Total new capital	$2,000	$1,500	$2,000	$500	$500	$500
Total capital	$2,000	$3,100	$4,480	$4,084	$3,767	$3,514
Depreciation	$400	$620	$896	$817	$753	$703
ITC	$0	$0	$0	$0	$0	$0
	Expense Model					
Year	1986	1987	1988	1989	1990	1991
No. employees	35	69	113	190	232	347
Net oper. exp	$1,400	$2,750	$4,500	$7,600	$9,263	$13,894

ful study of all the financial statements. The details of the cases are as follows:

Case 1: Common Stock

Common stock is issued in Years 1, 2, and 3 of operation. In Year 1, the stock is issued at $1 per share with 2 million shares; Year 2 at $2 per share and 1 million shares; and Year 3 at $3 per share with 500,000 shares. The founders have 1 million shares in all cases. This raises $6 million.

Case 2: Secured Debt

We assume that the company can get secured debt financing at a 15 percent annual rate. In this case, the balance sheet does not indicate the assets, but we'll assume that some benevolent benefactor was willing to sign for the debt. The debt is $2.5 million the first year and $3 million the second and third years for a total of $8.5 million, $2.5 million more than needed in the case of common equity funding.

Case 3: Preferred

This case assumes a preferred price of $2, $3, or $4 for each of the first three years, with 1.5, 1 and 0.5 million shares issued at a dividend rate of 12 percent. This raises a total of $8 million. It is important to remember that dividends are paid after taxes and not before.

Case 4: Convertible Debentures

In this case, $2.5, $2.0 and $2.5 million are raised through convertibles, with conversion prices of $2 for each year. The interest rate is 10 percent. We assume that the debentures are converted in the fifth and sixth years.

Case 5: Preferred and Convertibles

This is a more typical case. Convertible debt of $1 million in the first and $2 million in the third year are made at a conversion price of $1 per share, with conversion in Year 5. Preferred is issued in Years 1 and 2 at $2 and $3 respectively, for 1 million in Year 1 and the same number in Year 2. This raises a total capital of $8 million.

Case 6: Debt and Warrants

This is also a typical case. Here the debt is at 12 percent and is $2.5, $2.5 and $2.5 million for the first three years. Warrants are issued at $1 per warrant in the amounts of 1 million for each of the years. A total of $10.5 million can be raised in this case, yet the latter $3 million occurs at the exercise of the warrants in Year 5.

Tables 9.5 through 9.16 present the income statements and balance sheets for these six cases. Table 9.17 presents the key financial factors comparing the six cases. Before proceeding, assume that the company goes public in Year 6 and that the founders still have their one million shares. The payout to the founders under these cases is the baseline to evaluate the impact of the financing schemes. The results of these different types of financing on the performance of the firm will vary in terms of the mar-

TABLE 9.5 Income Statement: Case 1 ($000)

Year	1986	1987	1988	1989	1990	1991
Revenue	$1,000	$2,500	$5,000	$9,500	$14,250	$21,375
Expense	$1,400	$2,750	$4,500	$7,600	$9,263	$13,894
NOI	($400)	($250)	$500	$1,900	$4,987	$7,481
Margin %	−40%	−10%	10%	20%	35%	35%
Depreciation	$400	$620	$896	$817	$753	$703
Profit before int	($800)	($870)	($396)	$1,083	$4,234	$6,778
Margin %	−80%	−35%	−8%	11%	30%	32%
Interest	$0	$0	$0	$0	$0	$0
Profit before tax	($800)	($870)	($396)	$1,083	$4,234	$6,778
Margin %	−80%	−35%	−8%	11%	30%	32%
Taxes	$0	$0	$0	$0	$1,593	$3,321
Dividends	$0	$0	$0	$0	$0	$0
Profit after tax	($800)	($870)	($396)	$1,083	$2,641	$3,457
Margin %	−80%	−35%	−8%	11%	19%	16%

TABLE 9.6 Balance Sheet: Case 1 ($000)

Year	1986	1987	1988	1989	1990	1991
Assets						
Current Assets						
Cash	($47)	$130	$667	$1,875	$4,876	$8,904
Short-term invest	$0	$0	$0	$0	$0	$0
Accts receivable	$205	$514	$1,027	$1,952	$2,928	$4,392
Inventory	$100	$155	$224	$204	$188	$176
Tot cur assets	$259	$799	$1,918	$4,032	$7,993	$13,472
Capital plant-dep	$1,600	$2,480	$3,584	$3,267	$3,014	$2,811
LT invest	$0	$0	$0	$0	$0	$0
Sundry assets	$0	$0	$0	$0	$0	$0
Total assets	$1,859	$3,279	$5,502	$7,299	$11,006	$16,283
Liabilities						
Current liabilities						
Accts payable	$559	$699	$1,068	$1,332	$1,605	$2,366
Accrued liab	$100	$250	$500	$950	$1,425	$2,138
Taxes payable	$0	$0	$0	$0	$319	$664
Tot cur liab	$659	$949	$1,568	$2,282	$3,348	$5,168
Long-term debt	$0	$0	$0	$0	$0	$0
Other noncur liab	$0	$0	$0	$0	$0	$0
Total liabilities	$659	$949	$1,568	$2,282	$3,348	$5,168
Owners' Equity						
Shares @ par	$0	$0	$0	$0	$0	$0
Adtl paid-in cap	$2,000	$4,000	$6,000	$6,000	$6,000	$6,000
Retain earnings	($800)	($1,670)	($2,066)	($983)	$1,658	$5,115
Tot owners' equity	$1,200	$2,330	$3,934	$5,017	$7,658	$11,115
Tot liab/own equity	$1,859	$3,279	$5,502	$7,299	$11,006	$16,283

TABLE 9.7 Income Statement: Case 2 ($000)

Year	1986	1987	1988	1989	1990	1991
Revenue	$1,000	$2,500	$5,000	$9,500	$14,250	$21,375
Expense	$1,400	$2,750	$4,500	$7,600	$9,263	$13,894
NOI	($400)	($250)	$500	$1,900	$4,987	$7,481
Margin %	−40%	−10%	10%	20%	35%	35%
Depreciation	$400	$620	$896	$817	$753	$703
Profit before int	($800)	($870)	($396)	$1,083	$4,234	$6,778
Margin %	−80%	−35%	−8%	11%	30%	32%
Interest	$375	$813	$1,209	$1,159	$1,152	$684
Profit before tax	($1,175)	($1,683)	($1,605)	($76)	$3,081	$6,095
Margin %	−118%	−67%	−32%	−1%	22%	29%
Taxes	$0	$0	$0	$0	$0	$2,272
Dividends	$0	$0	$0	$0	$0	$0
Profit after tax	($1,175)	($1,683)	($1,605)	($76)	$3,081	$3,823
Margin %	−118%	−67%	−32%	−1%	22%	18%

TABLE 9.8 Balance Sheet: Case 2 ($000)

Year	1986	1987	1988	1989	1990	1991
Assets						
Current assets						
Cash	$0	$0	$0	$0	$0	$0
Short-term invest	$0	$0	$0	$0	$0	$0
Accts receivable	$205	$514	$1,027	$1,952	$2,928	$4,392
Inventory	$100	$155	$224	$204	$188	$176
Tot cur assets	$305	$669	$1,251	$2,156	$3,116	$4,568
Capital plant-dep	$1,600	$2,480	$3,584	$3,267	$3,014	$2,811
LT invest	$0	$0	$0	$0	$0	$0
Sundry assets	$0	$0	$0	$0	$0	$0
Total assets	$1,905	$3,149	$4,835	$5,423	$6,130	$7,379
Liabilities						
Current liabilities						
Accts payable	$559	$699	$1,068	$1,332	$1,605	$2,366
Accrued liab	$100	$250	$500	$950	$1,425	$2,138
Taxes payable	$0	$0	$0	$0	$0	$454
Tot cur liab	$659	$949	$1,568	$2,282	$3,030	$4,958
Long-term debt	$2,422	$5,058	$7,730	$7,681	$4,558	$56
Other noncur liab	$0	$0	$0	$0	$0	$0
Total liabilities	$3,080	$6,007	$9,298	$9,963	$7,588	$5,014
Owners' equity						
Shares @ par	$0	$0	$0	$0	$0	$0
Adtl paid-in cap	$0	$0	$0	$0	$0	$0
Retain earnings	($1,175)	($2,858)	($4,463)	($4,539)	($1,458)	$2,365
Tot owner equity	($1,175)	($2,858)	($4,463)	($4,539)	($1,458)	$2,365
Tot liab/own equity	$1,905	$3,149	$4,835	$5,423	$6,130	$7,379

TABLE 9.9 Income Statement: Case 3 ($000)

Year	1986	1987	1988	1989	1990	1991
Revenue	$1,000	$2,500	$5,000	$9,500	$14,250	$21,375
Expense	$1,400	$2,750	$4,500	$7,600	$9,263	$13,894
NOI	($400)	($250)	$500	$1,900	$4,987	$7,481
Margin %	−40%	−10%	10%	20%	35%	35%
Depreciation	$400	$620	$896	$817	$753	$703
Profit before int	($800)	($870)	($396)	$1,083	$4,234	$6,778
Margin %	−80%	−35%	−8%	11%	30%	32%
Interest	$0	$0	$0	$0	$0	$0
Profit before tax	($800)	($870)	($396)	$1,083	$4,234	$6,778
Margin %	−80%	−35%	−8%	11%	30%	32%
Taxes	$0	$0	$0	$0	$1,593	$3,321
Dividends	$360	$720	$960	$960	$960	$960
Profit after tax	($1,160)	($1,590)	($1,356)	$123	$1,681	$2,497
Margin %	−116%	−64%	−27%	1%	12%	12%

TABLE 9.10 Balance Sheet: Case 3 ($000)

Year	1986	1987	1988	1989	1990	1991
Assets						
Current Assets						
Cash	$593	$1,050	$627	$875	$2,916	$5,984
Short-term invest	$0	$0	$0	$0	$0	$0
Accts receivable	$205	$514	$1,027	$1,952	$2,928	$4,392
Inventory	$100	$155	$224	$204	$188	$176
Tot cur assets	$899	$1,719	$1,878	$3,032	$6,033	$10,552
Capital plant-dep	$1,600	$2,480	$3,584	$3,267	$3,014	$2,811
LT invest	$0	$0	$0	$0	$0	$0
Sundry assets	$0	$0	$0	$0	$0	$0
Total assets	$2,499	$4,199	$5,462	$6,299	$9,046	$13,363
Liabilities						
Current Liabilities						
Accts payable	$559	$699	$1,068	$1,332	$1,605	$2,366
Accrued liab	$100	$250	$500	$950	$1,425	$2,138
Taxes payable	$0	$0	$0	$0	$319	$664
Tot cur liab	$659	$949	$1,568	$2,282	$3,348	$5,168
Long-term debt	$0	$0	$0	$0	$0	$0
Other noncur liab	$0	$0	$0	$0	$0	$0
Total liabilities	$659	$949	$1,568	$2,282	$3,348	$5,168
Owner's Equity						
Shares @ par	$0	$0	$0	$0	$0	$0
Adtl paid-in cap	$3,000	$6,000	$9,000	$11,000	$11,000	$11,000
Retain earnings	($1,160)	($2,750)	($4,106)	($3,983)	($2,302)	$195
Tot owner's equity	$1,840	$3,250	$4,894	$7,017	$8,698	$11,195
Tot liab/own equity	$2,499	$4,199	$6,462	$9,299	$12,046	$16,363

TABLE 9.11 Income Statement: Case 4 ($000)

Year	1986	1987	1988	1989	1990	1991
Revenue	$1,000	$2,500	$5,000	$9,500	$14,250	$21,375
Expense	$1,400	$2,750	$4,500	$7,600	$9,263	$13,894
NOI	($400)	($250)	$500	$1,900	$4,987	$7,481
Margin %	−40%	−10%	10%	20%	35%	35%
Depreciation	$400	$620	$896	$817	$753	$703
Profit before int	($800)	($870)	($396)	$1,083	$4,234	$6,778
Margin %	−80%	−35%	−8%	11%	30%	32%
Interest	$250	$450	$700	$700	$700	$0
Profit before tax	($1,050)	($1,320)	($1,096)	$383	$3,534	$6,778
Margin %	−105%	−53%	−22%	4%	25%	32%
Taxes	$0	$0	$0	$0	$221	$3,321
Dividends	$0	$0	$0	$0	$0	$0
Profit after tax	($1,050)	($1,320)	($1,096)	$383	$3,313	$3,457
Margin %	−105%	−53%	−22%	4%	23%	16%

TABLE 9.12 Balance Sheet: Case 4 ($000)

Year	1986	1987	1988	1989	1990	1991
Assets						
Current Assets						
Cash	$203	($70)	$267	$775	($2,826)	$1,476
Short-term invest	$0	$0	$0	$0	$0	$0
Accts receivable	$205	$514	$1,027	$1,952	$2,928	$4,392
Inventory	$100	$155	$224	$204	$188	$176
Tot cur assets	$509	$599	$1,518	$2,932	$290	$6,044
Capital plant-dep	$1,600	$2,480	$3,584	$3,267	$3,014	$2,811
LT invest	$0	$0	$0	$0	$0	$0
Sundry assets	$0	$0	$0	$0	$0	$0
Total assets	$2,109	$3,079	$5,102	$6,199	$3,304	$8,855
Liabilities						
Current liabilities						
Accts payable	$559	$699	$1,068	$1,332	$1,605	$2,366
Accrued liab	$100	$250	$500	$950	$1,425	$2,138
Taxes payable	$0	$0	$0	$0	$44	$664
Tot cur liab	$659	$949	$1,568	$2,282	$3,074	$5,168
Long-term debt	$2,500	$4,500	$7,000	$7,000	$0	$0
Other noncur liab	$0	$0	$0	$0	$0	$0
Total liabilities	$3,159	$5,449	$8,568	$9,282	$3,074	$5,168
Owner's Equity						
Shares @ par	$0	$0	$0	$0	$0	$0
Adtl paid-in cap	$0	$0	$0	$0	$0	$0
Retain earnings	($1,050)	($2,370)	($3,466)	($3,083)	$230	$3,687
Tot owner equity	($1,050)	($2,370)	($3,466)	($3,083)	$230	$3,687
Tot liab/own equity	$2,109	$3,079	$5,102	$6,199	$3,304	$8,855

TABLE 9.13 Income Statement: Case 5 ($000)

Year	1986	1987	1988	1989	1990	1991
Revenue	$1,000	$2,500	$5,000	$9,500	$14,250	$21,375
Expense	$1,400	$2,750	$4,500	$7,600	$9,263	$13,894
NOI	($400)	($250)	$500	$1,900	$4,987	$7,481
Margin %	−40%	−10%	10%	20%	35%	35%
Depreciation	$400	$620	$896	$817	$753	$703
Profit before int	($800)	($870)	($396)	$1,083	$4,234	$6,778
Margin %	−80%	−35%	−8%	11%	30%	32%
Interest	$100	$100	$300	$300	$300	($450)
Profit before tax	($900)	($970)	($696)	$783	$3,934	$7,228
Margin %	−90%	−39%	−14%	8%	28%	34%
Taxes	$0	$0	$0	$0	$1,054	$3,542
Dividends	$240	$600	$600	$600	$600	$600
Profit after tax	($1,140)	($1,570)	($1,296)	$183	$2,280	$3,086
Margin %	−114%	−34%	−26%	2%	16%	14%

TABLE 9.14 Balance Sheet: Case 5 ($000)

Year	1986	1987	1988	1989	1990	1991
Assets						
Current Assets						
Cash	$613	$1,090	$727	$1,035	($3,933)	($124)
Short-term invest	$0	$0	$0	$0	$0	$0
Accts receivable	$205	$514	$1,027	$1,952	$2,928	$4,392
Inventory	$100	$155	$224	$204	$188	$176
Tot cur assets	$919	$1,759	$1,978	$3,192	($816)	$4,444
Capital plant-dep	$1,600	$2,480	$3,584	$3,267	$3,014	$2,811
LT invest	$0	$0	$0	$0	$0	$0
Sundry assets	$0	$0	$0	$0	$0	$0
Total assets	$2,519	$4,239	$5,562	$6,459	$2,198	$7,255
Liabilities						
Current Liabilities						
Accts payable	$559	$699	$1,068	$1,332	$1,605	$2,366
Accrued liab	$100	$250	$500	$950	$1,425	$2,138
Taxes payable	$0	$0	$0	$0	$211	$708
Total cur liab	$659	$949	$1,568	$2,282	$3,241	$5,212
Long-term debt	$1,000	$1,000	$3,000	$3,000	($4,500)	($4,500)
Other noncur liab	$0	$0	$0	$0	$0	$0
Total liabilities	$1,659	$1,949	$4,568	$5,282	($1,259)	$712
Owner's Equity						
Shares @ par	$0	$0	$0	$0	$0	$0
Adtl paid-in cap	$2,000	$4,000	$7,000	$7,000	$7,000	$7,000
Retain earnings	($1,140)	($2,710)	($4,006)	($3,823)	($1,543)	$1,543
Total owner equity	$860	$1,290	$2,994	$3,177	$5,457	$8,543
Tot liab/own equity	$2,519	$3,239	$7,562	$8,459	$4,198	$9,255

TABLE 9.15 Income Statement: Case 6 ($000)

Year	1986	1987	1988	1989	1990	1991
Revenue	$1,000	$2,500	$5,000	$9,500	$14,250	$21,375
Expense	$1,400	$2,750	$4,500	$7,600	$9,263	$13,894
NOI	($400)	($250)	$$500	$1,900	$4,987	$7,481
Margin %	−40%	−10%	10%	20%	35%	35%
Depreciation	$400	$620	$896	$817	$753	$703
Profit before int	($800)	($870)	($396)	$1,083	$4,234	$6,778
Margin %	−80%	−35%	−8%	11%	30%	32%
Interest	$250	$500	$750	$750	$750	$0
Profit before tax	($1,050)	($1,370)	($1,146)	$333	$3,484	$6,778
Margin %	−105%	−55%	−23%	4%	24%	32%
Taxes	$0	$0	$0	$0	$123	$3,321
Dividends	$0	$0	$0	$0	$0	$0
Profit after tax	($1,050)	($1,370)	($1,146)	$333	$3,361	$3,457
Margin %	−105%	−55%	−23%	4%	24%	16%

TABLE 9.16 Balance Sheet: Case 6 ($000)

Year	1986	1987	1988	1989	1990	1991
Assets						
Current Assets						
Cash	$203	$380	$667	$1,125	$3,052	$7,374
Short-term invest	$0	$0	$0	$0	$0	$0
Accts Receivable	$205	$514	$1,027	$1,952	$2,928	$4,392
Inventory	$100	$155	$224	$204	$188	$176
Tot cur assets	$509	$1,049	$1,918	$3,282	$6,169	$11,942
Capital plant-dep	$1,600	$2,480	$3,584	$3,267	$3,014	$2,811
LT invest	$0	$0	$0	$0	$0	$0
Sundry assets	$0	$0	$0	$0	$0	$0
Total assets	$2,109	$3,529	$5,502	$6,549	$9,182	$14,753
Liabilities						
Current Liabilities						
Accts payable	$559	$699	$1,068	$1,332	$1,605	$2,366
Accrued liab	$100	$250	$500	$950	$1,425	$2,138
Taxes payable	$0	$0	$0	$0	$25	$664
Tot cur liab	$659	$949	$1,568	$2,282	$3,054	$5,168
Long-term debt	$2,500	$5,000	$7,500	$7,500	$0	$0
Other noncur liab	$0	$0	$0	$0	$0	$0
Total liabialities	$3,159	$5,949	$9,068	$9,782	$3,054	$5,168
Owners' equity						
Shares @ par	$0	$0	$0	$0	$0	$0
Adtl paid-in cap	$0	$0	$0	$0	$6,000	$6,000
Retain earnings	($1,050)	($2,420)	($3,566)	($3,233)	$128	$3,585
Tot owner's equity	($1,050)	($2,420)	($3,566)	($3,233)	$6,128	$9,585
Tot liab/own equity	$2,109	$3,529	$5,502	$6,549	$9,182	$14,753

TABLE 9.17 Returns on Cases of Investment ($000)

Case Ownership	Market Value	Founders Value	Founders Rate of Return
1	$52,456	$11,540	22%
2	$65,257	$65,257	100%
3	$30,856	$30,856	100%
4	$55,026	$12,105	22%
5	$38,056	$8,372	22%
6	$60,799	$15,199	25%

ket value of the company, the value of the founders' share at the time of liquidation, and the percent ownership of the founders.

The key observation you can make by examining Table 9.17 is that, if they could secure and carry all the debt, the return from this form of financing is the greatest for the owners. This is the typical motivation for the entrepreneurs who perform leveraged buy-outs (LBO) of existing companies. However, the risk with this type of financing is the greatest. The second observation is that convertibles and warrants dilute ownership in a significant fashion.

Unfortunately, the venture companies do best with the Case 6 scenario, in which the venture capital firm effectively generates a hedge against failure. This truth is best shown in Tables 9.18 and 9.19. Here the material is expanded to include the payback for the investor. As indicated, the highest value is to the Case 6 scenario, wherein the investor gets a 118 percent annualized return. The lowest is the pure debt issue and, as expected, the risk is less since it is secured by the assets of the firm. The case of common stock is also one of the lower returns due to the long-term payback required. Also note that we assumed that the company would buy back the preferred at a multiple of 10 times its initial price. This typically is the only way preferred holders can cash in their preferred stock.

SEQUENCED FINANCING

As indicated in the last section, many types of financing have different impacts on the investor and the entrepreneur. The con-

TABLE 9.18 Detailed Comparison of Investment Alternatives

Case	Market Value	Founder Percent	Founder Value	Investor Percent	Investor Value
1 (Common)	$51,854	22%	$11,523	78%	$40,331
2 (Debt)	$57,339	100%	$57,339	0%	$0
3 (Preferred)	$37,454	25%	$9,363	75%	$28,091
4 (Convertible)	$51,854	22%	$11,523	78%	$40,331
5 (Prefd & Cnvrt)	$46,296	22%	$10,288	78%	$36,008
6 (Debt&Wrrnts)	$51,854	9%	$4,824	91%	$47,030

cept of sequenced financing is based upon the supposition that the entrepreneur will have the capability to select the means, methods, and times at which financing will occur.

The sequences follow the approaches that we discussed in the development of first and subsequent rounds of financing. The plan should consider the effects of these sequenced financing schemes on the overall value of the business. One word of caution on financing in this mode: certain companies or brokers bring companies public at the first round, which is a very dangerous strategy and often backfires. For example, one company was brought public at a $9 million valuation, leaving the entrepreneur with 30 percent, or $2.7 million. The company raised $3 million.

The first problem was that the company needed a minimum of $3 million in capital. However, the broker took $250,000 for filing fees, $250,000 for legal fees, $500,000 for a finder's fee, a payment of $6,000 per month for three years for the broker and three friends for consulting, plus 30 percent of the company.

Of the $3 million, only $1.7 million was left, forcing a second round at much lower rates. The founder held only 4 percent after the second round, with the company valued at only $9 million. A third round was still needed. The founder was bought out after three years for only $100,000 in cash.

CONCLUSION

The most sensitive part of business negotiations develops around financing, including the valuation and the sophistication

TABLE 9.19 Impact of Investment Option on Company Performance ($000)

Factor	Case 1	Case 2	Case 3	Case 4	Case 5	Case 6
IRR (%)	45%	27%	33%	40%	35%	39%
NPV (@ 18%)	$9,413	$3,859	$5,779	$8,366	$6,955	$8,293
PAT	$18,602	$18,602	$17,642	$18,602	$18,231	$18,602
PAT %	17%	17%	16%	17%	17%	17%
REV	$108,211	$108,211	$108,211	$108,211	$108,211	$108,211
Book Val	$54,958	$46,204	$51,198	$47,530	$50,905	$53,428
PNCF	($5,333)	($8,500)	($7,373)	($6,733)	($7,273)	($6,833)
PNCCF						
Year	3	3	3	3	3	3
CCF Turn	6	8	7	6	7	6

317

of the entrepreneur. The most important piece of advice is to think out the total financing strategy and to value the company properly. Then and only then can the wealth generated by the entrepreneur be retained.

In this chapter, we have looked at a model and framework for generating a set of alternative financing proposals for the new business. These proposals can then be evaluated for the impact on the return to both the entrepreneur and the investors. This approach allows for more equitable and balanced negotiating between the entrepreneur and the investor. We have continually stressed the need for being prepared with alternative scenarios that are backed by detailed financials on their respective performance. The intent of this chapter was to provide the entrepreneur with that set of tools.

10

CONCLUSIONS

In the preceding chapters, we developed the major concepts and presentations that enter into the business plan for a start-up company. As indicated at the outset, we have not presented an academic treatise—rather, we have discussed actual results from the experiences of many companies in this level of development. Once the company clears the first hurdle of getting started and becomes a living entity, it must meet a new set of challenges. By following the structured procedures and understanding the framework of the business development process, the start-up team should have a better insight into the successful business venture.

As the company grows through the idea and planning stage, it begins to take form as an organization. During this phase, the talents of the entrepreneur's team are tested in ways to which they have had very little, if any, exposure. It is during this phase that the principals are most vulnerable. The major risks come from the venture capitalists, who may be seeking their payout on too unrealistic a time schedule, or due to a one-product company that has no follow-through and a new set of competitors.

This conclusion focuses on the next steps that must be taken by the entrepreneur in the start-up company. We further assess the risks that may be faced and discuss ways to overcome them. Getting the business created and started is only the first step. It brings the players to a new threshold, fact to face with a new set of problems. If the principals can come to grips with these new problems and seek ways to manage them, they have the chance for future growth and success. The most important factor in this management effort is the establishment of a firm foundation in the business development phase discussed in this book.

DEVELOPING THE INFRASTRUCTURE

As we have continuously stressed, the essence of the business is people. The proper selection of people is the most important part of the business. The second most important part is the allocation of those resources into the infrastructure of the business. The manager must continually monitor the needs of the enterprise and reassign resources to meet the problems as they occur. No organization is static. In fact, the people in an entrepreneurial organization are often the most fluid in their abilities to flow from one position to another.

In fact, in one start-up company, the entrepreneur was the key technical person in the early days. He headed up the organization and took charge of all the technical developments. The company had a chairman who also handled the marketing role. As the business developed, it found that the technical president had so many contacts and had such a drive to sell the product that he evolved into the sales role, and the chairman took over the role of CEO. The company acquired a new technical person to focus on that area.

Change and redirection are important. Avoiding internal conflicts is even more so. Internal conflicts often arise between employees over their roles in the organization. To reduce these frictions, there must be a clean definition of these roles and a decisive communication of these roles to all employees. This is the simplest task. The CEO must also back up this organization with support of the key player in each role.

The second part of managing the infrastructure is the management of the board and investors. The board should be the responsibility of the chairperson, who should manage upwards. The chairperson should communicate freely with the board to ensure that there are no surprises.

With a tightly controlled board, this may not be a problem. With a venture capital-backed board, it can be a significant problem. Almost without exception, the companies that have gotten into trouble are those that have kept back facts from the board that reflect adversely on the business progress. If the board was chosen wisely, its assistance will be invaluable in times of stress. Aside from the legal implications, the board must be informed and its guidance sought. The board often operates on a shorter timespan and, in times of stress, may be less likely to weather the stresses. Management of the venture team is almost as important as managing the company.

MANAGING RISKS

The risks that will develop in the first few years are predictable. As we discussed in previous chapters, risks and risk strategies are key to survival. The risks that occur during the operations phase of the business are different from those arising during the development phase, however. They can be anticipated in general terms, and for the most part are predictable. These are the risks that result when the company is making revenue and may even be profitable. The following is a synopsis of those risks.

Risk 1: Unrealistic Goals

This occurs when the business was anticipated to be $100 million, with 50 percent pre-tax profit margins. It is now $4 million with a 7 percent pre-tax margin. A certain amount of over-enthusiasm accompanies a new business, but in some cases the business does not take off as rapidly as anticipated. Depending on the backers, many things can happen at this point. The venture people may seek to sell off the business, or the key players may get disillusioned with the returns for their time.

The managers should reassess their goals and reassess the strategies. Perhaps the business can become a $20 million-per-year business with some effort—not really a bad business. It may not make the venture people happy, but could make for a comfortable business base. One strategy: continually reassess the goals. If the venture backers get dissatisfied, a buy-out of their interests may be possible.

Risk 2: Only One Product

The problem with most start-ups is that they have one product. They may think about others, but there is only one in the stable. The problem occurs as the product life cycle comes to its end or when the revenue from that one product is saturated.

The time to plan for the second product is as the first one enters the development phase. Remember that products have life cycles and that the second product must follow in close step behind the first. Remember also that the second product may have less of a chance at success than the first. The classic example is the Apple computer line. The first product was the Apple II, followed by the Apple IIC, then the LISA, then the Macintosh. There was a clear progression of the product from the initial stage of conception to a continuing product introduction. What is essential is to have a vision of where the company will go and to develop a consistent product roll-out plan for that vision.

A key fact to reexamine is the question of the business the company is in, and to remember that the first product made is not the business. The product first introduced is only the initial manifestation of that business. The managers should strategically have a roll-out of other products that manifest the business.

Risk 3: The End of the Money

In the early phases, the money raised came from the the venture backers or their surrogates. In the more mature phase, the money must come in larger chunks and must be used for working capital and expansion needs. This is a new source of money from places that are less willing to take risk. With a good line of credit, the issue of raising capital is reduced to borrowing from banks on the basis of a secured debt. The management of this process is critical. Money is readily raised at favorable rates when least needed. Thus, it is imperative to have the financial expertise available at as early a stage as possible. This does not mean that the start-up company must have its own accountant or controller. It requires the presence of an experienced financial manager to set up the lines of credit and other necessary funds sources as soon as possible.

Risk 4: Not Enough People

As the business grows, the need for additional people grows significantly. This need is satisfied early on by contacts and the support of the Board members. The use of search firms may help for certain key people. As the business breaks through the 40 to 50 employee level, it gets more difficult to attract the right type of people. When there is no more equity to share, there may be no more challenges to make for day-to-day risks. However, the day-to-day challenges of managing a business remain.

The second element of this risk is the clash of cultures. The first group in the start-up company will think of themselves as pioneers in a wilderness and have a certain camaraderie. The next flow of people are really employees. They must be integrated and motivated, which will take a new set of talents. It will also require a new set of management structures. The actual acquiring and recruiting of these people will be difficult. The original sales pitch of working for a start-up is gone. Now these employees want competitive benefits and salaries. Recruitment firms may be necessary, which will increase the overhead since they charge 25 percent of the first year's salary as a finder's fee. This may be a big jump in expenses that was never anticipated.

Thus this risk has cultural, organizational, and financial elements that must be managed. These risks are the common second-phase risks that the business will experience. They are manageable, but they must be anticipated—and the organization must be prepared to respond to them.

BUDGET AND CONTROLS

The business develops along the line of meeting the many short-term goals that have been set for it. It must develop an effective budgetary and control system to manage expenses and growth.

This will include the strategic planning process, the budget process, and the management control systems that are typical of many larger corporations.

The biggest drawback that the company will experience in introducing products is that they take time and that the entrepreneurs have less time to do what they do best. The importance of these factors cannot be understated. They are the lifeblood of the business. The larger the business becomes, the longer the decision process and the greater the impact of those decisions.

The three elements that must be in place are:

Strategic Plan

This is an annual revival of the business plan. All of the material covered in this book must be duplicated in a structured form each year. The business must be re-evaluated and the products rediscovered. The process must be led from the top and must involve all the players in the business.

Budget

Based on the strategic goals of the business, the budget is a document that details the expenses and capital required to achieve those goals. It becomes the agreed game plan as to how much can be spent in what areas. It is a collaborative effort that requires the participation and consent of all the management team.

Management Control System

As we had discussed with the PMCS, there must be a continuing MCS that controls the budget expenditures and other uses of capital. The typical entrepreneur will have had little exposure to this process. It is in this area that a good controller is essential.

The net result of the above factors and risk areas is an expanding base of overhead functions that need to be provided as the business grows. These overhead functions were provided on an ad hoc basis during the development phase, but now have become institutionalized. It is at this point that the entrepreneur must be cautious to accept these factors and learn to live with them. These overhead functions encompass personnel functions, closer controller functions, increased management concerns, and more complex marketing efforts.

CONCLUSION

At this point the reader has developed an understanding of the fundamentals of the business development process. This process applies for the new business on a stand-alone basis, as well as for the new business in an existing corporation. This book has provided a framework to structure questions and decisions. It has stressed the importance of people as the major success factor in developing a new business. Finally, the process developed here is applicable as part of an ongoing process of evaluating an evolving, growing business.

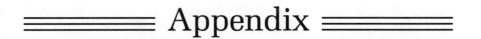

Appendix

SAMPLE BUSINESS PLAN

Bed-and-Breakfast
International

A Business Plan

EXECUTIVE SUMMARY

The bed-and-breakfast (B&B) industry—the fastest-growing segment of the lodging industry—is presently highly fragmented, with poor distribution. It markets its lodging services to a mostly upscale market looking for a unique vacation location and a more sophisticated set of services. The industry is composed of over 10,000 B&B locations with a total of over 80,000 rooms.

BBI was formed to provide a service to this growing industry segment in the areas of promotion, reservations, ratings, and ultimately franchising. The intent of the present business is to establish a base of B&B establishments as reservation subscribers on an exclusive basis, and to generate revenue through the reservation fee of 12 percent of the gross revenue.

At the present time no service exists to meet the demonstrated need. The business will start by establishing a rating guide and in the process sign up B&B subscribers. Through the rating service and other promotional means, the BBI service will provide a toll-free telephone number to allow for dial-in reservations to a computerized on-line reservation service.

The target market for the service is the top 30 percent of all B&Bs who cater to the upscale market on the consumer side. The key financial factors of the business are:

- Year 5 revenue potential of $63 million
- After-tax profit margin of 12 percent
- Peak negative cumulative cash flow of $2.7 million
- IRR of in excess of 40 percent
- NPV of $21 million at capital cost of 22 percent

The company has achieved the following:

- Incorporated in 1985
- President has 10 years' experience in industry
- Chairman has 20 years' real-time computer expertise
- Company has signed up 250 exclusive B&Bs

- Company has been funded internally
- President has been funded by Rand-McNally to develop rating service
- Company has agreement with TRW for proprietary terminal and network
- Computer system has been designed using DEC system

The financial needs of the company are for $3 million in development capital in three steps. The first step is $500,000 for market and system development, the second step is $1.5 million for implementation, and the third step for $1 million of working capital till positive cash flow. The company will provide the first-step investors with 20 percent equity for the initial capital infusion.

The risks of this business come in three areas: market development, technical operations, and rapid entry of competition. In the first area, the company seeks to reduce the risk by obtaining additional exclusive agreements to ensure a profitable business. In the second area, the company has secured the services of experienced technical expertise. In the third area, the company has an early entry and will have secured a market position with its agreements acting as a barrier to entry.

Section 1

BUSINESS DEFINITION

The bed and breakfast (B&B) industry provides lodging for vacation travelers who seek a unique European style of lodging, combining quality accommodations in a unique atmosphere along with a means to meet other vacationers in a setting unique to the locale. They are fashioned after the B&B establishments in Europe except that, in the United States, they have positioned themselves as more upscale accommodations rather than an alternative to hotels. Thus, they do not compete with the standard U.S. hotels or resorts.

The industry is relatively new, and has been receiving rapid acceptance as an alternative to hotels and motels. At present there are over 10,000 B&B establishments in the U.S., and the growth exceeds 20 percent per annum. The availability to them is restricted since they do not advertise extensively, nor do they belong to large associations. Other than via guides or word of mouth, no way now exists to make reservations.

BBI has recognized the B&Bs' need to establish a national rating and reservations service as well as the demand from the consumer for access to a similar set of information. BBI proposes to develop a computer-based reservations service that will allow the consumer to arrange for a set of reservations to a large national base of B&B establishments. The service will provide the participating B&Bs access to a computer terminal developed and serviced by TRW, including a credit card reader and verification system. BBI will operate a centralized computer system to provide for the reservation service. It will also operate a toll-free telephone number for consumers to make reservations.

BBI will provide a rating and routing service that will allow consumers to call into BBI and request a list and ratings of B&Bs. BBI will assist the consumer in establishing the reservations.

BBI has a threefold development strategy. First, it will develop the rating service, leveraged off the contract that it has with Rand-McNally. This will result in a published rating guide, which will also act as a lead generation for the B&Bs. Second, BBI will operate the on-line reservation service for the B&Bs. Third, BBI intends to extend its name recognition into a franchising of B&Bs in addition to the B&Bs that are on its client list. This third phase will be delayed until adequate market viability is established.

The service will operate as follows:

- BBI will establish a rating service operation funded separately.
- A national focused advertising and promotional effort using state agencies and other tourist services will be established to provide consumer awareness of the service.
- A toll-free telephone number will be available for the consumer to make real-time reservations in the desired B&B.
- BBI will receive the toll-free call and, using its computer system, make the reservation and electronically inform the B&Bs.
- The reservations will be guaranteed with a credit card.
- The B&B will receive a confirmation of the reservations.
- BBI will provide summary and audit information as well as market research data for the B&Bs.

This service has a clear set of benefits for both the consumer and B&Bs. The service increases the occupancy rates for the B&Bs, expands the market to include the upscale side, assures payment of reservations, and provides national promotion and recognition. For the consumer, the service provides support of reservations and scheduling of visits.

BBI has developed a strong management team that has experience in the industry, extensive operational experience in the real-time computer field, and competent, capable management teams.

Section 2

MARKET

The market for this business is composed of two elements: B&Bs and the consumer. BBI must be capable of providing support to the B&Bs and have access to the consumer base to generate leads and support sales of the B&B services.

TARGET MARKET

There are in excess of 10,000 B&Bs in the United States, with clustering in the Northeast and a generally even distribution in the remainder of the country. For the most part, these B&Bs have an average of eight rooms that are rented at $70 per night, and have an overall occupancy rate of 50 percent. This results in an annual revenue of $102,000 per B&B—just over $1 billion on a national basis.

The B&B consumer tends to be an upscale consumer seeking a different lodging accommodation for vacations. B&Bs are not used for business accommodations and for the most part provide a bundled package; they do not serve other meals or alcohol. Awareness of B&Bs is generally by word of mouth or through guidebooks specifically targeted at the B&B market.

The B&B operator is generally a professional who has decided upon an alternative lifestyle and has established a small business around the B&B operation. They are generally experienced in the business world and intend to use the B&B operation as a source of ongoing funds based upon their initial capital investment.

At the present time there are about 160 regional reservation services that provide a lead-generation service more than a real-time reservation service. They do not advertise extensively. They would not be a competitor in this business since they do not compete in the proposed service.

The target B&B market for the service can be quantified as follows:

- Those B&Bs on a national basis
- Having eight or more rooms
- With occupancy rates below 70 percent
- And room rates in excess of $60 per night

The target consumer market is segmented into two portions:

Segment 1

- 24–40 years of age
- Married professional with family
- Annual income in excess of $35,000
- With one or more children

Segment 2

- 55 years of age or older
- Married with professional background
- Annual income in excess of $30,000

The targeting of the B&B market is straightforward and can be performed from existing lists. The consumer market can be carefully targeted on a promotional basis using segmented publications such as *Travel and Leisure*.

NEEDS AND BENEFITS

The needs and benefits to the B&B segment are as follows:

- Increased occupancy rates
- Ability to gain greater market awareness
- Ability to raise rates as market demands increase
- Assured reservations for longer booking period
- Detailed market research data and support
- Shared information on promotional successes

On the consumer side:

- Ease of access of planning a total vacation package
- Assurance of quality locations
- Detailed travel information and itinerary information
- Guaranteed prices and accommodations
- Single source for all information
- On-road access to reservations service to provide flexible vacation plans

The service can be positioned as follows:

"The most extensive and easy-to-use service to provide national access to high-quality B&B reservations, ensuring service and full flexibility so as to enhance vacation travel."

MARKET SIZE

The target market size on the B&B side of the business is the top 50 percent of all B&Bs. This will amount to 5,000 B&Bs with eight rooms per for a total of 40,000 rooms. The growth rate in this segment is 25 percent per year. The target occupancy rate is 80 percent from a base of 50 percent. Of the total reservations made, it is estimated that 50 percent of the total can be made through the system.

The consumer target market exceeds the B&B capacity. In addition, it is estimated that the 25 percent growth rate can be maintained for a five-year period. Preliminary market research indicates that the positioning of the service will lead to a high acceptance rate, with over 25 percent of the target market showing a very high acceptance.

The market size is thus limited by room availability rather than consumer base availability.

SALES AND PRICING STRATEGY

There are two elements of the sales strategy. The first deals with the B&Bs:

- Using the rating service guide as a base, the company will target 400 B&Bs nationally to sign up on an exclusive basis. This will represent a core.
- Using 100 of the first B&B sign-ups as sales representatives, BBI will then provide these SRs with a commission of 10 percent of the first three years' revenue as an incentive to sign up other B&Bs in their locality. The strategy is similar to those of distributed sales organizations (DSOs), such as Avon and Tupperware.
- BBI will support and assist the sales representatives, SRs, as independent distributors of the service by national advertising and a direct mail campaign. The use of the SRs will reduce the need to develop a separate field sales force, and will provide a base of knowledgeable, motivated field personnel. The payout over three years will also provide a need for retention marketing and access to the updating of the rating service. A continuing need for quality and use of the system can be provided by this group.

The second element of the sales strategy is directed at the consumer market. The main objective is to raise awareness of the service and provide access to the toll-free telephone number. The sales strategy is as follows:

- Raise awareness through targeted advertising in such publications as *Travel and Leisure, Business Week,* and other targeted publications.
- Using a list of prior registrants, launch a direct mail campaign to assist in referrals and returns as well as scheduling in a set of new B&Bs.
- Publications of the rating guide will have notice of the toll-free number service. Updating the rating guide will provide ongoing presence.

The consumer will be provided with a toll-free number service to request reservations, and will have access to a toll-free "900" service to get on-line information of the rating service. The "900" service is charged at the rate of $0.50 per minute and will provide information on a selection of B&Bs. BBI will get 50 percent of that revenue stream, and the service will be run at cost.

The B&Bs will sign up for a three-year exclusive agreement and will be charged only a fee for those reservations made through the service. The charge will be 12 percent of the gross room rental rate, not including taxes. Credit cards will be used for all reservations; collections of the funds from the B&Bs will be made from an escrowed fund after arrival of the guest. Multiple night stays may be made at a B&B and also will be subject to the collection of a reservation fee. The SRs will provide a spot audit of reservations, and the B&Bs will agree to warrant payment of all leads.

REVENUE POTENTIAL

The revenue potential results from the following:

Number of B&Bs signed up
Number of rooms per B&B
Rate per room

TABLE A2.1 Revenue Model

| | Revenue Summary | | | | |
Year	1986	1987	1988	1989	1990
No. of B&B	4,000	4,400	4,840	5,324	5,856
Rooms/B&B	8	8	8	8	8
Rate/room (%)	$50	$55	$61	$67	$73
Occupancy rate (%)	85	85	85	85	85
B&B revenue ($000,000)	$496	$601	$727	$879	$1,064
No. rooms	32,000	35,200	38,720	42,592	46,851
% Penetration	10	20	30	40	50
No. B&B sold	400	880	1,452	2,130	2,928
% BBI allocation	55	65	70	70	75
No. rooms sold	1,760	4,576	8,131	11,926	17,569
Revenue base ($000)	$27,302	$78,084	$152,624	$246,233	$399,029
Reservation fee %	12	12	12	12	12
Revenue ($000)	$3,276	$9,370	$18,315	$29,548	$47,883

Percent of rooms obtained through BBI

Commission Fee

Table A2.1 depicts the revenue projections for this business for the first ten years. For example, in 1990:

- There are 5856 B&Bs in target market
- Occupancy rate of 85 percent
- Eight rooms per B&B
- 50 percent are obtained through BBI
- 12 percent commission
- Revenue of $48 million

The total revenue potential is $165 million by Year 10.

Section 3

COMPETITION

The business proposed in this plan provides for a two-step growth. The first step lies in the area of operating a national reservations service, the second in the area of franchising the concept on a national basis.

KEY SUCCESS FACTORS

To be successful in the business, the entrepreneur must address two major areas of success: marketing and technical factors. In the marketing area, the factors are:

Understanding and experience in the business

Recognition as a national entity

Access to a wide distribution capability for the product

The ability to provided a bundled set of service offerings

Points-of-sale support to the end user

On the technical side the following factors are important:

Experience in developing and operating a real-time computer system

Experience and capability in operating a national communications network

Understanding of credit validation systems

Software expertise in developing reservations systems

Experience in local terminal management for end users

These factors represent a broad range of expertise necessary for the success of the business. The emphasis is on both the marketing and technical sides. On the marketing side is the ability to blend large size with detailed understanding to gain the trust of the local B&B operator. Many growth factors are still undefined; it is necessary to develop a close relationship with the B&B operators to ensure that these factors are carefully developed.

COMPETITORS

The competitors for this business are divided into two major areas: hotel operators and transaction processors. In the former category, many chains such as Holiday Inn, Best Western, and Sheraton could, technically, provide the service. However, they would be perceived as the major operator of the business, and the B&B owners have a strong desire to stay apart from these entities.

The second class of competitors are the transaction processors such as American Express, GEISCO, ADP, and even MasterCard or Visa. All have national recognition and the technical expertise. Again, the B&B operators' main concern may be the service operator's lack of closeness to the business; that may cause them to decide not to support the service.

A third set of potential competitors—the present reservation services—enter the picture. However, they are not technically capable and are overly regional. They also have developed a very poor reputation and do not present a viable competitive threat.

DISTINCTIVE COMPETENCES

BBI has a unique set of distinctive competences that it believes matches the key success factors and provides a base to deal effectively with the competition. These competences are as follows:

- Eight years of direct experience in the operations of B&B establishments
- National recognition as a spokesperson for the B&B industry
- Extensive technical expertise in the development of consumer-based electronic transaction systems
- Skilled and competent corporate managers with proven track records
- A developed and workable transaction network

COMPETITIVE STRATEGIES

The business's success depends on developing a moderately fast entry into the marketplace with a moderately mature service offering. The company will target a set of upscale B&Bs using its leverage from the development of the reservation service. The company will also try to affiliate itself with a large transaction entity so as to increase national credibility as well as keep the relationships necessary to market to the individual B&Bs.

Section 4

DEVELOPMENT PROGRAM

The development effort will entail the development of the system, the service, and the customer base. It will also require the development of the management team and structure to support the ongoing sales and market support efforts.

PRODUCT DEVELOPMENT

The development of the product will encompass the following set of tasks:

1.0 Marketing

1.1 Commitment of a base of 400 B&B operators on a national basis for a prototype system

1.2 Development of local agents to market the service in the top ten regions in the United States; agents will have the responsibility of signing up follow-on B&Bs within an 80-mile radius

1.3 Development of a national promotional strategy and its implementation to reach the determined target market

1.4 Commitment of 2,000 B&B operators for the first operational effort

1.5 Development and implementation of a customer service support function

2.0 Technical/Operations

2.1   Development and implementation of the on-line reservation system

2.2   Telecommunications interface for the 400 prototype users

2.3   Specialized software development

2.4   Integration of the end user terminals

2.5   Development of administrative software support

2.6   Integration of credit card POS capabilities

SCHEDULE AND FINANCIALS

Table A4.1 depicts the schedule for the development program. The major benchmarks are as follows:

Sign up 400 B&Bs

Establish reservation system central facility

Place all end user terminals (400)

Initialize national promotion campaign

Sign up 2,000 B&Bs

Initiate national rollout promotion

Affiliate with card companies

ORGANIZATION AND MANAGEMENT

The development effort will be closely coupled with the company's East Coast and Western offices. The technical and operations development effort will be focused in the New Jersey office, allowing easy access to all technical support and telecommunications interface. The western office will focus on developing market relations and will manage the development of the field sales force. The New Jersey office will manage the promotional plan, drawing from the advertising agency relationships it has developed over the past several years.

The company management will consist of the following:

TABLE A4.1 Development Effort Schedule

Task No.	Jan	Feb	Mar	Apr	Jun	Jul	Aug	Sep	Oct	Nov	Dec
1.1	xxxxxx	xxxxxx									
1.2		xxxxxx	xxxxxx								
1.3			xxxxxx	xxxxxx							
1.4						xxxxxx	xxxxxx				
1.5						xxxxxx	xxxxxx	xxxxxx			
2.1	xxxxxx	xxxxxx									
2.2		xxxxxx	xxxxxx								
2.3			xxxxxx	xxxxxx							
2.4						xxxxxx	xxxxxx				
2.5					xxxxxx	xxxxxx	xxxxxx	xxxxxx	xxxxxx		
2.6						xxxxxx	xxxxxx	xxxxxx			

Chairman

Responsible for the East Coast office operations; an experienced entrepreneur with extensive computer development and operations expertise.

President

Located in the western office; responsible for the implementation and operations of the field forces. The positioning in this area will allow for national coverage.

Vice President, Engineering

An east coast position that will support the development of system operations. This executive will have had extensive experience with POS systems.

TABLE A4.2 Development Expenses

Element	Amount ($000)
Salaries	350
Travel	150
Overhead	200
Computer	100
Software	100
Advertising	350
Professional	150
Telecommunications	100
TOTAL	$1,500

Vice President, Marketing

An east coast position that will focus on the promotional areas.

The major operational and development expenses are as shown in Table A4.2.

RISKS

The development effort is phased, and the risks are manageable. The major risks are as follows:

- The service's acceptance by the B&Bs: The company has already tested this concept and feels that the risks are low.
- Slow market penetration: The business can be profitable at a low penetration due to the highly variable nature of the expenses and capital requirements.
- Technical delays: The company has a highly trained, experienced team that reduces this risk.
- Low consumer acceptance of the service: Perhaps the highest risk. After performing some preliminary research, the firm feels consumers will accept the service if awareness is high. By carefully targeting the market, the awareness can be met, but possibly at a higher price.

Section 5

OPERATIONS AND MANAGEMENT

The business will operate with a real-time computer system located in the East Coast, with its corporate offices located in Santa Fe, New Mexico and Florham Park, New Jersey. This section details the business operations and provides an outline of the management requirements. It also presents the details of the capital requirements as well as the expense model of the business.

OPERATIONS

The business will operate in the following fashion. It will perform:

Marketing and Sales

This function will include the remote sales force of sales representatives (SRs) managed by six regional representatives, who will be company employees. The sales force will function as the direct, day-to-day B&B contact. BBI will support a separate toll-free number for B&B interface and SR support.

The separate corporate marketing effort will focus on obtaining new B&Bs as well as preparing for the franchising effort. The marketing effort will also prepare the company promotional campaigns to target the consumer market.

A customer service facility, separate from the consumer interface, will be in place to handle B&B interface calls. It will be important to provide an ongoing marketing effort to support the B&B base, ensuring a low churn and high resale value of the exclusive franchise.

Billing and advertising are in this operations area.

Development

This technical area will support the operations and development of the real-time reservations service. It is composed of systems people, who provide high-level systems support functions, such as communications and database services; hardware people, who provide customer service support and who, in turn, interface with the TRW service company representatives; and the software group, which keeps the computer system developed and operational.

It will be important to continue to make modifications to the system; this goal is the major focus of the development group. It must also interface with the marketing people to ensure that the system meets operational requirements.

Operations

This area supports the real-time operations of the business. Its training effort provides direct training of the new B&B entrants in the use of the system. This training function is essential for the operations of the business and must be supported at the corporate level. It must be clear that the system is to be used, and that any failure to use it will result in reduced revenue. Thus, the training personnel will have close contact with marketing and the SRs.

The toll-free customer services telephone number for reservations also is supported in this operations area.

Field Service

The field service expense for the system may be supported from an TRW Service Company contract.

G&A

This area encompasses the overall management support functions.

The operations of the service will follow the flow in the diagram in Figure A5.1. Information will flow from the terminal in the B&B location, which will include a keyboard-type computer, a screen, a credit card device, and a printer. The terminal will be used to enter reservations received as well as to receive reservation requests from the central computer. The B&B will purchase

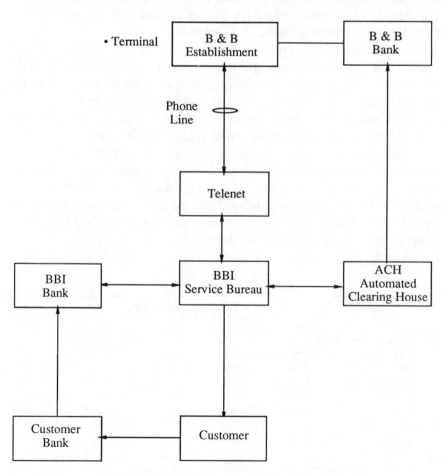

FIGURE A5.1 System Operations Diagram

the terminal equipment from Digital at an estimated price of $700, including an autodial modem for communications.

The terminal uses Telenet to communicate with the central computer, a Digital Equipment Corporation MICRO-VAX III machine with communications front-end software supporting a 56Kbps data modem. The MICRO-VAX will also support several video display terminals for the customer service workers who accept reservations. As reservations come in, they are recorded and then downloaded to the individual B&Bs.

The credit card validation on reservations can be done at this central facility. Once the customer arrives at the B&B, the B&B will inform the central facility of the arrival. No-shows will be billed on a guaranteed reservation basis.

The central facility will be able to provide audit trails and support statistics to all participating members. In addition, it will send monthly summary business status reports to all participating B&Bs so they can review the status of the business.

The expenses are depicted in Table A5.1. This expense breakout is derived along the functional lines just discussed. Note the revenue drivers, such as the total number of customers; the productivity factors, such as the number of customers per customer service rep; and cost factors of unloaded salaries per employee, which yield the number of employees in that functional area and the functional area's direct expense. Added to these are the overhead factors driven by the employee.

TABLE A5.1 Expense Model

Year	Expenses ($000)				
	1	2	3	4	5
M&S exp	$900	$1,200	$2,423	$3,722	$6,054
Engr exp	$340	$604	$1,234	$1,730	$2,313
Net O&M exp	$175	$384	$503	$738	$761
Plant O&M exp	$160	$352	$830	$1,217	$1,952
G&A exp	$219	$423	$764	$1,107	$1,587
OH exp	$1,770	$3,290	$5,876	$8,635	$12,577
Telcom exp	$448	$990	$1,637	$2,402	$3,309
NOE	$4,012	$7,244	$13,267	$19,551	$28,554

TABLE A5.2 Capital Summary

Year	Capital Model ($000)				
	1986	1987	1988	1989	1990
Initial capital	$0	$0	$0	$0	$40
Net capital	$0	$336	$672	$1,018	$1,384
Computer systems					
No. B&B	400	880	1452	2130	2928
CPU cap/B&B (MIPs)	1	1	1	1	1
Cap/CPU cap	$1	$1	$1	$1	$1
CPU cap	$400	$880	$1,452	$2,130	$2,928
New comm cap	$400	$480	$572	$678	$799
Comm equip					
No. B&B	400	880	1452	2130	2928
No. resvr/day/B&B	6	6	6	6	6
Hold time/rsvr	3	3	3	3	3
Arrival rate	7	15	24	35	49
No. data channels	2	4	7	11	15
Cap/channel	$10	$10	$10	$10	$10
Comm cap	$20	$44	$73	$106	$146
New comm cap	$20	$24	$29	$34	$40
Total new capital	$420	$504	$601	$711	$839
Total capital	$420	$840	$1,273	$1,730	$2,222
Depreciation	$84	$168	$255	$346	$444

The capital requirements are depicted in Table A5.2. As with expenses, they are driven by the revenue drivers. We have only two major capital requirements: computers and communications equipment. It is assumed that all other equipment is leased.

MANAGEMENT

Three key management positions are to be filled. They are:

President

The President and CEO must have the expertise of running a national reservations service business and must have a knowledge of the lodging business. The position requires a detailed knowledge of real-time computer operations as well as the ability to interface with a sales force.

Vice President, Marketing

This position will be responsible for all the marketing, sales, and customer service support. This person will have experience with a direct sales force operation as well as dealing with an extensive real-time customer service operation. This person must also be a demonstrated marketing executive.

Vice President, Operations

This position will be responsible for all computer operations as well as interfacing with all field service. This individual must be the key technical interface and must have a track record in operating a service bureau.

Section 6

FINANCIAL ANALYSIS

This section summarizes the results of the previous sections to present the financial analysis of the business opportunity.

INCOME STATEMENT

Table A6.1 presents the income statement for the business. The NOI margin is negative for the first year, indicating a need for initial capital to support development and sales. The margin grows to 40 percent, indicating a highly profitable service business. In such a business, an ongoing revenue stream supports continued growth. In addition, the cash will support the acquisition of B&Bs for the franchise operation.

CASH FLOW

Table A6.2 depicts the cash flow for this business. In the present analysis it was assumed that the financing included a debt service. This caused an additional $1.1 million in debt service, accounting for the $2.7 million negative cumulative cash flow. With all equity financing, this would be $1.5 million. The IRR is 97 percent, which is quite high and indicates that the business has significant leverage for price competition against competitors as it evolves. This factor will act as a barrier to entry. The

TABLE A6.1 Income Statement

Year	Income Statement $(000)				
	1986	1987	1988	1989	1990
Revenue	$3,276	$9,370	$18,315	$29,548	$47,883
Expense	$4,012	$7,244	$13,267	$19,551	$28,554
NOI	($735)	$2,126	$5,047	$9,997	$19,329
Margin %	−22%	23%	28%	34%	40%
Depreciation	$84	$168	$255	$346	$444
Profit before int	($819)	$1,958	$4,793	$9,651	$18,885
Margin %	−25%	21%	26%	33%	39%
Interest	$480	$720	$720	$240	$0
Profit before tax	($1,299)	$1,238	$4,073	$9,411	$18,885
Margin %	−40%	13%	22%	32%	39%
Taxes	$0	$0	$1,966	$4,611	$9,254
Dividends	$0	$0	$0	$0	$0
Profit after tax	($1,299)	$1,238	$2,107	$4,800	$9,631
Margin %	−40%	13%	12%	16%	20%

TABLE A6.2 Cash Flow

Year	Cash Flow Analysis ($000)				
	1986	1987	1988	1989	1990
NOI	($735)	$2,126	$5,047	$9,997	$19,329
Interest	$480	$720	$720	$240	$0
Taxes	$0	$0	$1,966	$4,611	$9,254
Dividends	$0	$0	$0	$0	$0
Capital	$420	$504	$601	$711	$839
LTD reduction	$0	$0	$0	$0	$0
Chg WC	($801)	($278)	($717)	($583)	($630)
Cash flow	($834)	$1,180	$2,478	$5,017	$9,867
Cumulative CF	($834)	$346	$2,824	$7,841	$17,708

TABLE A6.3 Sources and Uses Summary

	Sources and Uses ($000)				
Year	1986	1987	1988	1989	1990
Sources					
Beginning cash	$0	$6,166	$10,846	$13,324	$14,341
NOI	($735)	$2,126	$5,047	$9,997	$19,329
Senior debt	$0	$0	$0	$0	$0
Junior debt	$4,000	$2,000	$0	$0	$0
Equity (common)	$3,000	$1,500	$0	$0	$0
Equity (prefrd)	$0	$0	$0	$0	$0
Total sources	$6,265	$11,792	$15,893	$23,321	$33,670
Uses					
Purchase	$0	$0	$0	$0	$0
Capital req	$420	$504	$601	$711	$839
Int senior debt	$0	$0	$0	$0	$0
Int junior debt	$480	$720	$720	$240	$0
Taxes	$0	$0	$1,966	$4,611	$9,254
Dividends (com)	$0	$0	$0	$0	$0
Dividends (pref)	$0	$0	$0	$0	$0
Chg in junior debt	$0	$0	$0	$4,000	$2,000
Chng work cap	($801)	($278)	($717)	($583)	($630)
Chng in LTD	$0	$0	$0	$0	$0
Total Uses	$99	$946	$2,569	$8,980	$11,462
Net Cash	$6,166	$10,846	$13,324	$14,341	$22,208

NPV, at a cost of capital of 22 percent, is $21.5 million, which puts a large premium on this business from the outset.

Table A6.3 depicts the sources and uses for the business, re-phrasing the cash flow.

BALANCE SHEET

Table A6.4 shows the balance sheet for the business. We assume that all the cash generated is kept by the business. The receiv-

TABLE A6.4 Balance Sheet Summary

	Balance Sheet ($000)				
Year	1986	1987	1988	1989	1990
Assets					
Current Assets					
Cash	$6,166	$10,846	$13,324	$14,341	$22,208
Sht-term invest	$0	$0	$0	$0	$0
Accts receivable	$404	$1,155	$2,258	$3,643	$5,903
Inventory	$2	$4	$6	$9	$11
Tot cur assets	$6,572	$12,005	$15,588	$17,992	$28,123
Capital plant-dep	$336	$672	$1,018	$1,384	$1,778
LT invest	$0	$0	$0	$0	$0
Sundry assets	$0	$0	$0	$0	$0
Total assets	$6,908	$12,677	$16,606	$19,376	$29,900
Liabilities					
Current Liab					
Accts payable	$1,093	$1,910	$3,420	$4,996	$7,248
Accrued liab	$66	$187	$366	$591	$958
Taxes payable	$49	$141	$275	$443	$718
Tot cur liab	$1,207	$2,238	$4,061	$6,030	$8,923
Long-term debt	$4,000	$6,000	$6,000	$2,000	$0
Other noncur liab	$0	$0	$0	$0	$0
Total liabilities	$5,207	$8,238	$10,061	$8,030	$8,923
Owners' Equity					
Shares @ par	$0	$0	$0	$0	$0
Adtl paid-in cap	$3,000	$4,500	$4,500	$4,500	$4,500
Retain earnings	($1,299)	($61)	$2,046	$6,846	$16,477
Tot owner equity	$1,701	$4,439	$6,546	$11,346	$20,977
Tot liab/own equity	$6,908	$12,677	$16,606	$19,376	$29,900

ables and payables are kept short and do not lead to large working capital requirements.

The book value at Year 5 is $20 million and yields a ten times return on the initial investment in that period. The company provides an excellent opportunity for a sale after that period. In addition, there may be a public offering due to the continued growth.

REFERENCES

Abell, Derek and John Hammond.
[1] Strategic Market Planning, Prentice Hall, Englewood Cliffs, NJ, 1979

Andrews, Kenneth
[1] The Concept of Corporate Strategy, Irwin, Homewood, IL, 1971

Anthony, Robert and Glenn Welsch
[1] Management Accounting, Irwin, Homewood, IL, 1977

Athos, Anthony et al.
[1] Interpersonal Behavior, Prentice-Hall, Englewood Cliffs, NJ, 1977

Bellenger, Danny and Barnett Greenberg
[1] Marketing Research, Irwin, Homewood, IL, 1978

Boyd, Harper et al.
[1] Marketing Research, Irwin, Homewood, IL, 1981

Brealey, Richard and Stewart Meyers
[1] Principles of Corporate Finance, McGraw-Hill, New York, NY, 1984

Copeland, Thomas and Fred J. Weston
[1] Financial Theory and Corporate Policy, Addison-Wesley, New York, NY, 1983

Cox, James
[1] Sum and Substance of Corporations, CES Press, New York, NY 1982

Davis, Stanley et al.
[1] Matrix Management, Addison-Wesley, Reading, MA, 1977

Diamond, Stephen C.
[1] Leveraged Buyouts, Dow Jones Irwin, Homewood, IL, 1985

Drucker, Peter
[1] Concept of the Corporation, Mentor, New York, NY, 1972
[2] Innovation and Entrepreneurship, Harper & Row, New York, NY, 1985

Edwards, James D. et al.
[1] How Accounting Works, Dow Jones Irwin, Homewood, IL, 1985

Engel, James et al.
[1] Promotional Strategy, Irwin, Homewood, IL, 1979

Fishman, Katherine D.
[1] The Computer Establishment, Harper & Row, New York, NY, 1982

Fruhan, William
[1] Financial Strategy, Irwin, Homewood, IL, 1979

Galbraith, Jay R.
[1] Organizational Design, Addison-Wesley, Reading, MA, 1977

Gladstone, D. J.
[1] Venture Capital Handbook, Reston Press, Reston, VA, 1982

Griffin, Charles et al.
[1] Advanced Accounting, Irwin, Homewood, IL, 1977

Grove, Andrew S.
[1] High Output Management, Random House, New York, NY, 1982

Hamilton, R. W.
[1] Corporations, West Publishing, St. Paul, MN, 1982

Hoeber, Oalph et al.
[1] Contemporary Business Law, McGraw-Hill, New York, NY, 1982

Hopkins, Thomas
[1] Mergers and Acquisitions, Dow Jones Irwin, Homewood, IL, 1983

Keegan, Warren J.
[1] Multinational Marketing Management, Prentice-Hall, Englewood Cliffs, NJ, 1984

Kidder, Tracey
[1] The Soul of a New Machine, Avon, New York, NY, 1981

Kotler, Philip
[1] Marketing Management, Prentice-Hall, Englewood Cliffs, NJ, 1984

Kotter, John et al.
[1] Organization, Irwin, Homewood, IL, 1979

Kravitt, Gregory et al.
[1] How to Raise Capital, Dow Jones Irwin, Homewood, IL, 1984

Levinson, Harry
[1] Executive, Harvard University Press, Cambridge, MA, 1981

Levinson, Harry and Stuart Rosenthal
[1] CEO, Basic Books, New York, NY, 1984

Levitt, Theodore
[1] The Marketing Imagination, The Free Press, New York, NY, 1982

Liles, Patrick
[1] New Business Ventures and the Entrepreneur, Irwin, Homewood, IL, 1974

Lovelock, Christopher
  [1] Services Marketing, Prentice-Hall, Englewood Cliffs, NJ, 1984

Luck, David J. et al.
  [1] Marketing Research, Prentice-Hall, Englewood Cliffs, NJ, 1982

Luck, David J. and O. C. Ferrell
  [1] Marketing Strategy and Plans, Prentice-Hall, Englewood Cliffs, NJ, 1985

MacCracken, Calvin
  [1] Handbook for Inventors, Charles Scribner, New York, NY, 1983

Marren, Joseph H.
  [1] Mergers and Acquisitions, Dow Jones Irwin, Homewood, IL, 1985

Mayer, Martin
  [1] Bankers, Ballentine, New York, NY, 1974

McClellan, Stephen
  [1] The Coming Computer Industry Shakeout, Wiley, New York, NY, 1984

McDonald, John
  [1] The Game of Business, Anchor, New York, NY, 1977

Nash, Edward
  [1] Direct Marketing, McGraw-Hill, New York, NY, 1982

Nierenberg, Gerard
  [1] Fundamentals of Negotiating, Hawthorne Books, New York, NY, 1973

O'Flaherty, Joseph
  [1] Going Public, Wiley, New York, NY, 1984

Peters, Thomas J. and Robert H. Waterman
  [1] In Search of Excellence, Harper & Row, New York, NY, 1982

Peters, Thomas J. and Nancy Austin
  [1] A Passion for Excellence, Random House, New York, NY, 1985

Pooley, James
  [1] Trade Secrets, Osborne Press, Berkeley, CA, 1982

Porter, Michael
  [1] Competitive Strategy, The Free Press, New York, NY, 1980
  [2] Competitive Advantage, The Free Press, New York, NY, 1985

Raiffa, Howard
  [1] The Art and Science of Negotiations, Belknap Press, Cambridge, MA, 1982

Ries, Al and Jack Trout
  [1] Positioning, McGraw-Hill, New York, NY, 1981

Rogers, Everett and Judith Larsen
  [1] Silicon Valley Fever, Basic Books, New York, NY, 1984

Silver, A. D.
  [1] Up-Front Financing, Wiley, New York, NY, 1982
  [2] Venture Capital, Wiley, New York, NY, 1985
Sloan, Alfred
  [1] My Years with General Motors, Doubleday, New York, NY, 1963
Stern, Louis and Adel El-Asary
  [1] Marketing Channels, Prentice-Hall, Englewood Cliffs, NJ, 1982
Urban, Glen and John Hauser
  [1] Design and Marketing of New Products, Prentice-Hall, Englewood Cliffs, NJ, 1980
Welsch, Glenn and Robert Anthony
  [1] Financial Accounting, Irwin, Homewood, IL, 1977
White, Richard
  [1] The Entrepreneur's Manual, Chilton, New York, NY, 1977
Wilson, John W.
  [1] New Ventures, Addison-Wesley, Reading, MA, 1985

INDEX